BEST
AFRICAN AMERICAN
ESSAYS: 2009

BEST
AFRICAN AMERICAN
ESSAYS: 2009

GERALD EARLY, Series Editor
DEBRA J. DICKERSON, Guest Editor

BANTAM BOOKS

BEST AFRICAN AMERICAN ESSAYS: 2009
Bantam hardcover and trade paperback editions / January 2009

Published by Bantam Dell
A Division of Random House, Inc.
New York, New York

978-0-553-80691-5 (hardcover)
978-0-553-38536-6 (trade paperback)
978-0-553-90604-2 (e-book)

Printed in the United States of America
Published simultaneously in Canada

www.bantamdell.com

10 9 8 7 6 5 4 3 2 1
BVG

CONTENTS

ACTIVISM/POLITICAL THOUGHT

INTRODUCTION

During my life I cannot remember a time when black folk did not fuss, cuss, quarrel, and remonstrate with one another (and with whites) about their condition, about the world, about their humanity, about why we are here, and about what it all means. Probably because of the conditions that blacks had to endure for a good deal of their time in this country, they have always felt that in any public argument or debate about rights, freedom, or fairness, the stakes were especially high and "as serious as your life," to borrow a phrase from Valerie Wilmer. African Americans have been, if nothing else, a people of polemics, a people who have passionately argued in defense of themselves and against injustice and inequality. If at times their arguments were self-interested or self-serving, ethnocentric or chauvinistic, they served the best interests of the nation by forcing it to confront its own blood-soaked hypocrisy.

Since writing fiction so often seemed a luxury that the severity of their condition could hardly afford, African Americans have always vested a great deal of importance in writing nonfiction. And once upon a time blacks were more likely to read nonfiction. Nonfiction was the arena where arguments were made, facts amassed, ideology sharpened, statistics formulated, and corrections made. Within that arena the essay has long been a major weapon in the overall thrust and parry. Indeed, ever since the days of slavery, the essay has been the form of choice to carry the burden of black people's complaint with the visible world. The black essayist offers testimony, both for the religious (about God in an uncaring cruel world) and for the irreligious (about fate and how we are all predestined to lose). Black witnessing of the absurdity of life has given us both spirituals and the blues, allowing both God and the devil their due. Black folk have made their preoccupation with their condition a philosophical meditation on life itself. To express this meditation is why black people write essays.

When he was not producing various versions of his autobiography, Frederick Douglass was largely an essayist and journalist. W.E.B. Du Bois's *The Souls of Black Folk* (1903), the most highly regarded nonfiction work by an African American in American intellectual history, is a collection of essays. Du Bois also wrote books and monographs, such as the sociological treatise *The Philadelphia Negro* (1899) and the polemical *In Battle for Peace: The Story of My 83rd Birthday* (1952)—he even wrote novels. But he reached his audience primarily through the essays he published in magazines and newspapers. (Interestingly, Du Bois described one of his most important books, *Dusk of Dawn*, published in 1940, as "an essay toward an autobiography of a race concept," in short, a book-length essay. It reveals how important and how complex the concept of the essay was for him.) James Weldon Johnson, a contemporary of Du Bois, as well as a songwriter, diplomat, novelist, poet, and NAACP official, spent several years writing op-ed pieces for the *New York Age,* one of the great black newspapers of the early twentieth century. Early versions of Afrocentric thought were introduced to the black public back in the 1920s, through the columns of J. A. Rogers in black newspapers. George Schuyler became a sort of black H. L. Mencken through his 1920s magazine and newspaper essays. Black journalists like Carl Rowan and Chuck Stone became known to the world through their newspaper columns. Even Jackie Robinson spent time writing a newspaper column! And everyone should remember that Martin Luther King's most famous and influential piece of writing was an essay: "Letter from a Birmingham Jail" (1963).

As I learned in my teen years during the 1960s, nonfiction of all kinds—not just essays but autobiographies and political treatises—

was the arena where the most confident and tough-minded black writers were wont to tread. It was the age of argument and manifesto. Writers, I suppose, were trying to make sense of the chaos of their time. Perhaps writers have done this in all ages, as everyone's time is, to a greater or lesser extent, an epoch of chaos, cruelty, rude opportunity, and misunderstood change. But when I was a teenager in the 1960s, the explosion of black nonfiction, and especially of essay writing, struck me as heroic, as if some grand ideological, mythological shift was emerging right before my eyes, or as if explorers were discovering an uncharted frontier that would redefine us all. Significant works of fiction were produced during this time, including James Baldwin's *Another Country* (1962), and John A. Williams's *The Man Who Cried I Am* (1967), but the nonfiction overshadowed the novels. Two volumes of essays were among the most important books of the era: *The Fire Next Time* (1963) by James Baldwin and *Soul on Ice* (1968) by Eldridge Cleaver, the Black Panther Party's minister of information. And two landmark autobiographies by two very different men were highly influential best-sellers in 1965: *Yes I Can* by Sammy Davis Jr. and *The Autobiography of Malcolm X* by Alex Haley. Like Du Bois's *Dusk of Dawn,* the nonfiction works were being published not as books in the conventional sense but as book-length essays. For the essay had become an attempt to express something in prose—an idea, a feeling, an argument, an attitude, a proposition—that transcended its subject matter, and when it was successful, it took on the power of narrative. An essay is both searching and assertive, a contradiction that necessitates its artistry. Nonfiction prose, at its best, can do something for the mind, the heart, and the senses that is beyond the reach of other writing: it can make you doubt and believe at the same time. The essay especially seeks to achieve that end, to attain subtlety and suppleness, a daring nimbleness, to go beyond the mere conveying of information or description. Yet the essay never loses its accessibility, its charm, its magic, its ability to make ordinary language extraordinary, to induce the reader to see the visible anew. The essay, unlike poetry, aspires not to make the prosaic sublime but rather to make the prosaic complex and urgent. By the time I was sixteen, the world for me was not an epic poem to dream upon but an essay to be read and revised. For an essay is a trial that always invites another, better effort; it is the narrative of the road we're on and what we're thinking about that road at any given moment. It's a rough draft map that constantly needs to be reworked.

In 1967 *The Crisis of the Negro Intellectual* by Harold Cruse and *Black Power: The Politics of Liberation in America* by Stokely Carmichael and Charles V. Hamilton were the most talked-about books of the year, at least among black folk. I remember struggling to read them as a high school sophomore (a struggle I lost, finishing them only about ten years later) because they were the hip books to read among black nationalist types and college students who talked their fair share of revolutionary theory, everything from Maulana Ron Karenga's Kawaida Studies (which gave us Kwanzaa) to the Marxist-Leninist patter of Black Panthers like Huey Newton. This kind of work was not just some aberration of the 1960s, a time when radical political writing and ranting seemed to fall from the trees like leaves in autumn or bird droppings in the morning. Its origins go back as far as 1828, the year of David Walker's *Appeal* (a book made up of four essays), in which he argued that black folk had better get it together and that slaves were bound by Almighty God to rise up against their masters. We have been issuing nonfiction as jeremiads, warnings, and prophecies ever since. Among the most-read black books of the 1950s, for instance, when the United States was supposedly asleep and complacent, were E. Franklin Frazier's *Black Bourgeoisie* (1957), a lively diatribe against the superficialities of the black middle class, and Martin Luther King's *Stride Toward Freedom* (1958), the story of the Montgomery bus boycott.

The two most influential literary essayists of my time, indeed in black American history, were James Baldwin and Ralph Ellison. As highly literate and personal essayists, even old-fashioned belletrists in some respects, their reputations equaled, and in Baldwin's case exceeded, their renown as novelists. Baldwin's "Stranger in the Village" (1955) remains the best essay about the complexities of race ever written, and Ellison's "On Bird, Bird-Watching, and Jazz" (1962) remains one of the finest essays on American music. When I began writing essays nearly thirty years ago, my models were Ellison and Baldwin (along with George Orwell and Jacques Barzun, for clarity). As a teenager how I loved the essays of Amiri Baraka, wielding words as he did with the derring-do of a swashbuckler, the mad Pied Piper of black cultural nationalism. And Langston Hughes's Jess B. Simple pieces were always a treat to reread.

Because I had read so many great essays by black writers—I used to sit in the public library and read them by the hour—I wanted to write them too, convinced that being an essayist was as close as I would ever get to glory on this earth and to conversing with all the black writers I admired. Hughes, Zora Neale Hurston, and Richard Wright had all written seminal essays during their careers, as have Alice Walker, Toni Morrison, Charles Johnson, and the guest editor of this volume, Debra Dickerson. To me, the mark of greatness was not to write the great novel but rather to write a great essay, whether it was the length of a newspaper column or the size of a book.

My youngest daughter, when she was nine years old, discovered one day through a teacher at school that her father wrote essays, and she found this curious. When she came home, she asked me not what an essay was, but rather, "Daddy, why do you write essays?" It was a hard question, such as children are wont to pose, and it demanded a real answer because it was being asked completely without guile or any implication of an agenda. And embedded within it was her other question, "What is an essay?" which she chose to ask only indirectly, by asking about my connection to something that she did not understand. "I write essays," I said, "in order to say something that is worth saying in the best way that I can say it. That is why anybody writes anything that you would want someone else to read." That was the wrong answer. She looked puzzled, even a little distressed. I tried again. "I write essays because they are fun to write and people like them when I do them well." She grinned at that. "I'm glad they're fun because they sound hard," she said. "Well, sometimes even something that is fun to do can be hard," I laughed. "Is it fun when it's hard?" she pressed. "Sometimes, and sometimes it's just hard when it's hard," I said. And it was her turn to snicker. "I know what that's like," she said.

It is my hope that the *Best African American Essays* anthologies will remind the reading public that African Americans have a grand tradition in the essay. This new annual series is meant to showcase the range and variety of the essays we write: personal, literary, polemical, intellectual, comic, contemplative. Each volume will highlight a particular year. This first volume focuses on literature published in 2007. But it also contains two pieces from 2006, Kenneth McClane's deeply moving "Driving," and Brian Palmer's informative "Last Thoughts of an Iraq 'Embed,'" because Debra and I could not resist using them.

Also, I did not want future guest editors to feel that they could not include a piece or two from the year previous to the one that the volume is highlighting. Possibly, as these volumes continue, something may get overlooked, or one guest editor may value something that another guest editor does not. So including pieces from 2006 here is meant to serve as a precedent, to give future guest editors (and me) a bit of latitude.

The *Best African American Essays* series is intended to accomplish three goals:

1. to bring to the attention of a wide variety of readers the best essays published by African Americans in a particular year;
2. to bring to their attention some of the lesser-known sources that feature the African American essay; and
3. to offer an organic, ongoing anthology wherein, from year to year, one may observe shifts and changes, trends and innovations, in African American essay writing.

A point of clarification: What is an African American? This question has no obvious or even objective answer. For the purposes of these volumes, I choose a broad definition: an African American is any person of color from anywhere in the recognized African Diaspora who lives in the United States either temporarily or permanently, who writes in English, and who is published by an American-based publisher or in an American-based publication.

A second point of clarification: While the *Best African American Essays* series promises to feature writers of African descent, it will also, from time to time, reprint good writing by non–African Americans on African American subjects. Debra and I have included three such essays in this volume. Historically, black colleges—"oases of civility," as the historian John Hope Franklin once called them— admitted white applicants and hired white faculty members. The *Best African American Essays* series can do nothing less but follow this tradition of openness. Besides, I have learned over the years as much about African American life from non–African American writers as I have from African Americans: old-school Negro Studies scholars like August Meier and Melville Herskovits; more recent scholars like

Lawrence Levine, David Garrow, and William Van Deburg; and writers like Susan Straight, Peter Guralnick, and Brad Snyder. It takes a village to raise a child, goes the old cliché, and it apparently takes a village to tell a story as well, particularly the story of the village.

Finally, although all the selections in this volume are essays, the series is about presenting the best of black nonfiction writing. So future volumes may contain excerpts from nonfiction books as well as essays—whatever constitutes the best of that year. For this volume, we had a good number of strong essays from which to choose.

I wish to thank guest editor Debra Dickerson, an old sparring partner, for making most of the selections for this volume. I added a few more to round it out. Dickerson is the author of *The End of Blackness: Returning the Souls of Black Folk to Their Rightful Owners* (2004) and *An American Story* (2000). It was a pleasure to work with her. She works with great energy and care. I cannot think of any current nonfiction writer better suited to get this series off the ground. She is just the person you would want with you in a foxhole, surrounded on all sides by the enemy. She'll get you out alive. She is the last of the great fighters.

I wish to extend gratitude to Keya Kraft, Jian Leng, and Barbara Liebmann for all the work they did to make this volume possible. I very much appreciate their dedication and their support.

Gerald Early

Series Editor

INTRODUCTION

Black for No Reason at All

To be a minority is, among many other things, to live as a sort of cultural vampire: one is forced, by bad luck at birth, to subsist on the popular lifeblood of a majority which bogarts (if only by sheer force of numbers) the airwaves, bandwidths, museums, and performance halls. It's to search hungrily for your group's face in the zeitgeist's mirror and rarely find it there.

We at the margins hunger for glimpses of ourselves in the cultural viewfinder, for proof that we leave footprints in the earth, footprints that will still be visible in millennia to come when archaeologists, even extraterrestrials, comb through America's myriad scientific, cultural, and artistic layers to figure out who, what, and why the hell we were. How we long to see black footprints embedded in amber and not just in the shifting, momentary sands of fads like novelty rap, *Barbershop* movies, and gauche clothing lines. That search, subconscious though it may be—and more necessary because of it—is not even primarily for the "positive" images that blacks so justifiably demand to offset America's insatiable preference for encountering us via inner-city perp walks and welfare statistics. Rather it's the unexpected, off-topic encounters with ourselves for which we most long. Blacks climbing mountains. Arguing environmental policy. Composing symphonies.

Spelunking for lost treasures. Singing our children lullabies. Producing literature about the human condition. Blacks where you least expect to happen upon them and encounters that don't require our race, which should be the ultimate non sequitur, to be what matters most about us or, most daringly, even to matter at all.

Blacks, in other words, are human; and all humans are narcissists, enamored of their own existence and frustrated as hell not to be widely acknowledged as the fascinating creatures we, no less than every other self-absorbed group, most definitely are. *We're here. We're black. Get used to it.* Get used to it, and for the love of God, let us talk about something else for just a few minutes please. That, dear reader, is the purpose of this anthology.

Here, we are creating a space in which blacks may be unpredictable. Off message. Quirky. Individuals. Human. Black for no reason at all. Where better to happen upon ourselves than in the essay? Essays about life, essays about history, essays about nothing much. Essays by blacks, but not necessarily about *being* black, though that's all right, too. With this long overdue inaugural collection, we'll go spelunking for memorable essays, by or about *diasporic* blacks, on any subject at all. Anything. Whatever they happened to be thinking about that day and felt compelled to share with the world. With this series we announce the hunt for black essayistic art. Art—not protest or politics, unless those topics are rendered with transcendent, time-testing mastery. If you're interested in beautiful writing or thought informed by blackness but not required by it, this series is for you. *Best African American Essays* calls a time-out on the black artist's duty to his people, his country, or his livelihood and provides a place simply to be an artist. It's a place for the black artist to be free.

BLACKS LANDING ON THE MOON

In the 1960s, when blacks were first integrating television in real numbers, we set the phone lines asizzle, letting each other know whenever one of our own was on the small screen. As if the entire black community hadn't already planned Sunday dinner or the kids' homework around those pre-VCR, bated-breath events. Whenever Sammy Davis Jr. or Diahann Carroll was on TV, the streets of black America were deserted, just as they were during America's landing on the moon, both paradigm-shifting, fish-out-of-water events that changed American life as we knew it. For the entire half-hour of *The Flip Wilson Show* or *Julia*, Afro'd kids would sit entranced while adults just held the phone that connected them to another equally bemused Negro. All silently watched ourselves take part in America as artists and not, for once, as invisible, underpaid, much abused labor or—god help our psyches— as the all too visible "Negro problem."

Shaking our heads in prideful wonder at seeing ourselves in the tuxedoes and evening gowns of the day, finally invited into America's living rooms, blacks accepted that our public presence then had to be *qua* black people. We could not be simply the new neighbor—we had to be the new *black* neighbor that America could practice not calling a realtor at first sight of. We could not be the new co-worker, but the new *black* first-of-his-kind office mate, whose every utterance *had* to be wackily misinterpreted by well-intentioned whites (who *had* to be construed as well-intentioned, or integration was over) as racial protest, so that high jinks, neutered of any substantive politics, could ensue and be resolved before the credits rolled. It was Kabuki theater, a highly stylized enactment of catharsis whose preformatted, feel-good outcomes threatened the white psyche not at all and that achieved nothing but teaching whites that they could remain calm with us in the room without police protection. It was enough for us then—it had to be enough—simply to be allowed into the room.

Cultural encounters with us then, as America took baby steps toward racial tolerance, could include us only as the proverbial Other, extraterrestrials landed on Main Street. People who'd been here for centuries, people who'd both cared for and borne the children of the majority—the inscrutable, unpredictable strangers who'd lived in America since before it was America—were taking blackness for a wary stroll on the other side of the color line. It was a perp walk of a different kind, the kind intended to teach America it could encounter us as humans, fellow citizens. We were free but on our best credit-to-our-race, closely-monitored-by-both-sides behavior. Literal chains were replaced by existential ones.

Popular culture was the way America got to know its blacks—got used to its blacks—as something other than its volatile serfs; there was nothing then but for blacks to serve as the one-dimensional proxies via which America could confront its integrationist terrors: its terrors, its guilt, and its fear of justified confrontation. Hence the ritual thrashings from the overly but impotently politicized Negroes of *Maude*, *Good Times*, and *The Jeffersons*. Indeed, blacks then also felt a need for the existential training wheels of participation as symbols and tokens only, as refutations of innate white supremacy or black quiescence; our art, understandably, focused mainly on the black condition. In the 1960s, as we had for centuries, we primarily sought to answer the mind-strangling question that W.E.B. Du Bois implored us to resist: "How does it feel to be a problem?" As he did, black artists have either "smile[d] or [were] interested, or [were] reduce[d] to a boiling simmer, as the occasion [required]."*

But them days is over. Now, more than a century later, we've caught up to Du Bois: "To the real question, How does it feel to be a problem? [We] answer seldom a word."

That'll tick them off.

The question is, and always was, stupid, a subject-changer, not to mention ingeniously devised to keep us on the defensive, looking up at our interrogators, trying to figure out what they were thinking and what we could do to change it. But it's 2008. Let those determined to figure out what's so fundamentally wrong with blacks—and who require *us* to flail in vain for the answer to the wrong question, *their* question—spin their wheels on that racist, white supremacist, and *narcissistic* notion (i.e., "why do we find you, with your Quintellas and your swagger, to be so disturbing?"). However fascinated by the construction of blacks as problems, as defectives, as Other, the world might be, blacks have increasingly struggled uphill to change the bloody subject from their race to their minds. As late as 2002, the acclaimed sculptor Ed Hamilton, who labored in obscurity until his commemorations of black heroes like those of the *Amistad* and Booker T. Washington brought him prominence, had to unleash his frustration at race's constriction of his art. In an installation called *Confinement*, "faces peer out of holes in slabs, as if looking to break free . . . [his curator] Julien Robson sees in *Confinement* an African American artist

---

The Souls of Black Folk, pp. 43, 44. W.E.B. Du Bois, Signet Classic, Penguin Books. Introduction by Randall Keenan, 1995, originally published in 1903.

struggling to become visible on his own terms."* Unfortunately for him, a *Best African American Sculptures* is not likely in the offing.

Hamilton faces the same realities all black artists do: museums and editors industriously keep us on speed dial whenever "black" issues arise, but not when there's a mortgage crisis, an ecological issue, or a humanitarian disaster on another continent. We seldom occur to them except through our blackness. But art must take risks, and black artists have always done so; homes such as this collection will make that task a little easier. The only way to make the world see us as human is for us to act human—offering up, with great boldness, our two cents on whatever catches our fancy. Most excitingly, we hope this series will encourage more black writers to take a breather from the beaten path of the salable essay or the latest "black" controversy and ruminate on . . . life. Increasingly freed from the requirements of race, we have art to create and art already created to be unearthed from its non-race-related obscurity. In that regard, at least, the black writer has it easier than most of his brethren artists; we don't need twenty-foot ceiling heights and scarce gallery walls to be seen. Just anthologies like this one, which will hopefully inspire more editors to think of black writers for nonblack subjects and inspire more black writers to branch out.

In this inaugural volume, James Hannaham recounts for us an uneventful night out and about with his famous artist cousin, Kara Walker ("Coincidental Cousins"). Emily Bernard beautifully bangs her head against the wall over a friendship that has inexplicably, one-sidedly ended ("Fired"). Black but more than black. Art.

These essays will help the world understand that the culture produced by blacks must be understood as exactly that—as culture, not "black" culture. As long as racism does, black art as protest can, will, and should continue. "Jena, O.J. and the Jailing of Black America" (Orlando Patterson), "A Dream Lay Dying, Parts I, II, III" (Bill Maxwell), and "What IQ Doesn't Tell You About Race" (Malcolm Gladwell) are just a few examples of the internal, antiracist critique included herein. The time is long overdue, however, for blacks to abandon Du Bois's double consciousness—the impulse to understand and explain ourselves through white eyes and the strictures of race—and

*"History's Sculptor" by D. Cameron Lawrence, *American Legacy* magazine, Spring 2008, p. 31.

to explore what essayist Albert Murray describes as the "ambiguities and absurdities inherent in all human experience."* Whites can't move on until we do.

Writing in 1969 in his now canonical essay collection *The Omni-Americans*, Murray argued, among other things, that America's myopic reliance on bare statistics and the other tools of social science to "understand" its blacks was at best a dodge, and at worst a gambit designed to keep us "constructed" as a dysfunctional national problem. We were not neighbors, not humans, not fellow citizens, but a naked litany of negative "facts" in a vacuum that appeared to speak for themselves. Whites might be understood via Shakespeare and Milton, but for blacks, poll data alone sufficed. He wrote:

> The prime target of these polemics is the professional observer/reporter (that major vehicle of the nation's information, alas) who relies on the so-called findings and all-too-inconclusive extrapolations of social science survey technicians for their sense of the world [where blacks are concerned]. The bias of *The Omni-Americans* is distinctly proliterary. It represents the dramatic sense of life as against the terminological abstractions and categories derived from laboratory procedures. Its interests, however, are not those of a literary sensibility at odds with scientific method. Not by any means. On the contrary, a major charge of the argument advanced here is that most social science survey findings are not scientific enough. They violate one's common everyday breeze-tasting sense of life precisely because they do not meet the standards of validity, reliability, and comprehensiveness that the best scientists have always insisted on. As a result they provide neither a truly practical sociology of the so-called black community nor a dependable psychology of black behavior . . .
>
> [These essays] are submitted as antidotes against the pernicious effects of a technological enthusiasm inadequately

---

*Albert Murray, *The Omni-Americans*, Outerbridge and Dienstfrey, 1970. Da Capo Press paperback, Plenum Pub. Co., 1990, p. 5.

counter-balanced by a literary sense of the ambiguities and absurdities inherent in all human experience.*

Leave it to a Negro to believe that literature is more valid than statistics! But with a group as targeted as blacks have been, an overre-
liance on agenda-driven statistics, coupled with a profound lack of
interest in black interiority, can only lead us all astray.

Increasingly, blacks are secure enough in their civic identities to
resist the siren call of statistical debate and are instead striving to provide that "everyday breeze-tasting sense of [black] life." We want to
talk about ourselves as ourselves. Preoccupied as we've been trying to
survive, we're almost as much of a mystery to ourselves as we are
to others, something Dr. Carter G. Woodson well understood when he
wrote, "The most inviting field of discovery and invention, then, is
the Negro himself, but he does not realize it."† But he's beginning to,
as this collection will prove. With more opportunities to talk about
ourselves in our own right, we'll be discovering and inventing enough
to give white narcissism a run for its money.

No process of black self-discovery would be legitimate without
significant offerings from the black diaspora, so this collection ferrets
out non-American black voices from around the world. American
blacks can't understand, or encounter, themselves in isolation from
their cousins, however connected or disconnected the various groups
remain. We hope they'll be intrigued to learn how modern-day slavery works in a Ghanian-American's family ("A Slow Emancipation"
by Kwame Anthony Appiah), or how one African American encounters Israel ("Searching for Zion" by Emily Raboteau).

I'll leave you with a final quote, the one that drove the selection of
essays to include throughout this process, the one with which Albert
Murray opened *The Omni-Americans*:

The individual stands in opposition to society, but he is nour-
ished by it. And it is far less important to know what differen-

*Ibid., p. 5.

†Carter G. Woodson, *The Mis-Education of the Negro*, Africa World Press, Inc., 1990, The Associated
Publishers, 1933, p. 139.

tiates him than what nourishes him. Like the genius, the individual is valuable for what there is within him . . . Every psychological life is an exchange, and the fundamental problem of the living individual is knowing upon what he intends to feed.*

The essays chosen for this collection were written by writers (we assume they're all black but haven't inquired) who've chosen to feed on life, on art, and on their own humanity. They hunt for the nubbin of truth at the heart of any successful artistic enterprise. But that's an artistic truth, not a statistical one or an agenda-driven one. It's just one that makes you reread an essay, then share it with a friend—that kind of truth. However informed by their blackness, these writers would be equally arresting on topics that flowed from their Jewishness, their Ecuadorean-ness, or their Scottishness. They let us taste the breezes of life, and they nourish us.

Enjoy.

Debra J. Dickerson

Guest Editor

*André Malraux, quoted in *The Omni-Americans*, by Albert Murray, opening quotation.

BEST
AFRICAN AMERICAN
ESSAYS: 2009

Friends, Family

Fired

CAN A FRIENDSHIP REALLY END
FOR NO GOOD REASON?

Emily Bernard

On a Saturday morning at 10:00 a.m., Beverly and I planned a trip
to Long Island, just us girls, to celebrate my upcoming marriage.
By that evening, Beverly and I were no longer friends. But I didn't
know that yet. At 7:00 p.m. I was sure there had been some mistake,
some misunderstanding, some bizarre but absolutely explainable
crossing of wires—she hadn't gotten my messages, she had fallen into
bed with some new boy, she had been kidnapped. I would continue to
turn various scenarios over in my head for the next several months until finally I had to accept the truth—I had been fired.

Fired described anything or anyone Beverly could no longer tolerate. Other friends of mine use the word *tired* to describe what they find
tedious. To be fired is much worse. Something "tired" is wearisome
but tolerable if the occasion calls for it. Something "fired" is beneath
contempt. In Beverly's lexicon there was only one thing worse than
being fired, and that was being *so* fired.

Perhaps her cold, bureaucratic language should have warned me that Beverly would charge through our friendship with the take-no-prisoners attitude of a corporate downsizer. Even in the dismal state of the current corporate climate, euphemisms are employed to indicate the end of a career. Workers are laid off, let go, granted extended vacations. Only Donald Trump and other actors bark "You're fired!" at their employees. When Beverly fired me, it was not as if I came to work and the locks had been changed or someone else was sitting at my desk. It was as if I came to work and work wasn't there anymore.

Seven years later, I still mourn the loss of this friendship. I may never discover what happened to turn Beverly away from me, but I have learned something else: mourning the loss of a friendship elicits little sympathy from others. In our culture, it seems, friendships are generally considered to be incidental—garnishes on the plate of *important* relationships, like those between family members and spouses. There are no institutions, no common rituals to support either the initiation or termination of bonds between friends. Because I take my friendships as seriously as I do my marriage, I put together an anthology of writings about friendships, specifically interracial ones. At this point, it might be helpful for me to say that Beverly is white and I am black. This fact has nothing to do with why Beverly and I are no longer friends, even though I often pretend that it does. "You know how hard it is," I sigh when people ask me why Beverly and I are not friends anymore. I do this to spare myself and others the shameful truth, which is that Beverly dumped me. This is a fact more meaningful than our racial difference could ever be.

For a friendship that ended so recklessly, it had begun very carefully. Beverly (not her real name) was a student in the first class I ever taught—a section of a lecture course on 19th-century American literature. The first day of class, Beverly slumped down in her seat and stared past me. I took in the creamy red hair, the dull blue eyes, the turquoise sandals, and emerald toenails. She had a round, chubby face and long, muscular calves. Angry guitar chords floated around her as she walked in; Liz Phair, it turned out. Her mind was on other things besides 19th-century American literature. I would later learn what they were: her looks, which mostly displeased her; her family, always in some state of chaos; her future; a man who didn't want her, but should have; her friendships, shifting seismically as she approached her last year of college. I recognized this girl; she was someone I had been.

Looking at her slumped in her seat like that, I pegged Beverly as apathetic, and I was partly right. Still, what she accomplished without sweat was miles beyond what anyone else her age was capable of—at least anyone I knew. Her writing was stylish, enlivening, fearless. I was intimidated; she was benevolent. Beverly appeared to be amused by my attempts to behave like a grownup, but she generously helped me uphold the ruse.

At the end of the semester, I saw Beverly at a bar where graduate students hung out. She was the youngest, smartest, most interesting person at the table. Right next to her, I would later learn, sat the man who didn't want her, but should have. Beverly looked at me and said, "Should we start being friends now, or should I take your class first?" I had just found out that I would be teaching my very own seminar the following semester. That these words constituted the first personal exchange between Beverly and me did not feel strange. "Take my class," I said. "We have the rest of our lives to be friends."

She took the class. We were faithful to the boundaries prescribed by our respective roles until the day I handed in her final grade (an A). The next day, or very soon after that, we began a routine of hours-long phone calls, copious e-mails, and ponderous discussions during extensive walks. This routine continued for six years. Beverly could imitate anyone. She so accurately mimicked the voices and verbal tics of others that when I met the people in her stories, I had to keep my jaw from literally hitting the floor. Nothing could make Beverly laugh harder than to have someone say to her, "My jaw *literally* hit the floor." She loved language, and she delighted in the linguistic foibles of everyday speech. She constantly crafted and revised her own idiom. "This weather is beyond fired," she said as we looked out of her apartment window during a snowstorm. I nodded, giddy to be with her, eager for whatever she would say next.

I moved to Brooklyn, but Beverly and I still talked all the time. We watched the first season of *Big Brother* and at least one *Real World* marathon together on the phone. Early on, when I was dating someone I really liked, he and I set Beverly up with a friend of his, and that established a precedent. We played central roles in each other's romantic life, and she counseled me through numerous romantic disappointments. Years later, when I introduced her to the man who would become my husband, she made the pivotal observation, "I've never seen you be so much yourself with someone." When my husband met her, he used words like "exquisite" and "charming." He could see the rare jewel that she was, and that made me fall in love with him a little bit more.

Beverly was several years younger than I was, but I looked up to her. Once, as I sat in the passenger seat of her father's decaying blue Volvo, she passionately expounded on the parallels between the movie *Jerry Maguire* and the Horatio Alger myth, while deftly weaving in and out of rush-hour Manhattan traffic. "You're not afraid of anything," I blurted, feeling very much the child of the sleepy, suburban streets of Nashville, Tennessee, where I grew up. Beverly grew up in Manhattan, and her language and confidence seemed like the realization of my teenage fantasies about citizens of New York City. Maybe she became bored and alienated by how often I was awestruck by things about her that she considered utterly mundane.

I was not the first person Beverly fired. Earlier there had been a close friend in college whom Beverly suddenly and violently deemed her nemesis. Then, there was a co-worker who was one day an intimate and the next someone Beverly could no longer tolerate. Her reasons for rejecting her college friend seemed shaky to me, but her treatment of her co-worker I found chilling. Without explanation, Beverly stopped returning her phone calls and never opened a letter the woman sent her right after the phone calls ceased. Beverly was never particularly forgiving, but now she was trying on outright viciousness like a slick new suit. She would grow out of it, I thought.

I believed I was immune to Beverly's caprice. Like me, she had early on experienced ruptures in her most intimate relationships. Like her, I understood the irresistible, resonating power of silence. I learned about the power of silence where many people do: at home. In my family, feuds always ended in silence. Each and every argument clambered recklessly to a crescendo whose denouement was always the silent treatment. You knew in the fight that you had gone too far, but maybe you had actually gone somewhere even beyond that. You waited out the silence in fear that you would never be spoken to again. The fear was as terrifying as it was thrilling, like a roller coaster ride, only not nearly as safe.

At some point I developed an addiction to these sensations. For this reason, among others, I married a forgiving, even-tempered man who does not hold grudges. Before I met my husband, I nursed a serious crush on Jasper, a handsome postdoc from the Caribbean. We met through a mutual friend at about the same time I met Beverly. Jasper was worldly and vivacious and at times capable of a surprising sweetness. Jasper and our mutual friend, Steve, decided to share an apartment. Several weeks later Jasper kicked Steve out and never spoke a word to him again. He detailed his complaints about Steve, but none of them, I thought, justified such a radical act. Still, I believed Jasper when he looked me in the eye and assured me that he would never treat me that way. I was mistaken.

My experience with Jasper taught me two things. One: even minor relationships can end in ways that are devastating. Two: at the moment when someone makes the promise that he will never, ever betray you—particularly when you can see the carcasses of multiple, rashly aborted relationships right behind him—at that very moment, you should consider yourself betrayed.

Marriage to a compassionate man has encouraged me to rethink much of my own hasty behavior in past friendships. Not long ago I got back in touch with Jack, a white man who was once a close friend. We met in college and decided to attend the same graduate school. We found apartments within walking distance of each other. On most evenings one of us called the other and asked, "What are we doing for dinner tonight?"

I dumped Jack about a year into graduate school when I befriended several women with leftist convictions and feminist politics that I determined to adopt as my own. Jack was a good old boy who had a penchant for off-color jokes and impolite observations. I did as well, but I did not think these aspects of my personality would appeal to my new friends. So I put them in a grave alongside my friendship with Jack and sealed it.

I continue to be humbled by how easily Jack allows me back into his life after all these years. We have picked up as if my bad behavior never took place. When he expresses regret about how we "fell out of touch," I am too ashamed to confess that I dumped him deliberately and that I did so because one day I decided that he looked nothing like the person I was trying to become, and I resolved not to forgive him for that.

Beverly and I were friends for six years. In the last months of our friendship, I saw her go through the most remarkable transformation I have ever witnessed. First, she shed so many pounds that even my typically circumspect husband told her that he thought she was too thin. In truth, she was no thinner than any other conventionally attractive young woman out there, and I believed that was exactly what she was going for. She had chucked the weight as well as all the vestiges of eccentricity in her wardrobe. When she looked in the mirror, she used unforgiving words to describe her body and acted annoyed when I told her she was wrong. She began to lead a fabulous big-city life—the kind of life she used to mock, and she seemed to have buried her ironic distance from it. I sensed that she had lost the ability to laugh at herself altogether. She began to fantasize out loud about enhancement cosmetic surgery. It was around this time that she dumped her co-worker. She started dating a man she described as beautiful but dumb. I listened to her stories and pretended to understand whatever was happening. I thought if I just waited out this phase, she would come back to me. She said that the new man was not only dumb but also possibly racist. But he was beautiful. His teeth were perfect.

Beverly and I met at the opening of a friend's restaurant. I introduced her to two elegant, stately black women I considered role models. Beverly had heard me talk about them often, and I was pleased to have an occasion to introduce her to them. When I did, she pasted two index fingers together and pointed them at the women like a pistol. She said, "Okay, so which is which?"

The openness drained from the faces of the women. I admired

them so, and here I was bringing such rudeness, like the rotting carcass of a rat, right to their doorstep. I hated Beverly for a moment, but the moment passed. I knew she was nervous, nothing more. I steered her away, as quickly as I could, and later I apologized to the women, who graciously waved away my words of regret.

Sometimes I tell this story when people ask, "Who was that girl you used to hang around with? What happened to her?" Depending on my audience, I tell this story as a tale about racial difference, about the unbridgeable gap between black and white.

"You know how it goes," I say in conclusion. Sometimes I embellish the story, and make Beverly look more or less obnoxious, depending on my mood. But if Beverly hadn't dumped me, I would never have repeated this story to anyone, certainly not here.

What I have come to believe about interracial friendships is this: when a friendship ends between two people of different races, it is easy to point to race as the reason. It is easy, and it is misleading, as race itself is often misleading. I know that I hold on to the memory of that unfortunate moment because it puzzled and troubled me, but I also hold on to it because it is a convenient fixture on which to hang the pain and anger I feel about the fact that Beverly dumped me. This memory, like most memories, is as meaningful as it is meaningless.

Beverly and I talked honestly about race; it was part of the glue that bonded us. I loved her, in part, because she was not the kind of white person who saw race as the most significant aspect of an interracial friendship. She was also not the kind of white person who looked at black and white people and saw no difference. Beverly loved black cultural style for what was curious, appealing, and, to her, *different* about it. But she also saw me, too, for who I was, both within and beyond my racial identity.

"Membership has its privileges," I say when I walk down the street with a friend and exchange a nod or a greeting with a black stranger. Beverly had a black friend at her prep school who said this to her when she once asked the friend why she had nodded hello to a black stranger. I loved that Beverly noticed that her friend had said hello to a stranger who was black, that she recognized it as a custom among the black people she knew and observed, and that she had asked her friend about it. I loved that Beverly noticed the same thing about me and said out loud to me, "Membership has its privileges," one day when she saw me greet a black stranger. I loved that her comment caught me so much by surprise that I stopped and faced her, and we stood there and laughed unrestrainedly as a traffic light changed, and changed again. Maybe it is strange and possibly sad to reveal how much I treasured in a white person her interest in and ease around black people, but I have found it rare enough in my life to call it significant.

I thought that the ease between us meant that Beverly and I would always be friends. I never considered that it could be otherwise, and even now this realization surprises me. I grew up around adult women who believed that men had ruined their lives. Therefore, in romance, I have always proceeded with suspicion. In friendships, I have taken risks, been vulnerable, asked to know and be known. As a result, it has been in friendship that I have learned the pleasures and dangers of intimacy: the pleasures of loving openly and recklessly; the dangers of having it end before you are ready.

———————

Fired. In our sixth year of friendship, we met at the train station, and walked together down a New York street. She looked radiant, and I told her so. We sat in a restaurant and talked about men. I gave her advice. We planned a trip to Long Island. She gave me keys to her apartment and told me she had not checked them. She would be in town that night, she said, so I should call her cell phone if the keys didn't work. They didn't work. I called and called. It was raining, and I left self-pitying messages on her voice mail as I waited on the wet stoop. Eventually, I called another friend who offered me his couch, and I left a final, icy message for Beverly. "Don't bother calling back," I said. I turned off my cell phone to punish her. As I went to sleep, I imagined all the cooing, apologetic messages Beverly would leave on my voice mail. I was wrong. The next day, I boarded the train and headed back to Pennsylvania where I was living. I fumed for a few days, and then called Beverly again. She never called back.

Days turned into weeks. I worried. My husband wondered if she was depressed over something else, so I left a message reminding her how much I cared about her. "I'm here for you," I said. Weeks turned into months. Back then, my husband was my fiancé, and when friends threw us an engagement party, he slipped a note inside Beverly's invitation asking her to come. She did not respond. Months before, he and Beverly had shopped together for my engagement ring.

I sent her my own note, part accusatory, part humiliated, replete with outraged pride and sorrow, but ambiguous enough, I thought, so that she would see that reconciliation was not only possible, it was what I wanted. She did not respond. I did not send her an invitation to our wedding, not because I did not want her there, but because I believed one more round of silence from her would break my heart for good. But it didn't matter, really, because my heart was broken anyway.

It has been almost seven years since I last talked to Beverly. During these years I have reassured myself with memories of all the ways Beverly was obviously trying to transform her life. Maybe the demise of our friendship was just unfortunate fallout from the battle she was waging with herself. These days I am nearly satisfied with that explanation. But there were other days, not long ago, when I would get into my car to mourn her in private, where no one could judge me for missing my friend. One night I drove during a rainstorm for hours, crying and pounding on the steering wheel, startled by the depth of my grief and grateful that the rain and darkness shielded my display from other drivers. This is true. But it is also true that, over the years, I have heard from Beverly through other people, and I am still too proud to take up her indirect invitations to get back in touch.

Seven years. Periodically I come across the evidence of our friendship: unreturned books, birthday cards, the set of faulty keys. Then there are the memories that surface without invitation: sure hands on the steering wheel of a decaying blue Volvo; a cloud of guitar chords around a head of creamy red hair; a membership with privileges; two fingers pointed like a pistol.

I miss it all.

Gray Shawl

Walter Mosley

My mother is standing near the landing dock of a summer house in New Hampshire. There's a weather-beaten rowboat tied to the end of the quay.

"What did you say?" she asks me.

"The driver called, Mom. He's going to be late."

I think of the tall man in the black suit and the Lincoln Town Car on a dusty dirt road. Oddly, I feel sorry for him.

A bird somewhere on the lake makes a strangled cry, a call I once would have thought beautiful, and I remember the librarian wanting me to talk to urban teens about the expanded horizons they face.

"Say something inspirational," the woman on the telephone had said. "That's all."

"He's going to be what?"

"Late," I say to my mother. "He's run into traffic. Weekenders."

"Oh."

I turn away from the memory of the phone conversation and see that my mother has moved to the end of the dock. She's wearing the gray shawl that my grandmother wore after her husband, Harry, died and she moved to L.A. from New York.

My mother was a wonderful swimmer. As a child I watched her

cleave through the water not like a human being at all. No splashing or laughing, just long strokes and perfect parallel synchronicity.

"Where are they going?" my mother asks.

"Who?"

"The weekenders," she says, exasperated. After fifty-three years I know that even her frustration is not with me. "Always running and going this way and that way. Where do they think they're going anyway?"

A light mist is enveloping the houses across the lake. I wonder idly if our temporary dwelling looks as hazy to them.

Mom is sitting on the wooden ladder that leads down to the boat.

"Be careful."

"What?"

"You could fall."

"When is the driver coming?" she asks.

"In a little while."

"I used to swim like a fish," she says. "When I was younger than you I could swim across this lake in no time. I had long hair and so I had to wear a—a—what do you call it?"

"Swimming cap."

My mother smiles at me: a memory of a rubber hat and a summer camp and Harry who could walk on his hands and smell out pleurisy, heart disease, and walking pneumonia.

"You are most like my father," she says. "When is he coming?"

"Granddad?"

"The driver."

"He's late."

"My father was a diagnostician," my mother says, her left foot, now bare, kicking the green water. "He never used to touch a patient, just watch them and sniff the air."

"I'm sure he'll be here soon, Mom. Maybe you should come away from the water."

All kinds of things may loom on the horizon. I write these words on a yellow pad by the afternoon light.

My mother is in the boat now. The driver has called again. He's gotten lost somewhere at the Corners and has to retrace his route. He asked me if I knew the way. But I was driven to this cottage on the misty lake. On the drive my mother was nervous and I talked to her so that she wouldn't worry about the driver getting lost. Because of that I didn't pay attention to where we were going.

War, for instance, famine, fascism, disease . . .

My mother says something but I can't make it out.

My generation has broken this world . . .

"Can you hear me?" I think she says.

I put the pad under my arm and walk across the tar path toward the dock. My mother's rowboat is maybe eight feet from the edge.

"Pull me in."

I reach out as far as I can but the boat is farther still.

"I can't."

She grins, shaking her head at my impotence.

"Come in the water and pull me to shore."

The memory comes easily. My mother young and beautiful and me like a squiggly tadpole. She was in the water, at Santa Monica Beach, up to her waist. I had to stand on my toes to keep my nose in the air. I was laughing and frightened.

"Do you want to learn to swim?" she asked.

She put her hand under my diaphragm and all I knew were her breasts and arms. I grabbed on and laughed crazily.

Pushing me toward the shore she said, "You're too silly to learn how."

"I can't swim, Mom," I say. "And the water is too deep."

She grins again and shakes her head. "What will I do, then?"

"It's a small lake," I say. "Maybe the driver can swim."

"When is he coming?"

I come awake in a hotel room at 4:30 in the afternoon, in Philadelphia where 350 teenagers are coming to hear my inspirational words.

Children scare me. They want the truth, can't imagine anything else, and all the adults do is lie. The main lesson young people learn is that they are being lied to.

I'm tired and unprepared. What can I tell them, the children? I can say that their world is broken, that I broke it, that their horizons are crowded with dangerous prospects, that I and my generation will grow old and decrepit and expect them to make things right.

We will blame you for the wars we can no longer understand, I write on my yellow pad at the edge of the jetty.

"What time is it?" my mother asks.

"What?"

"What time is it?"

"He's about ten minutes late," I say. "It may take another hour."

The mist had lifted for a while but now I can't even see across to the other side. My mother is ten feet away floating in the lake, wearing a gray shawl that makes her look like a frog waiting for an unsuspecting fly.

"It's cold," she says.

"Can you paddle in with your hands?"

"Too cold. Can't you just dog-paddle out?"

The mist makes the lake seem vast. It's late in the season and most of the houses are empty.

My mother doesn't want to leave but she hopes that the driver will get here soon.

"What are you writing?" she asks me.

"Inspirations."

"Huh?"

"A talk that I have to give in Philadelphia."

"Oh."

"Do you want to hear it, Mom?"

"It's getting dark," she replies.

"You will inherit our mistakes," I read from the legal pages. "You will have to fix the world that we've broken.

"From the air you breathe to the tennis shoes you buy you will be responsible for the world that my generation has profited from. Your horizons will be China ascendant and Africa with its head bowed down. Your horizons will be India Indians taking jobs from you on the net and over the phone. Your horizon will be the extraordinary task of making peace with Islam."

"That's terrible," my mother says, cutting me off.

"What is?"

"I don't know," she says shifting in the boat, making it move far-ther from the shore. "Nothing works right anymore."

And I see her in my sleeping mind's eye swimming in the blue Pacific, sleek and true like a white dolphin.

———————

There's pornography on the pay-per-view TV in the hotel room. But the library is paying the bill and they want me to speak to children and so I take a shower instead.

My head hurts. The speech will never get written if I keep on sleeping. Maybe I should lie to them? What difference would it make?

———————

I dream now about the driver. Gray-haired and dignified, he's coming for my mother down the dirt roads through half-empty resort towns, around nameless lakes. In my dream he loves her, wants to take her away from me. She asked me to call him and now I don't want him to come. Neither do I want her to stay here in the boat in the water or in the cottage by the lake. My head hurts even here.

"Is that him?" my mother says.

A car is coming on the tar road. Its headlights illuminate the foggy mist with bluish white high beams. It rushes by us making the sound of the wind outside my room at night.

"It's a red car, Mom. Not him."

"When will he get here?" she asks.

I look out at the lake, which is now completely covered in fog. I can't see my mother, only hear her.

"Can you see me?" I ask.

"Yes . . . a little bit, I think. Yes. A little."

The phone in the cottage begins to ring.

"Who is it?" my mother asks. "Who's calling? Is it the driver?"

I jump up quickly at the edge of the small pier, dropping my pages into the lake.

"What was that?" my mother asks.

"Nothing," I say. The phone rings again. "I'm going up to the house a minute, Mom. I'll be right back. Don't worry. The lake's not very big."

"I'm not worried," she says as I run across the tar road toward the porch.

I miss the first stair and fall down hard.

My forehead feels wet like it's bleeding but I don't pay any attention to it. I get up and run into the house. The phone's still ringing.

"Hello?"

"The fog is so thick that I can't see the signs," the driver says. "I can't even tell where the signs are to stop the car and get out and read them."

"Where are you?" I ask.

"I don't know but I'll keep going. I know she'll be afraid without me there."

"It's okay," I say, peeved at his self-importance. "I'm here. I'm taking care of her."

"But she needs me to take her," he says. "You can't even drive."

I can't even swim.

"She's fine," I say. "You could go home and come back tomorrow."

"No. I better come now. She needs me."

"No. No she doesn't. She'd like to stay a day or two more."

"Let me talk to her," the driver says. "Let me see what she needs."

"No!" I shout. "No, no, no. She's my mother. She's my problem."

I'm yelling so loud that I wake myself up again. My head's killing me. There are yellow legal pages all over the bed. It's 5:01 and my semiconsciousness is like a stone dropped in the water.

"Who was that?" my mother asks.

My head is still bleeding. I don't even remember hanging up the phone.

"I love you, Mom," I call into the fog.

"Who?" my mother asks.

"You."

"Who was it?"

"I love you, Mom."

"I hear you. But who was it?"

"The driver."

"Is he all right?"

"He's fine. He's driving. I told him that you wanted to stay another day."

"But is he still coming?"

"Tomorrow. He'll come get you tomorrow."

"But will he come and stay the night?"

"No, Mom. We'll stay here together. You and me."

"I can't see you," she says.

I jump in the lake, splashing wildly, kicking and slapping the water.

"Are you all right?" she calls.

I hear these words and reach out for her voice. Nothing. I sink down. My nose fills with water. I come up gasping, panicked. I reach out again and this time I grab the edge of her rowboat.

My mother screams. "Help! The boat is turning, turning over!"

I hold on, rocking my aged mother's boat. She yells and cries out. "Help!"

"It's okay, Mom! It's settling down."

"What's wrong with you? You almost killed me," she says.

I can't see her. I can't even see the boat. I only feel the side that I've grabbed on to. I'm afraid to pull myself in, afraid that the rowboat will capsize and my mother, the white dolphin, will drown.

"What's wrong with you?" she asks from the foggy void. "Are you crazy, jumping in the water like that?"

The water is very cold and I have no sense of direction. I kick my legs and move the boat but the pier doesn't find my hand. I can hear the water lapping on the shore but I never reach it.

"Oh," my mother says every time I kick and the boat wobbles. "Oh."

"Mom?"

"What?" Her exasperation is with me now.

"I love you."

"Bring me to the pier then."

I want to do this but the void only grows larger. My arms and legs are cramping and at the same time going numb. I kick as hard as I can, reaching out.

Finally I grab on to reeds growing at the shore but my other hand has gone numb and lets go of the boat.

"Are you there?" my mother says.

"Yes," I say, shivering at the shore.

"I can't see you."

"Don't worry, Mom. I'm here."

"But I can't see you."

The fog is everywhere now. The tar road and the house are hidden in white vastness. I can hear the water and my mother, my own breath and the motor of a far-off automobile that doesn't seem to come any closer.

When I open my eyes I'm standing behind a blond wood podium in front of an audience of 350 adolescents. I'm giving a talk. It seems as if I've been here for a while, lecturing these children about things I don't know.

They are quiet on the whole, which surprises me. Many of them are looking at me as if they thought I had something to say.

". . . all we can do is love you and wish you well," I am saying.

The children break out into applause.

I scan the room for my young mother, a white dolphin among so many dark and eager faces. I am certain that she is there, somewhere, but hidden behind the children, plowed into their soil.

A woman touches my shoulder.

"Thank you," she says and puts light pressure on my arm.

Her smile says that it's time to go.

I pass from the stage alone.

REAL FOOD

~)))(o

Chimamanda Ngozi Adichie

I was nine years old, sitting stiffly at the dining table in my blue-and-white school uniform, and across from me sat my mother, who had come home from work at the university registry, elegant in her swishy skirt, smelling of Poison perfume and saying she wanted to watch me eat. I still do not know who told her that I was skipping lunch before school. Perhaps it was the houseboy, Fide. Perhaps it was my little brother Kenechukwu, who went to school in the morning and came home just before I left. The firm set of her mouth told me that I had no choice but to eat the *garri* and soup placed on the table. I made the sign of the cross. I plucked a morsel from the soft lump of *garri*. I lightly molded it with my fingers. I dipped it into the soup. I swallowed. My throat itched. I disliked all the variants of this quintessential Nigerian food, whether made from corn, cassava, or yams, whether cooked or stirred or pounded in a mortar until they became a soft mash. It was jokingly called "swallow," because one swallowed the morsels without chewing; it was easy to tell that a person chewing *garri* was a foreigner.

"Hurry up," my mother said. "You will be late for school." We had *garri* for lunch every day except Sunday, when we had rice and stew and sometimes a lush salad that contained everything from baked beans to boiled eggs and was served with dollops of creamy dressing.

The soups gave some variety to lunch: the yellowish *egusi,* made of ground melon seeds and vegetables; *onugbu,* rich with dark-green bitterleaf; *okro,* with its sticky sauce; *nsala,* with beef chunks floating in a thin herb-filled broth. I disliked them all.

That afternoon, it was *egusi* soup. My mother's eyes were steady behind her glasses. "Are you playing with that food or eating it?" she asked. I said I was eating. Finally, I finished and said, "Mummy, thank you," as all well-brought-up Igbo children were supposed to after a meal. I had just stepped outside the carpeted dining area and onto the polished concrete floor of the passage when my stomach churned and recoiled and the *garri* and soup rushed up my throat.

"Go upstairs and rinse your mouth," my mother said.

When I came down, Fide was cleaning up the watery yellowish mess, and I was sorry he had to and I was too disgusted to look. After I told my mother that I never ate *garri* before school, that on Saturdays I waited until nobody was looking to wrap my *garri* in a piece of paper and slip it into the dustbin, I expected her to scold me. But she muttered in Igbo, "You want hunger to kill you," and then told me to get a Fanta from the fridge.

Years later, she asked me, "What does *garri* really do to you?" "It scratches my throat," I told her, and she laughed. It became a standing line of family teasing. "Does this scratch your throat?" my brothers would ask. Following that afternoon, my mother had boiled yams, soft and white and crumbly, made for my lunch; I ate them dipped in palm oil. Sometimes she would come home with a few wraps of warm *okpa,* which remains my favorite food: a simple, orange-colored, steamed pie of white beans and palm oil that tastes best cooked in banana leaves. We didn't make it at home, perhaps because it was not native to our part of Igboland. Or perhaps because those we bought on the roadside from the women who carried them in large basins on their heads were too good to surpass.

I wish I ate *garri.* It is important to the people I love: My late grandmother used to want to have *garri* three times a day. My brother's idea of a perfect meal is pounded yam. My father once came home from a conference in Paris, and when I asked how it had gone he said that he had missed real food. In Igbo, another word for "swallow" is simply "food," so that one might overhear a sentence like "The food was well pounded, but the soup was not tasty." My brothers, with affectionate mockery, sometimes ask whether it is possible for a person who does not eat swallow to be authentically Igbo, Nigerian, African.

On New Year's Day of the year I turned thirteen, we went to my Aunt Dede's house for lunch. "Did you remember?" my mother asked my aunt while gesturing toward me. My aunt nodded. There was a small bowl of *jollof* rice, soft-cooked in an oily tomato sauce, for me. My brothers praised the *onugbu* soup—"Auntie, this is soup that you washed your hands well before cooking"—and I wished that I, too, could say something. Then my boisterous Auntie Rosa arrived, her wrapper always seeming to be just about to slip off her waist. After she had exchanged hugs with everyone, she settled down with her pounded yam and noticed that I was eating rice. "Why are you not eating food?" she asked in Igbo. I said I did not eat swallow. She smiled and said to my mother, "Oh, you know she is not like us local people. She is foreign."

ENTERTAINMENT, SPORTS, THE ARTS

HIP-HOP PLANET

⟿⟆⟲

James McBride

This is my nightmare: My daughter comes home with a guy and says, "Dad, we're getting married." And he's a rapper, with a mouthful of gold teeth, a do-rag on his head, muscles popping out his arms, and a thug attitude. And then the nightmare gets deeper, because before you know it, I'm hearing the pitter-patter of little feet, their off-spring, cascading through my living room, cascading through my life, drowning me with the sound of my own hypocrisy, because when I was young, I was a knucklehead, too, hearing my own music, my own sounds. And so I curse the day I saw his face, which is a reflection of my own, and I rue the day I heard his name, because I realize to my horror that rap—music seemingly without melody, sensibility, instruments, verse, or harmony, music with no beginning, end, or middle, music that doesn't even seem to be music—rules the world. It is no longer my world. It is his world. And I live in it. I live on a hip-hop planet.

HIGH-STEPPING

I remember when I first heard rap. I was standing in the kitchen at a party in Harlem. It was 1980. A friend of mine named Bill had just gone on the blink. He slapped a guy, a total stranger, in the face right in front of me. I can't remember why. Bill was a fellow student. He was short-circuiting. Problem was, the guy he slapped was a big guy, a dude wearing a do-rag who'd crashed the party with three friends, and, judging by the fury on their faces, there would be no Martin Luther King moments in our immediate future.

There were no white people in the room, though I confess I wished there had been, if only to hide the paleness of my own frightened face. We were black and Latino students about to graduate from Columbia University's journalism school, having learned the whos, whats, wheres, whens, and whys of American reporting. But the real storytellers of the American experience came from the world of the guy that Bill had just slapped. They lived less than a mile from us in the South Bronx. They had no journalism degrees. No money. No credibility. What they did have, however, was talent.

Earlier that night, somebody tossed a record on the turntable, which sent my fellow students stumbling onto the dance floor, howling with delight, and made me, a jazz lover, cringe. It sounded like a broken record. It was a version of an old hit record called "Good Times," the same four bars looped over and over. And on top of this loop, a kid spouted a rhyme about how he was the best disc jockey in the world. It was called "Rapper's Delight." I thought it was the most ridiculous thing I'd ever heard. More ridiculous than Bill slapping that stranger.

Bill survived that evening, but in many ways, I did not. For the next 26 years, I high-stepped past that music the way you step over a crack in the sidewalk. I heard it pounding out of cars and alleyways from Paris to Abidjan, yet I never listened. It came rumbling out of boomboxes from Johannesburg to Osaka, yet I pretended not to hear. I must have strolled past the corner of St. James Place and Fulton Street in my native Brooklyn where a fat kid named Christopher Wallace, aka Biggie Smalls, stood amusing his friends with rhyme, a hundred times, yet I barely noticed. I high-stepped away from that music for 26 years because it was everything I thought it was, and more than I ever dreamed it would be, but mostly, because it held everything I wanted to leave behind.

In doing so, I missed the most important cultural event in my lifetime.

Not since the advent of swing jazz in the 1930s has an American music exploded across the world with such overwhelming force. Not since the Beatles invaded America and Elvis packed up his blue suede shoes has a music crashed against the world with such outrage. This defiant culture of song, graffiti, and dance, collectively known as hip-hop, has ripped popular music from its moorings in every society it has permeated. In Brazil, rap rivals samba in popularity. In China, teens spray-paint graffiti on the Great Wall. In France it has been blamed, unfairly, for the worst civil unrest that country has seen in decades.

Its structure is unique, complex, and at times bewildering. Whatever music it eats becomes part of its vocabulary, and as the commercial world falls into place behind it to gobble up the powerful slop in its wake, it metamorphoses into the Next Big Thing. It is a music that defies definition, yet defines our collective societies in immeasurable ways. To many of my generation, despite all attempts to exploit it, belittle it, numb it, classify it, and analyze it, hip-hop remains an enigma, a clarion call, a cry of "I am" from the youth of the world. We'd be wise, I suppose, to start paying attention.

BURNING MAN

Imagine a burning man. He is on fire. He runs into the room. You put out the flames. Then another burning man arrives. You put him out and go about your business. Then two, three, four, five, ten appear. You extinguish them all, send them to the hospital. Then imagine no one bothers to examine why the men caught fire in the first place. That is the story of hip-hop.

It is a music dipped in the boiling cauldron of race and class, and for that reason it is clouded with mystics, snake oil salesmen, two-bit scholars, race-baiters, and sneaker salesmen, all professing to know the facts, to be "real," when the reality of race is like shifting sand, dependent on time, place, circumstance, and who's telling the history. Here's the real story: In the mid-1970s, New York City was nearly broke. The public school system cut funding for the arts drastically. Gone were the days when you could wander into the band room, rent a clarinet for a minimal fee, and march it home to squeal on it and drive your parents nuts.

The kids of the South Bronx and Harlem came up with something else. In the summer of 1973, at 1595 East 174th Street in the Bronx River Houses, a black teenager named Afrika Bambaataa stuck a speaker in his mother's first-floor living room window, ran a wire to the turntable in his bedroom, and set the housing project of 3,000 people alight with party music. At the same time, a Jamaican teenager named Kool DJ Herc was starting up the scene in the East Bronx, while a technical whiz named Grandmaster Flash was rising to prominence a couple of miles south. The Bronx became a music magnet for Puerto Ricans, Jamaicans, Dominicans, and black Americans from the surrounding areas. Fab 5 Freddy, Kurtis Blow, and Melle Mel were only a few of the pioneers. Grand Wizard Theodore, Kool DJ AJ, the Cold Crush Brothers, Spoony Gee, and the Rock Steady Crew of B-boys showed up to "battle"—dance, trade quips and rhymes, check out each other's records and equipment—not knowing as they strolled through the doors of the community center near Bambaataa's mother's apartment that they were writing musical history. Among them was an MC named Lovebug Starski, who was said to utter the phrase "hip-hop" between breaks to keep time.

This is how it worked: One guy, the DJ, played records on two turntables. One guy—or girl—served as master of ceremonies, or MC. The DJs learned to move the record back and forth under the needle to create a "scratch" or to drop the needle on the record where the beat was the hottest, playing "the break" over and over to keep the folks dancing. The MCs "rapped" over the music to keep the party going. One MC sought to outchat the other. Dance styles were created— "locking" and "popping" and "breaking." Graffiti artists spread the word of the "I" because the music was all about identity: I am the best. I spread the most love in the Bronx, in Harlem, in Queens. The focus initially was not on the MCs, but on the dancers, or B-boys. Commercial radio ignored it. DJs sold mix tapes out of the back of station wagons. "Rapper's Delight" by the Sugarhill Gang—the song I first heard at that face-slapping party in Harlem—broke the music onto radio in 1979.

THAT IS THE SHORT HISTORY

The long history is that spoken-word music made its way here on slave ships from West Africa centuries ago: Ethnomusicologists trace hip-hop's roots to the dance, drum, and song of West African griots, or storytellers, its pairing of word and music the manifestation of the painful journey of slaves who survived the middle passage. The ring shouts, field hollers, and spirituals of early slaves drew on common

elements of African music, such as call and response and improvisa-
tion. "Speech-song has been part of black culture for a long, long
time," says Samuel A. Floyd, director of the Center for Black Music
Research at Columbia College in Chicago. The "dozens," "toasts,"
and "signifying" of black Americans—verbal dueling, rhyming, self-
deprecating tales, and stories of blacks outsmarting whites—were defensive, empowering strategies.

You can point to jazz musicians such as Oscar Brown, Jr., Edgar
"Eddie" Jefferson, and Louis Armstrong, and blues greats such as
John Lee Hooker, and easily find the foreshadowing of rap music in
the verbal play of their work. Black performers such as poet Nikki
Giovanni and Gil Scott-Heron, a pianist and vocalist who put spoken
political lyrics to music (most famously in "The Revolution Will Not
Be Televised"), elevated spoken word to a new level.

But the artist whose work arguably laid the groundwork for rap as
we know it was Amiri Baraka, a beat poet out of Allen Ginsberg's
Greenwich Village scene. In the late 1950s and '60s, Baraka performed
with shrieks, howls, cries, stomps, verse floating ahead of or behind
the rhythm, sometimes in staccato syncopation. It was performance
art, delivered in a dashiki and Afro, in step with the anger of a bold and
sometimes frightening nationalistic black movement, and it inspired
what might be considered the first rap group, the Last Poets.

I was 13 when I first heard the Last Poets in 1970. They scared me.
To black America, they were like the relatives you hoped wouldn't
show up at your barbecue because the boss was there—the old Aunt
Clementine who would arrive, get drunk, and pull out her dentures. My
parents refused to allow us to play their music in our house—so my siblings waited until my parents went to work and played it anyway. They
were the first musical group I heard to use the N-word on a record, with
songs like "N—— Are Scared of Revolution." In a world where
blacks were evolving from "Negroes" to "blacks," and the assassina-
tions of civil rights leaders Malcolm X and Martin Luther King, Jr., still
reverberated in the air like a shotgun blast, the Last Poets embodied
black power. Their records consisted of percussion and spoken-word
rhyme. They were wildly popular in my neighborhood. Their debut
recording sold 400,000 records in three months, says Last Poet member
Umar Bin Hassan. "No videos, no radio play, strictly word of mouth."
The group's demise coincided with hip-hop's birth in the 1970s.

It's unlikely that the Last Poets ever dreamed the revolution they sang of would take the form it has. "We were about the movement," Abiodun Oyewole, a founder of the group, says. "A lot of today's rappers have talent. But a lot of them are driving the car in the wrong direction."

THE CROSSOVER

Highways wrap around the city of Dayton, Ohio, like a ribbon bow-tied on a box of chocolates from the local Esther Price candy factory. They have six ladies at the plant who do just that: Tie ribbons around boxes all day. Henry Rosenkranz can tell you about it. "I love candy," says Henry, a slim white teenager in glasses and a hairnet, as he strolls the factory, bucket in hand. His full-time after-school job is mopping the floors.

Henry is a model American teenager—and the prototypical consumer at which the hip-hop industry is squarely aimed, which has his parents sitting up in their seats. The music that was once the purview of black America has gone white and gone commercial all at once. A sea of white faces now rises up to greet rap groups as they perform, many of them teenagers like Henry, a NASCAR fanatic and self-described redneck. "I live in Old North Dayton," he says. "It's a white, redneck area. But hip-hop is so prominent with country people . . . if you put them behind a curtain and hear them talk, you won't know if they're black or white. There's a guy I work with, when Kanye West sings about a gold digger, he can relate because he's paying alimony and child support."

Obviously, it's not just working-class whites, but also affluent, suburban kids who identify with this music with African-American roots. A white 16-year-old hollering rap lyrics at the top of his lungs from the driver's seat of his dad's late-model Lexus may not have the same rationale to howl at the moon as a working-class kid whose parents can't pay for college, yet his own anguish is as real to him as it gets. What attracts white kids to this music is the same thing that prompted outraged congressmen to decry jazz during the 1920s and Tipper Gore to campaign decades later against violent and sexually explicit lyrics: life on the other side of the tracks; its "cool" or illicit factor, which black Americans, like it or not, are always perceived to possess.

Hip-hop has continually changed form, evolving from party music to social commentary with the 1982 release of Grandmaster Flash and the Furious Five's "The Message." Today, alternative hip-hop artists continue to produce socially conscious songs, but most commercial rappers spout violent lyrics that debase women and gays. Beginning with the so-called gangsta rap of the '90s, popularized by the still unsolved murders of rappers Biggie Smalls and Tupac Shakur, the genre has become dominated by rappers who brag about their lives of crime. 50 Cent, the hip-hop star of the moment, trumpets his sexual exploits and boasts that he has been shot nine times.

"People call hip-hop the MTV music now," scoffs Chuck D, of Public Enemy, known for its overtly political rap. "It's Big Brother controlling you. To slip something in there that's indigenous to the roots, that pays homage to the music that came before us, it's the Mount Everest of battles."

Most rap songs unabashedly function as walking advertisements for luxury cars, designer clothes, and liquor. Agenda Inc., a "pop culture brand strategy agency," listed Mercedes-Benz as the number one brand mentioned in *Billboard*'s top 20 singles in 2005. Hip-hop sells so much Hennessy cognac, listed at number six, that the French makers, deader than yesterday's beer a decade ago, are now rolling in suds. The company even sponsored a contest to win a visit to its plant in France with a famous rapper.

In many ways, the music represents an old dream. It's the pot of gold to millions of kids like Henry, who quietly agonizes over how his father slaves 14 hours a day at two tool-and-die machine jobs to make ends meet. Like teenagers across the world, he fantasizes about working in the hip-hop business and making millions himself.

"My parents hate hip-hop," Henry says, motoring his 1994 Dodge Shadow through traffic on the way home from work on a hot October afternoon. "But I can listen to Snoop Dogg and hear him call women whores, and I know he has a wife and children at home. It's just a fantasy. Everyone has the urge deep down to be a bad guy or a bad girl. Everyone likes to talk the talk, but not everyone will walk the walk."

FULL CIRCLE

You breathe in and breathe out a few times and you are there. Eight hours and a wake-up shake on the flight from New York, and you are on the tarmac in Dakar, Senegal. Welcome to Africa. The assignment:

Find the roots of hip-hop. The music goes full circle. The music comes home to Africa. That whole bit. Instead it was the old reporter's joke: You go out to cover a story and the story covers you. The stench of poverty in my nostrils was so strong it pulled me to earth like a hundred-pound ring in my nose. Dakar's Sandaga market is full of "local color"—unless you live there. It was packed and filthy, stalls full of new merchandise surrounded by shattered pieces of life every-where, broken pipes, bicycle handlebars, fruit flies, soda bottles, beg-gars, dogs, cell phones. A teenage beggar, his body malformed by polio, crawled by on hands and feet, like a spider. He said, "Hey brother, help me." When I looked into his eyes, they were a bottom-less ocean.

The Hotel Teranga is a fortress, packed behind a concrete wall where beggars gather at the front gate. The French tourists march past them, the women in high heels and stonewashed jeans. They sidle through downtown Dakar like royalty, haggling in the market, swim-ming in the hotel pool with their children, a scene that resembles Birmingham, Alabama, in the 1950s—the blacks serving, the whites partying. Five hundred yards away, Africans eat off the sidewalk and sell peanuts for a pittance. There is a restlessness, a deep sense of something gone wrong in the air.

The French can't smell it, even though they've had a mouthful back home. A good amount of the torching of Paris suburbs in October 2005 was courtesy of the children of immigrants from former French African colonies, exhausted from being bottled up in housing projects for generations with no job prospects. They telegraphed the punch in their music—France is the second largest hip-hop market in the world—but the message was ignored. Around the globe, rap mu-sic has become a universal expression of outrage, its macho pose bor-rowed from commercial hip-hop in the U.S.

In Dakar, where every kid is a microphone and turntable away from squalor, and American rapper Tupac Shakur's picture hangs in market stalls of folks who don't understand English, rap is king. There are hundreds of rap groups in Senegal today. French television crews troop in and out of Dakar's nightclubs filming the kora harp lute and tama talking drum with regularity. But beneath the drumming and the dance lessons and the jingling sound of tourist change, there is a quiet rage, a desperate fury among the Senegalese, some of whom seem to bear an intense dislike of their former colonial rulers.

"We know all about French history," says Abdou Ba, a Senegalese producer and musician. "We know about their kings, their castles, their art, their music. We know everything about them. But they don't know much about us."

Assane N'Diaye, 19, loves hip-hop music. Before he left his Senegalese village to work as a DJ in Dakar, he was a fisherman, just like his father, like his father's father before him. Tall, lean, with a muscular build and a handsome chocolate face, Assane became a popular DJ, but the equipment he used was borrowed, and when his friend took it back, success eluded him. He has returned home to Toubab Dialaw, about 25 miles south of Dakar, a village marked by a huge boulder, perhaps 40 feet high, facing the Atlantic Ocean.

About a century and a half ago, a local ruler led a group of people fleeing slave traders to this place. He was told by a white trader to come here, to Toubab Dialaw. When he arrived, the slavers followed. A battle ensued. The ruler fought bravely but was killed. The villagers buried him by the sea and marked his grave with a small stone, and over the years it is said to have sprouted like a tree planted by God. It became a huge, arching boulder that stares out to sea, protecting the village behind it. When the fishermen went deep out to sea, the boulder was like a lighthouse that marked the way home. The Great Rock of Toubab Dialaw is said to hold a magic spirit, a spirit that Assane N'Diaye believes in.

In the shadow of the Great Rock, Assane has built a small restaurant, Chez Las, decorated with hundreds of seashells. It is where he lives his hip-hop dream. At night, he and his brother and cousin stand by the Great Rock and face the sea. They meditate. They pray. Then they write rap lyrics that are worlds away from the bling-bling culture of today's commercial hip-hoppers. They write about their lives as village fishermen, the scarcity of catch forcing them to fish in deeper and deeper waters, the hardship of fishing for 8, 10, 14 days at a time in an open pirogue in rainy season, the high fee they pay to rent the boat, and the paltry price their catches fetch on the market. They write about the humiliation of poverty, watching their town sprout up around them with rich Dakarians and richer French. And they write about the relatives who leave in the morning and never return, surrendered to the sea, sharks, and God.

The dream, of course, is to make a record. They have their own demo, their own logo, and their own name, Salam T. D. (for Toubab Dialaw). But rap music represents a deeper dream: a better life. "We want money to help our parents," Assane says over dinner. "We watch our mothers boil water to cook and have nothing to put in the pot."

He fingers his food lightly. "Rap doesn't belong to American culture," he says. "It belongs here. It has always existed here, because of our pain and our hardships and our suffering."

On this cool evening in a restaurant above their village, these young men, clad in baseball caps and T-shirts, appear no different from their African-American counterparts, with one exception. After a dinner of chicken and rice, Assane says something in Wolof to the others. Silently and without ceremony, they take every bit of the leftover dinner—the half-eaten bread, rice, pieces of chicken, the chicken bones—and dump them into a plastic bag to give to the children in the village. They silently rise from the table and proceed outside. The last I see of them, their regal figures are outlined in the dim light of the doorway, heading out to the darkened village, holding on to that bag as though it held money.

THE CITY OF GODS

Some call the Bronx River Houses the City of Gods, though if God has been by lately, he must've slipped out for a chicken sandwich. The 10 drab, red-brick buildings spread out across 14 acres, coming into view as you drive east across the East 174th Street Bridge. The Bronx is the hallowed holy ground of hip-hop, the place where it all began. Visitors take tours through this neighborhood now, care of a handful of fortyish "old-timers," who point out the high and low spots of hip-hop's birthplace.

It is a telling metaphor for the state of America's racial landscape that you need a permit to hold a party in the same parks and playgrounds that produced the music that changed the world. The rap artists come and go, but the conditions that produced them linger. Forty percent of New York City's black males are jobless. One in three black males born in 2001 will end up in prison. The life expectancy of black men in the U.S. ranks below that of men in Sri

Lanka and Colombia. It took a massive hurricane in New Orleans for the United States to wake up to its racial realities.

That is why, after 26 years, I have come to embrace this music I tried so hard to ignore. Hip-hop culture is not mine. Yet I own it. Much of it I hate. Yet I love it, the good of it. To confess a love for a music that, at least in part, embraces violence is no easy matter, but then again our national anthem talks about bombs bursting in air, and I love that song, too. At its best, hip-hop lays bare the empty moral cupboard that is our generation's legacy. This music that once made visible the inner culture of America's greatest social problem, its legacy of slavery, has taken the dream deferred to a global scale. Today, 2 percent of the Earth's adult population owns more than 50 percent of its household wealth, and indigenous cultures are swallowed with the rapidity of a teenager gobbling a bag of potato chips. The music is calling. Over the years, the instruments change, but the message is the same. The drums are pounding out a warning. They are telling us something. Our children can hear it.

The question is: Can we?

WRITERS LIKE ME

❧

Martha Southgate

I am a 46-year-old writer of "literary" fiction. I've had three novels published—the first for young people, the last two for adults. All have won minor prizes, been respectfully reviewed and sold modestly. I've been awarded a few fairly competitive fellowships and grants. The business is full of fiction writers like me. With one difference: I'm black, born and raised in the United States. At the parties and conferences I attend, and in the book reviews I read, I rarely encounter other African-American "literary" writers, particularly in my age bracket. There just don't seem to be that many of us out there, and that's something I've come to wonder about a great deal. And so I got on the phone with some editors and African-American writers to talk about it.

For many writers, middle age is when they hit their stride. Robert Gottlieb of Knopf, who has been Toni Morrison's editor for many years, said, "Many very fine writers take time to get there." Looking at the white American fiction writers who have the most cultural prominence, one quickly sees a large group in their 40s or 50s (Michael Chabon, Jonathan Franzen, Rick Moody, Jane Smiley, Michael Cunningham et al.) who have generally had four or more major works of fiction published. Gottlieb points out that Morrison's first two books sold adequately, but it wasn't until her third novel, *Song of*

Solomon, published the year she turned 46, that she had a commercial breakthrough. "It was larger and more ambitious, demonstrating a new power and authority, and the world noticed," he said. "Some careers start with a bang—*Invisible Man, Catch-22.* Others take time to find a significant readership—Anne Tyler, Toni. And sometimes I feel that those are the healthiest ones."

But when you look at the careers of African-American writers, you don't always see that healthy arc. Ralph Ellison, for example, seemed to lose his way completely after *Invisible Man.* These days, there are only a few names of black authors born in the United States, beyond Morrison's, that the average reader of serious fiction might easily drop—Colson Whitehead, ZZ Packer, Edward P. Jones. Of these three, only Jones is over 40.

In some ways, the American literary scene is more racially and culturally diverse than ever. A few examples: Of the 21 writers on Granta's recent Best of Young American Novelists list, six (including Packer and Uzodinma Iweala) are people of color (many colors: black, South and East Asian, Hispanic), and seven were born or raised outside the United States. Indian writers born or educated here, like Jhumpa Lahiri, Vikram Chandra and Kiran Desai, win critical acclaim and big sales. "Girlfriend," "urban-lit" and other branches of commercial genre fiction by African-Americans have continued to enjoy a boom since the door-busting success of Terry McMillan's *Waiting to Exhale* in 1992. But black authors writing in an ambitious, thoughtful way about American subjects are harder to find—even when they do get published. Malaika Adero, a senior editor at Atria Books, said: "Literary African-American writers have difficulty getting publicity. The retailers then don't order great quantities of the books. Readers don't know what books are available and therefore don't ask for them. It's a vicious cycle."

Though the publishing industry remains overwhelmingly white, editors say they are always looking for good, marketable work by writers of any background. Morgan Entrekin, publisher of Grove/Atlantic, which recently published Michael Thomas's first novel, *Man Gone Down*—one of the few novels by an African-American to grace the cover of this publication of late—said: "I don't tend to approach the black writers we publish as African-American. I see them as writers first."

But there's colorblindness, and then there's blindness. Christopher Jackson, executive editor at Spiegel & Grau, a division of Random House, tells a story about being mistaken for Iweala at the launch party for Granta's Best of Young American Novelists issue—even though Iweala is more than 10 years Jackson's junior, had just left the stage as an honoree, and, frankly, doesn't look much like Jackson. Let's face it, something like that is awfully unlikely to happen to a white editor or writer. It's hard to say whether this obtuseness translates into a lack of interest in African-American work, but some black writers think it might. The novelist Tayari Jones, author of *The Untelling*, said: "I know that there are very few black authors who publish the fourth novel. Hardly any of us are considered prestige authors, so no one is going to sign us up for our names alone." Calvin Reid, a senior news editor at *Publishers Weekly*, who often covers African-American publishing, agrees that black writers stuck in the midlist face an uphill battle, but he sees it as a business reality, not a racial thing: "If you have two or three books out and you've never sold more than 3,000 copies, people make decisions based on that."

Things are tough all over, but arguably tougher for some. For many black writers, a writing life very rarely unfolds the way it does for so many white writers you could name: know you want to be a writer from the age of 10, get your first book published at 26, go on to produce slowly but steadily over a lengthy career. Even Morrison didn't follow that timeline: her first novel wasn't published until she was nearly 40 and had worked for a number of years as a teacher and then an editor at Random House. And she didn't quit that day job until urged to do so by Gottlieb in the mid-1970s, after *Sula* was published.

So what's holding us up? Sometimes it's just the ordinary difficulty of juggling family, writing and earning a living. But African-American writers also speak of a larger problem of what I'd call internal or cultural permission. It's just plain harder to decide to be a writer if you don't have a financial cushion or a long cultural tradition of people going out on that bohemian limb. Consider the case of Edward P. Jones. He published his first book, *Lost in the City*, in 1992 (he was 41 at the time) to much critical acclaim and a number of significant honors, if not huge sales. He returned to his day job at *Tax Notes* magazine, where he remained until he was laid off 10 years later.

He then wrote *The Known World* in about six months—though he told me he'd been thinking about it nearly those whole 10 years. The novel won the Pulitzer Prize.

When asked why he didn't make the leap to full-time writing sooner, Jones spoke firmly: "If you're born poor or you're born working-class, a job is important. People who are born with silver spoons in their mouths never have to worry. They know someone will take care of them. Worrying about not having a job would have put a damper on any creativity that I would have had. So I'm glad I had that job."

The problem isn't just money, says Randall Kenan, a 1994 Whiting Award winner who published two critically acclaimed books of fiction in 1989 and 1992, and two nonfiction books since 1999: "I think among middle-class black folk, it's still a struggle to validate literature as a worthy way to spend your time." ZZ Packer, the author of the story collection *Drinking Coffee Elsewhere,* who is currently at work on a novel, said the situation is somewhat different for those who are younger. (She is 34.) "People who came half a generation before us were the first ones to begin to go to elite colleges in larger numbers," she said. "They were beholden to a lot of their parents' expectations, namely, that if you go to a prestigious school, you're going to become a doctor or a lawyer, you're not going to 'waste your time' writing. People who are around my age have seen blacks in the Northeastern establishment for a while. . . . They don't always feel the same obligation to ditch their dream for something more practical."

It saddens me to think of the dreams that have been ditched, the stories that haven't been told because of racism, because of fear and economic insecurity, because that first novel didn't move enough copies. I hope to see the day when there are more of us at the party (and the parties), when the work of African-Americans who tell our part of the American story well receives the celebration, and the sales, it deserves.

Dances with Daffodils

Jamaica Kincaid

I wandered lonely as a cloud
That floats on
high o'er vales and hills,
When all at once I saw a crowd,
A host, of golden daffodils;
Beside the lake, beneath the trees,
Fluttering and dancing
in the breeze. . . .

Ten thousand saw I at a glance,
Tossing their heads
in sprightly dance. . . .

—William Wordsworth

When I was a child, a long time ago, I was forced to memorize this poem in its entirety, written by the British poet William Wordsworth. I had to memorize many things written by British people, since the place I was born and grew up in was owned by the British, but for a reason not known to me then, of all the things I had to memorize, I took an ill feeling to this piece of literature. And why should that have been so? Let me show you a picture of the little black-skinned girl, with hair strands curlier than wool, an imagination too vivid for the world into which I was born, my mind (whatever that meant and means) shining new and good, certainly good enough to know that there were things it was not allowed to know. The daffodil, for one: What was a daffodil, I wanted to know, since such a thing did not grow in the tropics.

In my child's mind's eye, the poem and its contents (though not its author) and the people through whom it came were repulsive. I had no rational or just way of arranging and separating the people who created the things to memorize from the people who made me memorize wonderful things, whether they were about daffodils, heaven and hell or just the river Thames. And so for me, "I Wandered Lonely as a Cloud" became not an individual vision coolly astonishing the mind's eye but the tyrannical order of a people, the British people, in my child's life.

And yet, given all of that, what has the daffodil become to me, for memory is not set, no matter how we wish it to be so, and the past will intrude on the present new and fresh. I now live in a climate that has four seasons. When I was a child and memorizing the British literary canon, I lived in a climate of eternal summer, and the reality that, in England, four different climates existed filled me with sadness, succeeded by longing and, inevitably, curiosity.

Last fall I planted, without qualms, 2,000 daffodil bulbs, "Rijnveld's Early Sensation," in my lawn. This cultivar came on the market in the 1940s, and it is the only one I can find in any catalogue that brings to my mind that host that danced in the breeze. For 20 years now I have lived in Vermont, a state that falls in a climate suitable for this genus. For many of those 20 years I have gone back and forth with the daffodil: I love it, I do not love it. But I live in this place where there is true spring, a place where the four seasons repeat themselves one after the other in the usual order and the sight of the daffodil is a true joy. In any case, I view spring itself as such pleasure that I have come to believe that the earth and its workings are meant to result in this season, spring.

The 2,000 daffodils have joined 3,500. That is a little more than half of 10,000, but my aim is not Wordsworth's number, my aim is to cover my entire lawn and beyond that every nook and cranny that will receive some sun. I want to walk out into my yard, unable to move at will because my feet are snarled in the graceful long green stems supporting bent yellow flowering heads of daffodils. I will not have to come upon them suddenly; I have planted them myself, dug (with some help from a man named Paul) the 200 holes myself, placing 10 in each hole, making sure the holes are lined up just so for a visual show.

Somewhere I read that Wordsworth worried about misreadings of his poem. It can't be that he worried about the uses to which his countrymen would employ the product of his genius (they were busy trading slaves, not educating them). I believe it possible, though, that with his sensibility, so finely tuned to the unknown in the human realm, so finely tuned to our universal confusions and misunderstandings, he was, when worrying about misreadings, thinking of someone like me. There is no record as far as I can tell of Wordsworth and his sister, Dorothy, frantically planting daffodils anywhere hoping to be in touch again with that moment when they came upon them on their walk in the woods.

THE COINCIDENTAL COUSINS

A NIGHT OUT WITH ARTIST KARA WALKER

James Hannaham

Every night out has its bizarre themes, tiny lights of synchronicity that flash in conversations, a certain irrational logic. All the possibilities in New York City pile up to form a devilish consciousness.

A few nights ago, you leave the office with an immense coffee-table book about Chuck Close and another about the Wooster Group. You drop the books at home, forget about them, head to the Bowery to meet up with Kara.

You've seen a lot of your artist cousin Kara recently. Yes, that Kara—Kara Walker. The MacArthur genius whose cutout-silhouette installations of "sex pickaninnies," as you once called them, have generated accolades, anger, and sales. Her career is ablaze—again. Whitney retrospective (through February), *New Yorker* cover, *New Yorker* profile, *Time*'s 100 Most Influential People. Her humility is hilarious, though. About illustrating the *New Yorker* cover, she says, "See, I can do something else, in case this gallery stuff doesn't work out." Only half-joking. You're like, "If this isn't 'working out,' what is?"

Your relationship in seven words: She amazes you, you make her laugh. It started in junior high. This year you spent a semi-vegetarian Thanksgiving at her place, and the following Sunday was her birthday party. Tonight your significant others are busy, so you hit the opening of the New Museum of Contemporary Art's new building, reminiscent of a stack of gray books, then go off to see *Sister's Keeper,* a thriller at the African Diaspora Film Festival.

You get to the museum before Kara. In the stark lobby, lit by flat-screen TVs, a boyish caterer holds out a tray of glasses filled with golden liquid. "What is this?" you ask, expecting to hear "Chardonnay" or "Sauvignon Blanc." "White wine," he replies. Is this racial profiling? You just say thanks.

Despite the cavernous spaces in the New Museum, it still feels cramped. The offices have low ceilings, the galleries no windows. A truly claustrophobia-inducing staircase squeaks down from the sixth floor. You make it to the seventh floor, lured by the promise of hors d'oeuvres. Up there, the DJ is hooked on AOR—songs in ⅞ time, wtf?* The hors d'oeuvres disappear fast—seared salmon on a potato lattice with a hint of orange flavor. Kara, characteristically dressed down, emerges from the elevator with her pal Eungie Joo, director of education programs at the museum.

Soon, art historian Robert Hobbs—who has written about Kara and wants to write lots more—corners her. The one thing Kara isn't good at is ending conversations assertively. "I need you," Eungie says, almost angrily grabbing Kara's forearm. Eungie leads the two of you through the inaugural exhibition, "Unmonumental." Most of the works are large-scale sculptures made from cheap materials: a mountain of chairs, rags bound together. Eungie points out her favorite piece: four pieces of sandpaper balanced on a pair of two-by-fours. "My grad students at Columbia are making work like this," Kara says, "perhaps trying to avoid something, like content." She decides we'll come back later. At the coat check, she rips a fiver by accident. "What should I do about this?" she asks. "Tape it back together?" "It's the least we owe Marse Lincoln," you say.

Honey-voiced performer Kyle deCamp recently hepped you to the charms of the passé restaurant—quiet, empty places with good food and no wait—in particular the nearby Rialto, on Elizabeth Street.

*What the fuck?

Tonight the front room is relatively full; only two tables open. "They're coming out with this huge Chuck Close book," Kara starts. The same one you brought home. "And Robert wants to put a similar one out for me, but I don't need another book right now." Earlier in the evening, you'd referred to Robert as her remora, the fish that attaches itself to a shark and feeds on its crumbs. Then again, you qualify too.

You talk a lot about astrology. All your intense, volatile relationships are with Cancers, hers with Tauruses. You order a thick pork chop with polenta; she has a stack of grilled veggies. "This dish only lacks one thing," she says. "Flavor."

A guy at the next table looks like Philip Roth. His friends all lean in to listen to him, which seems like proof. "That reminds me of a tryst I had with a downtown performer, in college, when I was working in that bookstore in Atlanta." Another Kara habit: blurting out things she might not want to see in print. A Sagittarius trait, supposedly. "Er, who? If I promise not to print it, will you tell me?" She tells you. It's another coincidence from your day. "I was investigating something about myself," she explains. "That must have made two of you," you respond. She describes her mother's sex-ed lesson: "Men don't like the feel of condoms. That's how we got you."

Outside it's crisp, and golden leaves skitter everywhere through the streets. The two of you dash to Anthology Film Archives, and you're soon watching a film with 20 other black people.

Kent Faulcon stars and directs this thriller, *Sister's Keeper,* a stylish yet low-budget movie about a hired killer who falls in love with the woman he's supposed to murder. Think *Soul Food* meets *Shadowboxer*—if you dare. The heroine mistakes the assassin for her estranged brother. Hints of incest, a rifle-toting grandma, a cameo by Eric Roberts. "Can I leave?" Kara whispers, maybe sickened by the female lead's perkiness. "Only if you tell me why," you say. She stays; the film gets more absorbing—even the actress—though it's literally murky. Black people in the dark have only been shot this haphazardly by the NYPD. "These are some silhouetted Negroes," you say to Kara. "Who was the cinematographer? You?"

During the film, Kara whispers, "I have never seen a black woman in a film that I wanted to meet in person—except Beloved," and writes on your scratch pad: "I am going to make a feature!" You thought of the shell-shocked fogies you watched leave the room at the Whitney where her short film *8 Possible Beginnings* is still on view. They had just witnessed a scene of interracial gay sex and male pregnancy, followed by the difficult birth of a cotton-ball ghost-child. Nicole Kidman will not star in the upcoming feature version.

The screening ends at midnight, but Kara wants a nightcap. You wander through the Lower East Side, appalled by the fratty atmosphere of the East Village Yacht Club. A comparatively empty video bar, the Blue Seats, has about 30 flat-screen TVs embedded in its walls. You order a sidecar, she a mojito. You turn to the handsome, lost-looking white man next to you—whose last name turns out to be Whitman—and ask, "Wanna meet a famous artist?" He's polite but clearly has no clue who Kara is. Coincidentally, he's waiting for his cousin, who seems to have stood him up. Kara, born in Stockton, recognizes in him a specific Northern California privilege. "Don't you just want to fuck the entitlement out of him?" you ask. "That's the danger," she says. "My whole career started out as revenge on ex-boyfriends."

After the one drink, she considers going dancing. Most people with kids are in bed by now, if not asleep. But she's only considering. You put her in a northbound cab, and then have trouble finding one yourself.

The next morning, Eric Roberts appears in a saccharine AIDS film on TV, his lover soothing him into the next world by describing a scene on a ski lift. You watch him slowly die.

MUSIC

BODIES IN PAIN

~⧟⧟◯

Mark Anthony Neal

In his brilliant and demanding book, *In the Break: The Aesthetics of the Black Radical Tradition,* theorist Fred Moten describes Billie Holiday's *Lady in Satin* as a "record of a wonderfully articulate body in pain." Recorded as Holiday's body was literally falling apart, *Lady in Satin* lacks the robustness and sassiness that marked so many of Holiday's earlier recordings. Here, Holiday is defiant, though, embracing death in the full bloom of her imperfection(s). As Moten writes, Holiday "uses the crack in the voice, extremity of the instrument, willingness to fail reconfigured as a willingness to go past . . ." The same could be said for Soul singer Linda Jones who recorded her most famous tune, "Hypnotized," a decade after Holiday's death. What links Holiday and the largely obscure Jones is the violence they enacted—lyrically and musically—within the realm of their vocal performances. This was a violence that, in large part, was a response to that which their own bodies bore witness to—

Born in Newark, NJ, in 1944, Jones spent much of her childhood and early adulthood struggling with a debilitating case of diabetes, which as writer Becca Mann suggests, "lent her career an urgency." The disease led to Jones's early demise at the age of 28—she was in the midst of a successful week-long engagement at the Apollo Theater in Harlem at the time of her death in 1972. Vocally, Jones's style can only be described as "fits of melisma"—melisma being that particular style of vocal performance that is marked by the singing of single syllables across several pitches—and it is likely one of the reasons, including lack of national distribution, Jones never found a mainstream audience for her music. Though some found Jones's performances as overwrought, that was exactly the point; Jones performed songs like "That's When I'll Stop Loving You" or "For Your Precious Love" not simply as performative gestures, but as if she knew she was dying.

Linda Jones's music demanded an emotional investment—specifically, in the lives of Black women—that mainstream audiences, I'd like to argue, were likely incapable of making at the time. While Aretha Franklin is a seemingly clear example of a Black woman who attracted a broad mainstream audience in the late 1960s, I would argue that Jones's performances were inspired by a depth of pain that Franklin's music more actively attempted to transcend. While Jones had peers in this regard—the tragic career and life of Esther Phillips being a prime example—few could match her vocal calisthenics. As *Rolling Stone* critic Russell Gersten once commented, Jones sounded like "someone down on her knees, pounding the floor, suddenly jumping up to screech something, struggling to make sense of a desperately unhappy life."

What distinguished Jones from a figure such as Holiday was the extent that Jones made palpable the influence of the Black Church on her vocal style. As such, Jones was of a generation of vocalists who were making the transition from the gospel choirs of their youth onto the secular music charts. Sam Cooke was of course a tremendous influence in this regard and in Jones's case that influence can be clearly heard on her soul-stirring performance of "That's When I'll Stop Loving You" on the live recording *Never Mind the Quality . . . Feel the Soul*. Cooke's singing was a model of control and restraint, performed under the guise of aesthetic risk-taking—Cooke arching to reach that high note, only to float seamlessly across a phrase. Jones, in comparison, had no interest playing to the fiction that she was in control of anything—the music, her voice and at times her own body. Both artists had the ability to present an aura of vulnerability that made their music so palpable to audiences—Cooke's emotiveness was particularly striking for a male singer—but in Jones's case she was vulnerable and each performance was an attempt to grasp a slither of the humanity that was slowly departing from her.

Jones, like Cooke and others including Franklin and Sly Stone (Sylvester Stewart) helped secularize African-American gospel ritual in the late 1950s and 1960s. In his work on the tradition of African-American gospel quartets (the specific tradition that helped produce Cooke), Ray Allen writes, "in its ritualized context, gospel performance promises salvation for the believer in this world as well as the next. Chanted narratives remind listeners of their past experiences, collective struggle, common southern and familial roots, and shared sense of ethnic identity." (*The Journal of American Folklore*, Summer 1991.) Such rituals likely allowed Jones to provide her audience with some language to better interpret the aspects of her performance that were simply beyond language. In this regard, Jones literally had to talk through those aspects of her pain—testifyin' as it were—in order to better galvanize her audience, which was largely African-American, around her pain and by extension the pain uniquely experienced by African-American women.

Jones's desire to give tangible meaning to her pain is evident during her performance of "Things I Been Through." Ostensibly a song about a woman surviving the infidelity of a partner, Jones's sermonic break midway through the song transforms it into a performance of (Black) women-centered resistance in which Jones seemingly relishes her literacy of African-American church traditions. Speaking directly to her audience, Jones says,

> I don't believe you people out there know what I'm talking about/I hear people say that it's a weak women that cries/But I do believe that there are very few women that can stand up under all of this pressure without at least shedding one tear/I do believe that some of you out there have had heartaches and pain of some kind . . ./now if you have, I just want you to raise your hand and say with me just one time . . ./now mercy, mercy, mercy, mercy, whoo, whoa

The irony for Jones is that it was never about simply "shedding one tear," but a cavalcade of shrieks, screams and cries that found its place in the violence she did literally to each note she sang. As Elaine Scarry observes in her now classic book *The Body in Pain* (1985), one of the dimensions of physical pain is "its ability to destroy language, the power of verbal objectification, a major source of our self extension, a vehicle through which the pain could be lifted out into the world and eliminated." (p. 54)

"Things I Been Through" highlights the ways that Jones's music was transgressive, particularly with regards to the connections between the Black preacher and African-American musical idioms. According to jazz scholar Robert O'Meally, the "Black preacher presents a rhythmically complex statement in which melisma, repetition, the dramatic pause, and a variety of other devices associated with Black music are used," noting that the "man or woman of the Word," often "drops words altogether and moans, chants, sings, grunts, hums, and/or hollers the morning message in a way that one of [Ralph] Ellison's characters calls the 'straight meaning of the words.'" (*Callaloo*, Winter 1988.)

Writing in the late 1980s, O'Meally's analysis captures a more progressive notion of the gender politics of the Black pulpit, but when Jones was recording in the late 1960s, the idea of a Black female preacher—and there were many—was still a fairly radical concept, especially during an era when many still presumed Black men of the cloth to be the logical public voices of Black communities. (Think here of James Brown's deliberate marketing of Jones's contemporary Lynn Collins as the "female preacher.") "Things I Been Through" is notable because it is one of the best examples of the ways that Jones employed the Black preacher tradition—historically one of the most prominent sites of Black patriarchal power and privilege—in the service of addressing Black female pain and struggle. Consider the way, for example, that Jones disturbs assumptions about the relationship between physical emotiveness and weakness stating that there are "very few women that can stand up under all of this pressure without at least shedding one tear."

Jones's music was also transgressive because of the way that it exploited African-American religious rituals for distinctly secular concerns. The same could be said about the Black liberation struggle of

Jones's era, which consciously utilized the discourses of Christianity to address the political and social realities of the Black masses. But in this regard, Jones's music was concerned with the more immediate concerns of pleasure and joy amidst the physical pain that largely defined Jones's life; Jones's rendition of "For Your Precious Love," popularized by Jerry Butler, exemplifies these desires. Like "Things I've Been Through," Jones's version of "For Your Precious Love" features a sermonic break, though Jones also provides a spoken introduction to the song. Midway through the song Jones addresses the women in her audience ("you know something ladies. It's especially you ladies I'd like to speak with"):

> Sometime I wake up in the midnight hours, tears falling down my face/And when I look around for my man and can't find him/I fall a little lower, look a little higher/Kind a pray to the Lord, because I always believe that Lord could help me if nobody else could/But sometimes I think that he don't hear me/So I have to fall a little lower on my knees, look a little higher/kind of raise my voice a little higher . . .

Here Jones suggests that the "Lord" was not fully attentive to her needs. Though this could be read as a rejection of religious practice, I'd like to suggest that, given Jones's use of the African-American gospel ritual, she was instead rejecting the distinctly masculine concerns ("he don't hear me") which often frame such practices. In other words, Jones is suggesting that if such practices were fully cognizant of the lives of Black women, as embodied in Jones's voice, the emotional and sexual desires of Black women would be addressed. In Jones's case the desire for companionship, in the midnight hour, was infused with the knowledge that any midnight could be her last.

A CASE OF THE RUNS: A CONSIDERATION
OF KEYSHIA COLE

Whereas the Soul singers of Linda Jones's era often strategically deployed their use of melisma, it can be said that many contemporary R&B singers have a case of the runs. For example, what often marked the best performances of seminal R&B singer Luther Vandross was his ability and willingness to leave his audiences anxious in wait for the deep runs that he was noted for. With a flair for the dramatic, Vandross often held out those runs towards the end of a song as a form of artistic denouement—a final pronouncement, if you will, of his singular vocal genius. In the case of Vandross and others of his generation (think here of Whitney Houston at her peak), these moment were to be cherished—a grand gesture for the audiences that supported his music.

Such subtleties have largely been lost on the contemporary crop of R&B singers, who often break into frantic riffs and runs midway through the first verse, in the process cheapening the integrity of the lyric as well as audiences' investment in their craft. And it's not necessarily the fault of the singers, at a moment when so-called "urban" music is being driven by producers whose skill set is largely related to making beats and many young singers are simply not getting the vocal direction that they deserve. For example producers such as Jerry Wexler and Tom Dowd were seasoned veterans when they worked with Aretha Franklin upon her move to Atlantic Records in 1967 after languishing at Columbia Records for a few years. In the case of Patti LaBelle, another vocalist well known for her histrionics, one of her most popular recordings as a solo performer—"If Only You Knew" (1983)—was the product of her collaboration with Kenneth Gamble and Leon Huff. The duo had worked with LaBelle a decade earlier on Laura Nyro's "Gonna Take a Miracle" and thus knew how to rein in her voice to produce, what remains, her most nuanced performance. Too often contemporary R&B singers are working with producers who have been in the game only a few years longer than they have.

This lack of experience by producers and vocalists often adds to the dissonance that resonates in the vocal quality of figures like Mary J. Blige or Faith Evans, who have become easy targets for a generation that is regularly thought to be out of tune—musically, morally, and politically—with the Soul singers of the 1960s and 1970s. But I'd like to suggest that such dissonance is not simply the product of a generation of singers who are out of pitch—and lacking the training to know so—but a response to the ways that post–Civil Rights generations hear the world. The nostalgic harmonies of the Civil Rights Generation (and their parents, many of whom are in their 80s) strike discord in the lives of post–Civil Rights generations, notably Generation Hip-Hop, which have never had a tangible relationship to concepts such as "freedom" and "liberation" that some in the old guard presumed were transferable. Issues like the crack cocaine epidemic, the prison industrial complex, police brutality, voter disenfranchisement largely based on race and class, wage depression, lack of access to quality and affordable healthcare, misogyny, the failing infrastructure of public schooling, homophobia, as well as a populism of common sense (which by definition is stridently conservative and anti-intellectual), have often left post–Civil Rights generations grasping for straws, much the way Keyshia Cole—who I offer for your consideration—seems to frantically grasp for notes in virtually every song that she sings.

In the case of Cole, her singing style really is the embodiment of her ongoing desire to hold together a life that has been fragmented by an absentee-father, a drug addicted and incarcerated mother, a difficult stint in foster care and her years as a runaway. Cole's debut recording *The Way It Is* (2005) provides some context for her near-tragic back-story, which became the basis of a reality show (production on season two is about to begin) which captures Cole's attempts to find some closure to her relationship with her mother and the hard-scrabble Oakland community that reared her. And though none of Cole's songs, many of which she co-wrote, speak directly to the struggles of her childhood and teenage years, those difficulties are implicit in lyrics like "I used to think that I wasn't fine enough/And I used to think that I wasn't wild enough" (from "Love") which powerfully attest to Cole's desire to be loved—by any somebody—and the desire to matter in society that has shown little love for young, poor, and homeless Black girls.

It was in fact a demo copy of Cole's "Love" that found its way to industry executive Ron Fair in 2003 and became the stimulus for his signing of Cole to Interscope A&M Records. As Fair recently noted, "When [Cole] sings, there's a real feeling in the notes . . . There's pain in her voice that is coming from reality." (*LA Times,* 4.20.06) Much of the drama in "Love" pivots on Cole's utterances of the words "found/find" throughout the song's chorus ("Love, never knew what I was missing, but I knew once we start kissing I fouououououounnd, love"). In the context of the song, found is the virtual space where Cole finds some emotional and psychic grounding. But as the tortured nature of the performance suggests, this space offers little solace—if Cole relaxes one bit, the performance literally falls flat—as Cole is symbolically in constant turmoil with the melodic terrain that she is largely responsible for creating.

With a successful reality series in rotation and relative mainstream visibility for her music, Keyshia Cole has access to an audience that Linda Jones couldn't even imagine. What the two artists share is a willingness to make plain, musically, the pain that has defined their lives, in the process creating a sensual and spiritual space which gives voice to the wide-ranging desires and fears of Black women—even as so many simply want to render their music as little more than noise.

When Tyra Met Naomi

RACE, FASHION, AND RIVALRY

~~ℓℓ⊙

Hawa Allan

One of the last places I expected to hear an engaging antiracist and feminist critique of the fashion industry was on *The Tyra Banks Show*. But on a January 2006 episode, there was Banks, sitting couch-to-couch with fellow supermodel Naomi Campbell, discussing the forces that years ago had pitted the two women against each other on the assumption that America had room for only one black top model.

I sat rapt on my futon, munching potato chips and settling in for what I had expected to be a legendary catfight between the catwalk titans. Instead, Banks, at times fighting back tears, dedicated much of her sit-down with Campbell to spelling out the dearth of opportunities for black models in the fashion industry. She concluded the very special episode with a segment calling on women to stop competing with one another and unite: "One of the reasons I wanted to do this show is because sisterhood is so important to me. I feel like women hate on each other—we're jealous—and it has to stop."

Banks, who hoped her confrontation with Campbell would bring "healing" for both women, attributed their painful 14-year rift to a narrow-minded fashion industry and the media that covers it. "Back then, there were 10 top models but there was an unwritten rule that only one of them could be black," Banks said. "And Naomi was that one black girl." Indeed, upon her spectacular rise to prominence soon after being discovered at age 17 by a model scout, Banks was hailed as the "new Naomi Campbell" and a Campbell "look-alike." Such race-based comparisons are nothing new for black models. In a 2003 *Time* article, Somali supermodel Iman said that, upon arriving in New York in 1975, she realized she was being pitted against Beverly Johnson. She recalls quickly learning "that magazines would only use one black girl at a time, and they were trying to create a competition between us." It's needless to say that neither Iman and Beverly nor Tyra and Naomi look much alike.

As far back as 1994, Banks resented the comparisons between her and Campbell, as she told *People* in a rare comment on her supposed competitor: "Why do I have to knock Naomi out to be successful? With white models they don't do that." Nonetheless, in one oft-recounted incident, Campbell had Chanel designer Karl Lagerfeld ban Banks from appearing on the fashion giant's runways; she also reportedly tried to force her then-agency, Elite Model Management, to choose between her and Banks. Banks decided to leave Elite for IMG in order to ease the tension. (Campbell was later dismissed from Elite after founder John Casablancas declared the model to be "crazy, irrational, and uncontrollable.")

Banks eventually quit high-fashion catwalks and photo shoots and found refuge in mainstream gigs—like modeling for the Victoria's Secret catalog and posing for *Sports Illustrated*'s swimsuit issue—that make room for more voluptuous (in modeling terms, anyway) figures like hers. This has been her official story for years—but, as she revealed to Campbell on her show, "that's only 50 percent of it." Banks was also "tired of the comparison" and "tired of constantly hearing that I got canceled from this job or this magazine was called and [told] not to use me." Ultimately, Banks grew tired of walking in Campbell's shadow, so she ceded the haute couture battle to her.

Prior to the talk-show sit-down, the most Banks had been willing to publicly say about Campbell was that she doubted they would ever be friends. However, on the show, Banks elaborated on their strained relationship, offering specific examples of unpleasant moments between the two, and pointedly asking Campbell why she had treated her so badly. Campbell, for her part, stopped short of outright denying Banks's allegations, opting for an Oliver Northian failure to recollect. Responding to Banks's recounting of one particular incident, Campbell said: "I know the person that I am and I'm not someone to go and give myself away and say that to anybody. But if that's what you remember, I accept that, but it doesn't sound like me." Campbell also conceded that she was emotionally unstable during the period in question and was being advised by the wrong people.

Indeed, the two women were embedded in an industry that yanks adolescent girls from anxiety-ridden obscurity to magnify their assets and flaws for worldwide assessment. Given this backdrop, it's not difficult to imagine Campbell's distress at having to contend with a younger model who was literally being groomed to replace her. Campbell's own career was launched in 1986 when she landed the cover of *Elle* in place of another black model who had canceled. Having established her livelihood on the missed opportunity of "another black model," Campbell must have learned an indelible lesson and would not allow herself to be so easily displaced.

Though the *Tyra* episode ended with the requisite apology from Campbell ("However I've affected you or you've felt that I've affected you, I take my responsibility. I must say I'm very proud of you. You've been a powerful black woman. . . . Please continue") and tears from Banks, its real strength was that Banks framed her enmity with Campbell as a result of the larger institutional and social forces that pitted the two models against each other in the first place. The story had all the elements of talk-show pathos—the tears, the accusations, the confessions of emotional agony—but, to her credit, Banks refused to make the story purely a personal one, reminding the audience throughout the show that "the press had cast Naomi and [me] as rivals before we ever met each other." She could easily have made Campbell the sole villain—given the model's history of petulance, anger-management issues and resulting lawsuits, most of the work was already done for her—but instead she chose to focus on both systemic racism in the modeling industry and internalized sexism among women.

The issue of race and modeling goes far deeper than Tyra vs. Naomi, of course. Hot on the heels of the televised showdown came a

May 2006 *Slate* article by J. E. Dahl that wondered, "Is Tyra Banks Racist?" In it, Dahl notes that on *America's Next Top Model*, Banks reserves her harshest criticisms for the black wannabes. Taking Banks to task for "discouraging any behavior that could be considered 'too black,'" Dahl cites some of *Top Model*'s biggest controversies—Banks's disapproval of season-three runner-up Yaya's Afrocentric head wraps; her many admonitions to recent winner Danielle that her accent was "too country"; and her now-infamous "Tyrade" (as Television Without Pity dubbed it) against season four's ghetto-fabulous Tiffany, in which Banks's usually composed persona gave way to unbridled rage at the contestant's seemingly indifferent attitude toward the competition. The diatribe reiterated the kind of rhetoric about self-reliance and individual responsibility often directed at black Americans in general, and Dahl argues that these and other actions suggest Banks's own internalized racism—a criticism similar to that lodged against Bill Cosby, who in 2004 publicly lambasted black Americans marginalized by poverty for, among other things, not speaking proper English.

But it's worth arguing that Banks is not so much racist as she is both aware of racism and dedicated to ensuring that future black models arm themselves with the sensibilities and postures necessary to compete in a stubbornly unreflective and homogeneous industry. Surely Dahl has heard of the phenomenon wherein members of marginalized groups are tougher on their own, instilling the "twice-as-good" attitude among protégés within their group to ensure that they thrive in the mainstream. Just as Cosby critics aptly retorted that the comedian should save his scathing tongue for the systemic injustices that drive urban black poverty, Dahl would have done better to balance his critique of Banks with a stark assessment of the modeling industry.

Yes, Banks's criticism of black contestants on *Top Model* works to reproduce the Eurocentric notions that impede the success of blacks in the fashion industry at large. But it also acknowledges the endemic racism in her industry—and not just the modeling industry, but also that of reality television. For example, Banks warned season-three contestant Eva that she was in danger of not being cast simply because Banks didn't want "another black bitch" on the show. Banks's statement reflected an awareness of reality television's "Omarosa complex," where black women are represented as haughty divas with attitudes in order to heighten drama—and, subsequently, ratings. In petitioning for black models (and reality-show contestants) to change their behavior rather than for a systemic overhaul, Banks opts to reform black models rather than to revolutionize either industry.

Banks is obviously not the first to verbalize this resignation to the fashion world's limitations. Legendary fashion editor André Leon Talley—the lone recognizable black face at *Vogue*—has long acknowledged the dearth of opportunities for black models in the industry. In a 2003 *Essence* interview, he admitted: "We have regressed. I often sit at a show and see not one black model on the runway. Can't they find some black girls?" Talley, who has also noted this frustration in his monthly "Stylefax" column for *Vogue*, explained in the same interview that he has written notes and made suggestions to designers and editors, stating that he "can't believe it when [they] say, 'I couldn't find anyone' or 'She didn't look right in the clothes.'" However, when pressed for a solution to this problem, as well as the one of a scarcity of black editors at fashion magazines, he replied matter-of-factly: "*Vogue*, Condé Nast, that's not our world. We are not the majority."

But neither Talley nor Banks nor Dahl addresses the intransigence of this "world." In his *Slate* article, Dahl tags Banks as a kind of reactionary without considering the rigid context in which she operates. We all know that the fashion industry is hardly progressive in its representations of womanhood. And where race is concerned, the industry has largely sidestepped the issue by reducing the significance of skin color to the aesthetic—black models are reportedly in higher demand during spring and summer seasons because their skin color contrasts well with the brighter shades in such collections. Just as purple can be in one season and out the next, so can, say, Asian models. (In a 2003 article on the fashion industry titled "The Role of Race," IMG agent Kyle Hagler told *Time*, "A while ago, every show had to have an Asian girl, but that seems to have passed.") The modeling industry, shrouded by notions of subjective aestheticism, is one realm that has remained largely untouched by gender- or race-based identity politics. Physical appearance, even if racial or ethnic, can be embraced or disregarded by the industry as capriciously as Marc Jacobs tulip pants.

The April 2005 issue of *Vanity Fair* echoed this sentiment with its cover story, "Slavs of Fashion," about the influx of models from former Communist countries. Among the women profiled in the piece is Natalia Vodianova, who succinctly interpreted the so-called invasion of models from the old Soviet Bloc as such: "We have beautiful skin, beautiful faces and the Brazilians are finished!" Vodianova was referring to the erstwhile craze in the modeling industry for Brazilian models like Gisele Bündchen. But, unfortunately for Bündchen and her bronzed crew, the newer crop of Eastern European and Russian models, according to *Vanity Fair,* exude a kind of "toughness or seriousness" that's apparently more in vogue than the "fun-loving Gisele thing." (Such toughness was attributed to hard times endured under the Communist regime. Frolicking Brazilians are out and poised ex-Soviets with an aura of stoicism are in—just another day in fashion.)

Though the prominence of different ethnicities or nationalities often swells and subsides within the modeling industry according to the whims of its decision makers, with race—and with black models in particular—such transient recognition has tended to be more singular than group-based. Sensations like Naomi or Tyra or Iman are singled out for individual success rather than as one of a crowd or stable of black models ushered into prominence.

There have, however, been waves of wider acceptance. In the 1970s, Iman, Pat Cleveland, and Beverly Johnson—the first black woman to appear on the cover of *Vogue*—were all catapulted onto the fashion stage. In the early-to-mid-'90s, opportunities for nonwhite models seemed to open up once again, as not only Banks and Campbell but also Karen Alexander, Tyson Beckford, Beverly Peele, Jenny Shimizu, Veronica Webb, Alek Wek, and Roshumba Williams became highly visible figures. It was a short-lived period, though, one that Webb herself explored in a 1996 *Essence* article, "Where Have All the Black Models Gone?" After noticing that the runways were overwhelmingly populated with very pale blonds, she took it upon herself to talk to industry insiders about the reason for this shift. Webb's interviews with designers, photographers, and fashion-magazine editors inspired an orgy of finger-pointing, with photographers claiming that they shoot models chosen by the magazines who hire them, editors saying they tap the runway for models to appear in their magazines, and designers replying that they look to magazine pages to scout modeling talent for their collections.

Chicken-and-egg conundrum aside, magazines do have a commercial incentive to keep nonwhite models off their covers, as an *Allure* editor admitted to Webb: "Sales are significantly lower when we put a person of color on the cover." But why? Gary Younge investigated this hard-and-fast dictum in a 1999 piece for the U.K. *Guardian* after seeing only three black models out of a total of 41 in *Vogue*'s millennium issue showcasing the magazine's all-time favorite faces. Both sources he consulted—one a spokesperson for designer Jean-Paul Gaultier and the other a magazine editor—blamed the biases of the general reading audience, with the former stating that magazine sales can drop as much as 20 percent when a black woman is on the cover. "I would not say the fashion industry is racist; it's the world which is racist," the spokesperson said. "It is people who buy fashion and people who buy magazines and they seem to prefer the white woman." The editor had a more generous interpretation of the apparent tastes of magazine buyers: "The person you put on the cover has to be somebody that readers can aspire to aesthetically. You want to look at the picture and say: 'I want to look like that.' I'm not saying that couldn't happen if the reader is white and the model is black. But it is more difficult."

Even Campbell recently voiced her own displeasure with the paucity of black models, telling *Vogue*: "I remember a time when there were at least eight black girls working. And now, in 2006 . . . it's shocking!" Nonetheless, any nonwhite model who takes legal action in the U.S. claiming employment discrimination on the basis of race can be easily trounced by the counterclaim that she was not "qualified" or hired for the position solely due to an aesthetic, not racist, judgment. Certainly, the fashion industry is one site where aesthetics and politics shall never meet.

It is important to note that race is less of a determining factor in magazine sales when black celebrities rather than models are the ones mugging on covers. The seminal example, of course, is *O*, the sales of which have consistently increased despite (or, indeed, due to) the fact that Oprah Winfrey is on every single cover. Winfrey, of course, is no regular celebrity, but a national phenomenon who, incidentally, has also appeared on the cover of *Vogue*. However, as legal scholar and author Patricia Williams wryly observed, given that *Vogue* is "the province of Helmut Lang's spiky, emaciated teenagers in white lipstick, cashmere underwear, and shoes designed for those who have little occasion to ride the subway . . . [i]n that space, Oprah appeared so . . . unusual." Seeing a full-figured black woman on the cover of a high-fashion magazine, even when the woman in question is Oprah Winfrey, is somewhat bizarre.

Given that we all know that fashion-mag standards of female beauty are hopelessly skewed and endlessly limited, why should we even bother critiquing the race or the height or the bustlines of the few women chosen to exemplify this absurd standard? It's an old question, one that's been explored by everyone from Toni Morrison to Eve Ensler to Oprah. Morrison, in the epilogue to her novel *The Bluest Eye*, pondered why black beauty needed "wide public articulation in order to exist." She concluded that "the assertion of racial beauty was not . . . a humorous critique of cultural/racial foibles common in all groups, but against the damaging internalization of assumptions of immutable inferiority originating in an outside gaze."

Indeed, black models whose own beauty has achieved this "wide public articulation" frame their success as not only an individual one, but as something to be shared by other black models and black women more generally. Despite Banks's tough-love approach to black contestants on *Top Model*, she's acting with the hope that more black models will persevere in the industry and perhaps ease the path for their successors. Banks, who cites Sonia Cole and Iman as inspirations, has a sense of historical lineage; she sees herself as a descendant of those who came before and as a trailblazer for those who will come after. As she told *Essence* in 1995: "I think things will change for the Black models who come after us. They won't have to feel so insecure about losing their spots. They'll benefit from our pain." Current Ethiopian sensation Liya Kebede, the first black model to sign a multimillion-dollar contract as the face of Esteé Lauder, has a similar take. Discussing the contract and her overall success with *Time*, Kebede said, "I'd love it if young girls can see me and say, 'She's done it, and so can I.'"

Banks and Campbell, along with their predecessors, are noteworthy pioneers in the representation of nonwhite beauty. Banks was the first black model to appear on the covers of *GQ* and *Sports Illustrated*'s swimsuit issue; Campbell was the first black model to appear on the covers of French and British *Vogue*, not to mention the first black woman to be considered a "supermodel." Granted, *GQ*, *Vogue*, and the like are problematic turf on which to wage the battle for women's self-esteem. But, for women of color of all shapes and phenotypes, the fact remains that many can and do see a part of themselves in the few nonwhite models designated as representatives of Beauty. Therein lies the conundrum of being a black spectator of American culture—seeing diversity as a tiresome mantra masquerading for tokenism and, at the same time, as a worthy principle pushing society to rectify persistent racial exclusion. Thus, while diversity practiced as tokenism creates a scenario whereby Tyra must replace Naomi or the Slavs displace the Brazilians, those who believe in diversity on principle are shoehorned into supporting new recruits despite the rigid context in which opportunity is supposedly being equalized. The danger of this situation is that instead of continually widening new opportunities—or, in the case of the modeling industry, expanding popular notions of beauty—certain token diversity slots are created and jealously guarded by persons occupying them, who rationally fear being ousted for the next exotic trend. Such is the predicament of nonwhite models roaming the frontier of identity politics in an industry both zealously fickle and unwavering in its devotion to Eurocentric beauty.

The hope in all this is that expanding opportunities for models of color will eventually put an end to the kind of jealous protectionism that created the rift between Banks and Campbell in the first place. The increasing prominence of mixed-race models suggests a subliminal wish for a postrace hybridity that, once and for all, discounts race as an arbitrary and illusory category.

What's more encouraging is that celebrities of all casts and dyes are displacing professional models in both cosmetic endorsements and glossy fashion spreads. The implication of this move is that, more and more, having a certain kind of look will not be sufficient for models to successfully compete for such exposure; a personality might also be required. Supposed role models are being sought after to a greater extent than fashion models, with women like Halle Berry chosen to represent Revlon, Beyoncé for L'Oreal, and Queen Latifah as the face of Cover Girl. Lionizing celebrities isn't necessarily a solution, but a focus on beauty that's more than one-dimensional might help reduce the racial tokenism and exoticism that runs rampant on fashion's rarefied catwalks.

Still, such a move won't eradicate competition between models, whoever those models are. (For all we know, Halle beat out Beyoncé for that Revlon spot.) Jealousy and protectionism will always be a function of any commercial industry, and perhaps more so in one where catty women are the most visible agents. So, if race becomes a less salient factor in pitting future Naomis against future Tyras, something else will inevitably rise up to spur competition in its wake among other dubious elements alongside weight and height and the symmetry of one's facial features. In the end, understanding models as rational economic actors rather than as insecure waifs protracting their claws is crucial to seeing hidden strains, pressures, and biases apparent in their cutthroat market—and changing them for the good of us all.

Dancing in the Dark

RACE, SEX, THE SOUTH, AND EXPLOITATIVE CINEMA

Gerald Early

*There is nothing, absolutely nothing, calculated to
raise the goose-flesh on the back of an audience more
than that of a white girl in relation to Negroes.*

—D. W. Griffith

*To get at the ultimate secret of the Southern rape complex,
we need to turn back and recall the central status that
Southern woman had long ago taken up in Southern emotion—
her identification with the very notion of the South itself.
For, with this in view, it is obvious that the assault on the South
would be felt as, in some true sense, an assault on her also,
and that the South would inevitably translate its whole
battle into terms of her defense.*

—W. J. Cash, *The Mind of the South*

1

THE SOUTH AS THE HEART
OF THE COUNTRY

For many years I was puzzled over why the United States fought a Civil War. The whites of both the North and South were united by a common language (English), a common religion (Christianity, albeit with many variations), similar beliefs in free markets, representative democracy, individualism, and, of course, white supremacy. So why, exactly, was there a war between the whites over the presence of black slaves, especially since virtually no one in mid-nineteenth-century America liked African-descended people, and most thought bondage not a terrible fate for them?

I suspect that buried in that question is something revelatory about what made the South different from, and fascinating to, the North. The South has always captured the imagination of that segment of the country—indeed, the entire country. (Conversely, the South has never been obsessed by the North, although it has been obsessed about itself to nearly the same extent that the North has been obsessed about it.)

In the end, perhaps what was key about the distinction between the antebellum geopolitical regions of the United States was merely that, as an economic necessity, the South chose to live with Africans. The result was a strange cultural advantage in which Southern whites kept blacks down in perversely inventive and horrendously creative ways. This was one case where familiarity did not breed mere contempt but a form of smug and stunning insanity.

———————

With *The Birth of a Nation*, D. W. Griffith single-handedly created the cinematic South, and it might be argued that all other Southern films have been, in various ways, responses to that 1915 epic. For instance, *Gone With the Wind* (1939), the other major Southern cinematic powerhouse, attempted to retell *The Birth of a Nation* from the modernist point of view of an emancipated woman during the creation of the

New South. But *Gone With the Wind* was conflicted about the South in a way that *The Birth of a Nation* was not.

Griffith's film dramatized the burden of reactionary white Southern history. His film was made at a time when African Americans were a socially inferior caste: a powerless, impoverished, segregated, and largely rural population. By the time David O. Selznick filmed *Gone With the Wind*, African Americans had become a more urban and politically influential group that, though still segregated, had rising expectations. So the burden of reactionary white Southern history began to be dramatized somewhat differently. Unlike *The Birth of a Nation*, in which whites played all the major black parts, black actors had significant roles in *Gone With the Wind*. Selznick even hired Walter White, the executive secretary of the NAACP, as a consultant—a collaborator of sorts. (The NAACP had fought Griffith's film strenuously when it was released, so the reversal here is not without irony.) White helped to shape a film that depicted the slave population as loyal and childlike—and thus politically less troublesome since they ceased to be central to the drama of the South's rise and fall. This was an even more simplistic rendition than found in *The Birth of a Nation*, where at least the blacks could be evilly ambitious, like all great megalomaniacal villains. *Gone With the Wind* gave white Southern viewers all the romance and emotion of the Lost Cause without giving them the Cause itself. *The Birth of a Nation* never let viewers forget the nature of the Cause for a single minute.

The Birth of a Nation, in its genius, pointed in two different directions simultaneously: to its cheap, pulp-racial, potboiler source, the rabidly racist novels of Thomas Dixon (*Gone With the Wind* was a far better novel in virtually every respect than anything Dixon wrote, and, despite Dixon's approval of Margaret Mitchell's work, was somewhat anti-Dixon in sensibility) and to a sort of Shakespearean historical drama whose grand pretensions would go so far as to move President Woodrow Wilson, a former academic, to say of the film version that it was "all so terribly true." As Griffith biographer Richard Schickel argues, Griffith had the historians of the era on his side because they too believed Reconstruction was a tragic mistake and that white redemption of the South was a political and moral necessity. For students today, Reconstruction is still seen as a mistake, but for failing on its promise of producing a truly multicultural, pluralist society of equality and democratic virtue. White Southerners who want to be PC can't get too hot and bothered about how insulted they were about "being ruled by blacks" and "the excesses and incompetence of the Reconstruction governments," at least not in mixed company. The Lost Cause is truly lost these days.

It was not merely that for a time Griffith was able, through the suspect vehicle of movies, to make many people believe that bad novels make spectacular history (which is often true) but that—and this is true for all of Griffith's Southern race films—the racialized South itself was synonymous with history and myth. The South for Griffith was always larger than America, larger than life itself. So the South's imaginative sources were cheap, vulgar, pulp nonsense combined with the only majestic touch of tragedy that the white race has ever experienced on the American continent: losing a war and being briefly ruled by servile, stupid, sly, lusty blacks. This self-conscious contradiction of the high and low clearly made the South different from anywhere else.

To get the full sense and sweep of Griffith's mythological vision of blacks and the South, *The Birth of a Nation* must be seen together with two earlier Griffith films, *His Trust* and *His Trust Fulfilled,* both made in 1911. These films, which were set during the Civil War and its aftermath, have white actor Wilfred Lucas adopting blackface to play George, the old black family retainer. When the master leaves for war, George accepts the responsibility of looking after his left-behind wife and child. In this vision of Southern family happiness, the slaves, who whoop and celebrate like children when the Confederate soldiers leave their families to defend the homeland, are stirred by the pageantry but less aware of the larger stakes. After the master dies heroically in battle, George remains with the master's now poverty-stricken family. Union soldiers loot and burn the homestead, but the faithful black servant risks his own life and enters the burning house to save both the child and the master's sword.

The second reel, the Reconstruction reel, begins with the mother's heartbreak and death. And so hard have times become that at one point George is tempted to steal a wallet, but he resists and, in the end, secretly underwrites the daughter's education. The girl happily marries without ever knowing what George has done for her, thinking, in fact, that it was neighboring whites who came to her rescue. By confirming the order of the universe, and sweetly affirming the place of the lowly, this touching bit of *Great Expectations*–type homespun could have been as easily a class-based Russian, Italian, or Indian story of aristocracy and its privileges.

In asserting this myth about the loyal black slave, a myth that was central to the South's claim as a unique and especially humane civilization during the days when slavery was defended, Griffith was supported by the most important black leader of the era, Booker T. Washington, who said, when speaking to Southern whites in the 1895 speech that made him a national figure:

> Cast [your bucket] down among the eight millions of Negroes whose habits you know, whose fidelity and love you have tested in days when to have proved treacherous meant the ruin of your firesides. . . . While doing this, you can be sure in the future, as in the past, that you and your families will be surrounded by the most patient, faithful, law-abiding, and unresentful people that the world has seen.

For Washington to demand such loyalty from his black followers seems a striking form of political impotency. Here was a Southern black man whose claim to leadership and legitimacy was the endorsement of a myth of loyalty, a myth that blacks were a race of natural retainers. How far could a leader go with the message of reminding weak people that they were weak?

It is an indication of his considerable political and rhetorical skills that Washington was able to exercise deep influence with blacks while espousing something so blatantly unpalatable. In all his books, Washington insisted that he was always sincere in the expression of his beliefs, which means he believed that most people figured that no rational person could possibly be sincere under such circumstances. In the age of black minstrelsy, when black men had to black up to play parodies of themselves, maybe Washington was passing as a black man playing a white man's version of a black man. But it must be remembered that Walter White and the NAACP—the organization created in opposition to Washington's accommodationism—sanctioned the same myth of black loyalty with *Gone With the Wind*.

Griffith's 1911 *Trust* films celebrated the sentimental South of hearth and home where white women relied on old, self-sacrificing black men like George, who gave the appearance of being celibate and strangely alienated from their own race. Wilford Lucas's blackface character was simply another manifestation of the minstrel-stage version of Uncle Tom, a character fashioned from the exquisite marginality of his own isolation, a haunting archetype of emasculation and deracination. Without the Victorian piety and racialized mannerisms, the character becomes an almost perfect embodiment of modern existentialism, a point that James Baldwin sensed, although he could not fully articulate it, when, in one of his notable essays, he compared *Uncle Tom's Cabin* to Richard Wright's *Native Son*.

After *His Trust* and *His Trust Fulfilled,* the full fury of Griffith's vision of the horrors of miscegenation is made more vivid four years later in *The Birth of a Nation,* where uppity blacks want to have sex with and marry white women (as black heavyweight champion Jack Johnson, the most famous black man in America, had been doing at the time the film was conceived and made). Dixon's novels emphasized rape more than marriage but from the white Southerner's perspective consent was irrelevant.

The sheer grotesqueness of the miscegenation scenes in *The Birth of a Nation* gives the film a particular compulsive power. Like a Peeping Tom watching something verging on taboo, the more one sees, the more one wants to see. Similarly, an implicit moral rage within the deranged American racial conscience shouted out that this ought not to happen—while perversely hoping that it will. The anxiety of the Progressive Age was that the two political archetypes declaring their emancipation from the past—the New Negro and the New Woman—were not only emerging together, but seemingly colliding.

Big, burly black men diddling tiny white women (and the two offended white women of *The Birth of a Nation* certainly seem small and the pseudo-black men—white actors in blackface—seem big) is still close to how interracial pornographic films are advertised and sold today on the Internet. Yes, interracial sex can somehow always be pornographic, especially when it is associated with the South.

It is, however, in the vision of an intransigent white Southerner like Griffith that white men do not diddle black women as a perk of their lordly status. Griffith's cinematic South is a peaceable kingdom of different races, inferior and superior, living in intimacy but without border-crossing sex. His was the South that, on the one hand, celebrated the interracial clan and, on the other, celebrated the racial-purity enforcement of the Klan. (Margaret Mitchell, too, does not entertain this idea of white men bedding black women in her novel, and the film, having consigned interracial sex to the trash bin of the prurient and the politically risky, does not even hint at any lust for black women by white men. Whence, then, the mulatto, like Booker T. Washington, who always believed and was told that his father was white?) But always this immaculate arrangement between the races is threatened by lurching and lurking miscegenation, a hidden danger symbolizing the possibility of a black politics that won't accept as the reality of Southern family happiness the mythology of the black retainer and his loyalty and self-sacrifice.

The New South meant and boasted of was mainly a South which would be new in this: that it would be so rich and powerful that it might rest serene in its ancient positions, forever impregnable.

—W. J. Cash, *The Mind of the South*

It is said that the camera cannot lie, but rarely do we allow it to do anything else, since the camera sees what you point it at: the camera sees what you want it to see. The language of the camera is the language of our dreams.

—James Baldwin, *The Devil Finds Work*

2

AMERICAN GOTHIC

With the arrival in the 1950s and '60s of the sexploitation films of Russ Meyer, Doris Wishman, Michael and Roberta Findlay, and Dave Friedman—whose subjects ran the gamut from nudist colonies, strip clubs, and suburban swinging to prostitution and the illegal drug trade—emerged a category of movies that combined interracial sex and the South. What drove D. W. Griffith's fascination with Reconstruction drove sexploitation filmmakers' fascination with the Civil Rights Movement (in effect, the second Reconstruction): big, burly black men diddling tiny white women in a South where, traditionally, burly black men swung from trees for doing such a thing.

At least one of these films was made by an artistically ambitious European and thus, as with Griffith and his potent technique, we have the crossing of the idea of cinema as profound art, with pretensions to history, with the idea of cinema as pop trash, voyeurism, and melodramatic slop. Of course, the big difference here was that non-Southern whites who presumably had no interest in defending the white South or trying to empathize with the strange, hypocritical form of conservatism that rationalized its contradictions, made the film. As a result, a certain kind of cynicism pervades French director Michel Gast's *I Spit on Your Grave*. Whatever commercial impulses propelled the European, his was a liberal's reinterpretation of the South's own pop-culture typologies and clichés. The European thought himself above the parochial preoccupation of thinking of black-and-white sex as sensational or threatening. (After World War II, the white South's racial reactionaryism had become, for sophisticated or moral thinkers, insupportable, an inconvenient tribalism.) He thought black men were liberated by diddling white women and white women were liberated by it, too. But the European could never forget that interracial sex between black men and white women was a persistently perverse fascination in American culture. To some it seemed as if the Civil Rights Movement and the sexual revolution had, at the cost of the white South's traditions and power, simultaneously unleashed the libidos of black men and white women. (The libidos of black women were always free, according to the white mind, whenever anyone gave a thought to their libidos at all.)

So the final heterosexual taboo—miscegenation—was about to be broken by a revolution in this New Emerging South and by a cinematic style that combined the skepticism of film noir with the amateur ineptitude of the grindhouse. Gast's *I Spit on Your Grave* (originally released in France in 1959, and in the United States in 1962) is based on French writer Boris Vian's pseudo-American potboiler novel, *J'irai cracher sur vos tombes* (published in France in 1946). Vian, a white jazz musician, writer, and hipster/iconoclast, wrote the novel pretending to translate into French a novel by a fictional black American writer named Vernon Sullivan—another instance of a white man passing for black or for what he thinks is black. (Vian, supposedly, was so outraged at an advanced showing of the film that he dropped dead after seeing the first few scenes, which, if true, possibly makes this film unique in the annals of filmmaking.)

I Spit on Your Grave is about a light-skinned black man named Joe Grant (played by a white actor)* who decides to pass for white when his much darker brother (played by a black actor) is lynched for having an affair with a white woman. (In the novel, the darker brother, who also teaches at an all-black school, is named Tom, and is "meek and resigned.") Joe Grant goes to another town, where he seduces several white women, all of whom find him irresistible, which suggests that his black blood serves as a sex magnet.† Perhaps your daughter may not wish to marry one—the favorite question among white Southerners at the time was, "Would you want your daughter to marry one?"—but, according to this film, she sure is determined to sleep with one. (In the novel, Grant not only seduces but murders two white women.) As James Baldwin points out in his discussion of both the novel and the film in *The Devil Finds Work*, the fantasy here is of a white man who acts like a black man—that is, acts like black men "according to the white imagination which has created them." This is a different take from Griffith's, where white women find sexualized black men to be nightmares. But these are merely two sides of the same pulp coin: the white Southern interracial sex obsession and the idea of a white man pretending to be a black man in order to do to white women what whites imagine that black men want to do.

---

*Many post–World War II American "problem" films about race and passing featured white actors playing blacks, including *Pinky*, *Lost Boundaries*, *I Passed for White*, *Kings Go Forth*, *Raintree County*, *Imitation of Life* (the second version), and *Band of Angels*. In this respect, things hadn't progressed very far from the days of Griffith.

†The idea of a black man seeking revenge against whites by having sex with white women is not unusual in sexploitation or pornographic films. Melvin Van Peebles used a variation of this idea with his black stud as revolutionary in his landmark independent film *Sweet Sweetback's Baadasssss Song* (1971). More recently, in the hard-core arena, JM Productions has put out over twenty-five volumes of *White Trash Whore*. In each film, one or two white women are gang-banged by five or six black men in scenes that are nearly unwatchable for anyone who does not have a strong stomach for the most tasteless, savage depictions of sex. Those scenes are tantamount to a glorified dramatization of hate crimes.

There is a small bit of nudity in *I Spit on Your Grave* as well as the obligatory decadent party scene of lesbian and homosexual stereotypes that are standard for sexploitation cinema of this period. Joe Grant's true identity is eventually discovered but not before he falls in love with a rich white woman who also loves him.

In this instance of passing, a black man who looks like a white man diddles and wants to diddle white women. To anyone watching, it would look like two white people coupling so the crime of interracial sex could only be actualized here if the perpetrator confesses that he is black. Absent any other proof, one simply has to take his word for it, which begs the question: What sane white man would say that he was black? Yet from the time of minstrelsy white men have constantly pretended to be black as a masquerade ritual and an art form. The film seems to say that race is merely rhetorical or vocal (Joe Grant was always afraid that his "black voice" would give him away) or a fantasy projection, but it does not seem to be anything else. Race is what we say any difference can be when we want it to be that.

Michel Gast made two endings for the film: In one, both Grant and the white woman are killed trying to escape the town. In the other, they succeed in escaping.

————————

Another racial sexploitation film of this period is Larry Buchanan's *Free, White, and 21* (1963), a surprisingly impressive, almost documentary-like dramatization about interracial rape. In *Free, White, and 21,* a white woman from Sweden named Greta goes South to join the Civil Rights Movement and become a freedom rider. (Is there a racy pun in her being a freedom rider that is the inside joke of the film?) She is seemingly raped in a rundown black hotel by a black man, Ernie Jones, a local businessman who leases the hotel and is a sleaze artist on the hunt for models. A great deal of ambiguity surrounds the rape. The courtroom drama, played out somewhere in Texas, has the white prosecutor, who is officially pressing Greta's case, glad to see Ernie Jones acquitted. The prosecutor dislikes Greta, because she is a Civil Rights worker, more than he dislikes uppity blacks. Later, it is revealed that Greta passed a lie-detector test, so she was almost certainly telling the truth. The irony also complicates the audience reactions: Whites are less inclined to come to Greta's defense because she socializes with blacks, while blacks feel that liberal whites and racist whites are the same—Greta's charges against the black man are typical of those used by racist whites to bring black men down and keep them in their place. The film is striking because the black defendant is not admirable. Unlike mainstream films of the period about race (compare the black man accused of rape in this film with Brock Peters's noble character in *To Kill a Mockingbird,* a film made at nearly the same time), there is never any overt or implied theme of uplift or "let's do something good for race relations." Greta is portrayed more sympathetically, but she, too, is flawed in her naïveté and her racial innocence, which borders on being a form of racism itself.

Despite the suggestive title and the sensational subject matter, the film is almost oddly restrained in most respects.

Murder in Mississippi (1965), shot mainly in Philadelphia, Pennsylvania, and directed by J.P. Mawra, who also directed *All Men Are Apes* (which particularly haunted me as a teenager because my friends told me that the film ends with a woman having sex with an ape), is another racial sexploitation film about the Civil Rights Movement and one that is as wildly gruesome as *The Birth of a Nation.* The film features murder, castration, beatings, and a brief relationship between a black Civil Rights worker and, again, a naive white woman drawn to the Movement. Seedy as *All Men Are Apes* but less comically cynical, *Murder in Mississippi* tries for an unusual and discordant happy ending by showing the white woman, who'd been tempted to leave the Movement, returning to the South to register black voters (the film's final moments are from the March on Washington in 1963).

I remember these films very well from my childhood for they were targeted to black audiences. As a child in Philadelphia, I went to the downtown theaters only on special occasions, such as when my Sunday School class was taken to see *Ben-Hur, Barabbas, The Ten Commandments, The Story of Ruth,* or *King of Kings.* Otherwise, I saw movies at a black theater with black audiences. In this sense, I usually experienced films as if I had been living in the South—in a segregated setting. This deeply affected the range of movies that was available for me to view (Elvis Presley movies never played at the black theater I attended), and *how* I understood them, because the audience's reaction to various films was often different than might have been expected. Although I did not realize this until I was much older and watched films with mostly white audiences, in black theaters people frequently laughed at gangster and horror films, openly disdained Doris Day comedies, acted out swatches of dialogues, or conversed with characters on the screen. I "misread" several mainstream films as a child because I watched them with a black audience.

I didn't attend these racial sexploitation films as a child or an adolescent because they were considered adult fare and my mother would not permit me to see them. Since the films frightened and unnerved me, I did not have the courage to defy my mother, although I could have as she did not closely police my leisure time. Instead, I experienced racial exploitation through the trailers that appeared before routine, safer movies. These trailers caused me to squirm and fidget. I thought them unnatural and pornographic, almost like the stories I might read of debauched Hollywood actors, crazy murders, and hideous diseases in, say, *The National Enquirer* (a paper that was very popular with the black kids with whom I grew up). The black men in those trailers were always blacker than any blacks in real life and the white women always whiter (and better-looking). This, I suppose, was the intended effect.

In one trailer, a white woman kissed a black man, and the image, both fascinating and terrifying, stayed with me for several days. My poor stricken brown face—I had heard that black boys in the South were killed for such things! What made her so special to die for? (Those pictures in *Jet* magazine of Emmett Till in his coffin had terrorized me in the darkness of my bedroom. His misshapened face had seemed to rise up in front of me even with my eyes tightly shut.) "White women fart and belch, too," my mother told me after she saw how disturbed I was by the trailer. I was relieved to know that white women were human. At the time, white women seemed either a desire or a curse but nothing else.

The exploitation film I remember better than any other is *Black Like Me* (1964), based on the famous journalistic account of white

Southerner John Howard Griffin's travels through the South disguised as a black man. When I saw the trailer, I thought it was a horror movie. James Whitmore, who played the Griffin character, was simply covered in burnt cork. He did not seem like a black person at all to me but rather like someone disfigured or monstrous. It made me think that perhaps this is how a black person looks to whites. Years later, when I watched the film again, he was to bring to mind the white actors who passed for black with the use of blackface in Griffith's films, and perhaps that was a point of this film, to remind us very blatantly of that tradition. But I could not understand how anyone in the movie could possibly think he was a black person. No white person in blackface could ever fool me into thinking he or she was black. Instead, Whitmore was something alien, a projection in the minds of whites. I remember the trailer showed his white wife and asked, with the usual luridness of implied interracial sex, *Could she love him now that he was a Negro?* But since he was not a black person at all, how could that be a real question? Didn't Al Jolson's white wife love him even though he put on burnt cork and made a living pretending to be a black man? And, of course, it took place in the South, where black people were lynched and whites were evil, a place I never planned to visit, a place my mother feared that my sister would go to because she had joined SNCC and had become, in college, a devoted Civil Rights worker.

Everyone in America at the time seemed to be living on the edge of both the familiar and unreal and it all seemed rooted in the weird playing-out of the fantasy of integration in the South.

But *Black Like Me* was an exploitative film only because it was so cheaply made; it was, in reality, a leftist film, an anti-Griffith, anti–*Gone With the Wind* drama about the New South, made by the Marxist husband-and-wife team of film editor Carl Lerner, who directed the film, and Gerda Lerner, who wrote the script (and who would become a noted pioneer scholar in feminist studies). What better way for whites to be convinced of how terribly blacks are treated than by becoming black? The book is certainly empathetic and has become the standard text for exploring the meaning of "becoming the other." Griffin was a devout, liberal Catholic who had entertained thoughts of becoming a composer or musicologist. He went blind for several years after World War II but miraculously regained his sight. *Black Like Me* is like a Catholic vision of the Southern race problem:

piety combined with social witness of the Dorothy Day sort. The film
uses incidents from the book, emphasizing the peripatetic nature of
Griffin's exploration of the South, making it, in effect, a road movie.
Whitmore's Griffin is far angrier on the screen than in the book
version—at times, he's like a Northern black man who has come
South. Indeed, in one scene, he nearly kills a white man who wants to
see the size of his penis. Nothing like this happens in the book, as
Griffin makes it a point to be humble and seems more shocked and depressed than angered by his treatment as a black man. A white man
does ask to see his penis but Griffin simply demurs. There is a good
deal of talk about interracial sex in the book and this is carried over
into the film but with more sensationalism. Making Griffin angrier and
prone to violence is not simply a result of the leftist filmmakers' more
radical vision of how blacks ought to be portrayed but also a reflection
of the gap of three years from the publication of the book to the release of the film. Between 1959, when Griffin was in the South, disguised as a black man, collecting material, and 1964, when the film
played in black theaters in cities like Philadelphia, blacks had become
more publicly militant and violence hung, miasma-like, over the
American landscape. The film was made after the assassination of
John Kennedy and shows us the kind of militant black Civil Rights
workers who were not present in the South of 1959 but surely existed
by the time of the Mississippi Freedom Democratic Party of 1964.

Black Like Me came out one year after *To Kill a Mockingbird* (1963),
probably the most celebrated liberal film about the South and race ever
made. It was, of course, based on Harper Lee's novel, now a classic
book for schoolchildren.

On one level, the novel and the film free the white South of its
gothic past with the symbolic murder of the bad, racist Bob Ewell (the
evil father) by innocent Boo Radley (the ghost of the haunted
house)—ushering in a truly new New South. The New South was liberated from defending its past and harsh but courtly conservatism,
which had been nothing more than a reactionary revolt against modern life. At its core, the story seems built around interracial sex between a black man and a white woman and the charge of rape, the

Griffith obsession that became the raison d'être of the cinematic de-
piction of the South. The film, which schoolteachers took me to see as
a child, is sophisticated in that it disarms a viewer by re-pathologizing
rape not as interracial but as incestuous, the real secret sin of the South
that everyone accepted readily enough (Southerners, like that nutty
Jerry Lee Lewis, are always going around marrying their teenaged
cousins), and by making the Southern miscegenation movie into a redemptive story for children to grow by. But the liberalism of *To Kill a
Mockingbird* was smug and that made it all too easy. Virtue was virtu-
ous and evil was, alas, evil, a reflection of the same hollow, obvious art
that drove not the Griffith of *The Birth of a Nation* but the Griffith of
His Trust and *His Trust Fulfilled*. Besides, in giving the viewer the slut-
tish, poor, victimized white girl (who wanted to be diddled by a black
man, as only a poor slut who had been having sex with her father
would) and the noble black victim (who would not stoop to having sex
with a half-deranged, stinky white girl), *To Kill a Mockingbird* was toy-
ing with, in an exploitative, knowing way, a white paternalist variation
of the contradictory fantasy that seems at the center of the American
consciousness: either black men want to diddle white women above all
else or resist such temptation with an emasculatory zeal that seems
saintly.

By the time I was twenty, I thought *To Kill a Mockingbird* was absolutely the worst film about the South I had ever seen, contrived piety
and innocence, dishonesty and schoolmarm nonsense about uplift and
brotherhood, a lot of sentimental flapdoodle about "good white people and their conscience," which ought to have been blasted off the
screen by the white Southern male madness of *The Birth of a Nation*,
the film that defined America, and which has yet to be defeated or
erased by its counter or its other.

Modern-Day Mammy?

Jill Nelson

Would all the big-boned, all-suffering, all-nurturing, asexual sisters please step away. Ditto to all you loud, ignorant, obese, sexually voracious, potentially violent sisters with too much attitude. All y'all, take your neck-rolling, eye-cutting, sassy selves elsewhere—what follows is not for you.

What, all you sisters still reading? I guess you don't see yourself in these images. Then who are the models for the Black women who appear so often in popular culture?

I wasn't the only woman offended by ads for the movie *Norbit* depicting Eddie Murphy as an obese Black woman in a pink fur-trimmed baby doll negligee straddling Murphy's Norbit, the skinny nerd. The horrified expression on his face was no match for the greedy one on hers, and we all know the meaning of the film's tagline, "Have you ever made a really big mistake?"

Call me naive, but I'd like to believe the real mistake was Murphy putting on drag and hauling out tired jokes about body fat and flatulence. But *Norbit* was No. 1 at the box office in its opening weekend, earning $34.2 million, more than twice as much as its closest competitor.

Murphy's not alone in ridiculing big dark-skinned women for fun and profit. He joins a list of Black comedians—Flip Wilson, Jamie Foxx, Martin Lawrence—in strapping on oversize breasts and buttocks and exhibiting an obnoxious personality. These modern-day mammies are desexualized figures, like Lawrence's Big Momma or Tyler Perry's Madea, or desperate predators, à la Murphy's Rasputia and Foxx's Wanda.

They join an advertising culture that perpetuates similar stereotypes of Black women, although it's some consolation that at least real Black women get a paycheck for these commercials. Still, whether we're selling ice cream or hemorrhoid cream, too often we're broad caricatures: the dominatrix with an attitude or the long-suffering know-it-alls guaranteed to confront, humiliate or both. These images of us aren't rooted in reality but are exaggerated, demeaning composites.

Some researchers believe that such images contribute to an increase in eating disorders among girls and women. A study published in 2000 in *Archives of Family Medicine* found that binge eating or vomiting is a current problem among both Black and White women.

I'm certainly not advocating obesity, but since when did having some meat on your bones become a negative among Black people? When did it become acceptable to mock hefty brown-skinned women and exalt light-skinned women with thighs the diameter of a wrist? It's time for those of us in the vast middle to say "Enough!" We should demand with our purchasing power at the box office and in the marketplace that Black women be portrayed in all our shapes, sizes and colors, not as stereotypes. It's the twenty-first century and past time for us to reclaim our images.

Broken Dreams

⤳⧬⧬◎

Michael A. Gonzales

The DeBarge family—El, Marty, Randy, and James, not to mention Thomas, Bobby, and baby brother Chico—were supposed to be Motown's follow-up to the Jacksons. But after a trail of dazzling '80s hits, behind-the-scenes drama threatened to bring the family down. From dating La Toya and Janet Jackson to allegations of sexual abuse and drug addiction—the DeBarge family has dealt with everything from prison time to AIDS. But even now, their music is sampled by the likes of Diddy and Polow Da Don, and some of the DeBarges are trying to resurrect their careers. Is it too late, though, to pick up the pieces?

The house lights dimmed on a humid summer evening in 1994, and El DeBarge floated across the cluttered stage of the now-defunct New York City nightclub Tramps.

"Respect to the old school!" screamed a drunk woman from the bar. El, then 33, gently grabbed the microphone and wrapped his feathery falsetto around a songbook of classic material from his family's R&B-pop group, DeBarge. Though he'd left the group in 1986, El opened with their heartbreaking 1983 hit "Stay with Me" (Gordy), which Sean "Puffy" Combs would sample for the Notorious B.I.G.'s 1995 smash remix of "One More Chance" (Bad Boy). As El sang, it seemed he was ready for another chance himself. Despite rumors that he was caught up in a fog of drug addiction, on this night, both El's voice and his wardrobe were sharp as nails.

An ex-child preacher at Bethel Pentecostal Church in Grand Rapids, Mich., Eldra DeBarge still knew how to work a crowd, baptizing the blissful audience simply by playing a few chords on his white keyboard. Born into a biracial—not hispanic, as many still believe—family of sublime vocalists, El became the brightest star of the eight singing DeBarge siblings.

DeBarge was part of Motown's second wave of soul-music stars after founder Berry Gordy Jr. fled the grit of Detroit for the glam of Los Angeles. Consisting of brothers El, James, Mark, Randy, and their elder sister Bunny, the group was transformed from Midwestern church singers to *Right On!* magazine teen dreams, complete with flashy 1980s fashions and beaming smiles. But by the late '80s, DeBarge's fame was fading.

Less than a decade later, El was in NYC to promote his new album, *Heart, Mind & Soul* (Warner Bros.), and perhaps to make a new start. Except for the huge hit he'd had with Barry White, Al B. Sure!, and James Ingram of 1990's Quincy Jones–produced "The Secret Garden (Sweet Seduction Suite)," El had been off the radar for years. He was already a throwback in a world dominated by new jacks like R. Kelly and Jodeci, but no one could have predicted that *H,M&S* would be El's last solo release for 13 years.

At Tramps, El closed his eyes and sang the tortured lyrics of "All This Love," a massive radio hit he wrote and produced in 1983: "I've had some problems," he sang. "And no one could seem to solve them." The poignant lines were a fitting synopsis of the turbulent life and times of the DeBarge family—the greatest story never told.

It began in 1975, when Barry White fired a crew known as White Heat, one of his many backing bands, which included pianist/singer Robert "Bobby" DeBarge Jr., the second oldest of the 10 DeBarge siblings. The whole DeBarge family loved music. They'd sing on Detroit radio on Sunday mornings and perform at talent shows. Bobby's talent always stood out.

"I've never heard anyone sound quite like him, and with so much ease," producer Bernd Lichters has said. "I knew I saw a star." Lichters worked with former White Heat members Bobby DeBarge and Gregory Williams (a schoolmate of Bobby's) to launch the pioneering soul-pop group Switch. Bobby co-wrote and co-produced much of the group's music, but behind his good looks and talent lurked a tortured soul.

Bobby's drug issues were common knowledge among the members of Switch, but his voice was too gorgeous to ignore. Still, Switch—which released five albums on Motown's subsidiary Gordy Records—almost bounded into the studio without his supple crooning. "I wasn't sure I wanted Bobby to be in the group because he was still on drugs," says Williams. But when a chance meeting in Los Angeles with Jermaine Jackson and his wife, Hazel (Berry Gordy's daughter), got them an audition with Gordy, Williams reconsidered.

Bobby was determined to kick his habit before reaching Hollywood, sweating the junk from his system on the bus ride west from Grand Rapids. By the time anyone from Motown met him, Bobby was clean. Switch—which consisted of Bobby and Tommy DeBarge, Williams, vocalist Phillip Ingram, Eddie Fluellan, and Jody Sims—was offered a contract.

Released in 1978, Switch's self-titled debut featured the ethereal "There'll Never Be," which rode the *Billboard* R&B charts for 19 weeks, peaking at No. 6. The album formed the sonic template for future groups like Jodeci and Mint Condition.

"The night we wrote 'I Call Your Name' was a strange one," says Williams of the achy slow jam, sampled in 2006 by Polow Da Don for Rich Boy's hit "Throw Some D's." "Bobby was dating La Toya Jackson," Williams says, "and she was the only girl on his mind. One night, he started fooling around on the Fender Rhodes. I started singing along, and next thing you know we had a song. I'm not saying the song was written for La Toya, but they were in love, and Bobby couldn't wait to play her the completed song."

While Bobby was working on the second Switch album, Mark and Randy DeBarge visited Los Angeles to see what their brothers were up to. Before long, Bunny, Mark, Randy, El, and James made the journey west. Lichters leased a five-bedroom house and took them to buy instruments. "Motown put us on salary because we were starving," says Bunny by phone from Grand Rapids. "Because he'd lost the Jacksons, we became [Gordy's] pet project." Motown encouraged the DeBarges to fire their managers and sign with De Passe and Jones

Management, which was affiliated with Motown. They eventually agreed.

While family acts like the Osmonds and the Sylvers had become passé after the Jackson 5 left Motown in 1975, the acclaim of DeBarge's 1982 sophomore album, *All This Love,* inspired a new generation of brothers and sisters—like 5 Star and The Jets—to bumrush the sibling scene. But DeBarge stood head and shoulders above the rest. Romantic, pop-friendly R&B jams like "All This Love," "I Like It," "Love Me in a Special Way," and their biggest pop hit, "Rhythm of the Night," from the 1985 Motown film *The Last Dragon* (Tri-Star Pictures), made the group crossover stars.

But the DeBarge family was ill-prepared for the challenges of celebrity. Back in the 1960s, when Gordy's hit factory was still run like a mom-and-pop shop, the "old" Motown was renowned for artist development that included everything from dance lessons to etiquette classes. The label's 1972 move to L.A. killed that tradition. "Coaching? What coaching? I haven't been fortunate enough to have people around to show me things," El told the *Los Angeles Times* in 1984. "Basically, I'm out there by myself."

That same year, James DeBarge, the second youngest of the group, married Janet Jackson. She was 18. He was 21. He was a rising star at Motown, and she was struggling to break away from a notoriously insular family. James met her because his brother Bobby was dating La Toya. "James and Janet started secretly seeing each other," says Bunny. "Then they came to Grand Rapids and eloped. For the Jackson family, it was a nightmare. Nobody knew how serious it was, but they were so young." The marriage was annulled after several months amid allegations of James' drug abuse. It's long been rumored that Janet gave birth to a baby girl who was raised by her older sister Rebbie. All parties involved have denied the story for decades. "They say the kid's in Europe or that one of my brothers or sisters is raising it," Janet said in the May 2001 issue of *Vibe.* "But no, I've never had a child."

It was also in 1984, during DeBarge's four-month stint as the opening act on Luther Vandross' sold-out "Busy Body" tour, when the family discovered just how famous they'd become. This was the era of Michael Jackson's *Thriller,* Prince's *Purple Rain,* and The Police's *Synchronicity,* but DeBarge was driving their fans every bit as crazy as those household names. "Girls would pull out our hair, tear off our clothes, and sometimes scratch off our skin," says James by phone from California. "It got even scarier when we stopped off in Detroit to perform at a record shop. The crowd broke down the barricades and smashed the windows. There were a lot of Beatles-type moments."

Nevertheless, in the Motown tradition of separating powerful lead singers from successful groups—Diana Ross from the Supremes, Michael Jackson from the Jacksons, Lionel Richie from the Commodores—it wasn't long before divide-and-conquer tactics apparently went down with DeBarge. "They made El think he was better than his brothers and sister," says El's 71-year-old mother, Etterlene. "Michael was the star of the Jacksons, but I thought my kids made them look like crap," adds the woman who refers to herself—even on her MySpace page—as Mama DeBarge. Speaking by telephone from her home in Grand Rapids, her voice is as soothing as peppermint tea, but she harbors bad memories of Motown, which she's channeling into a book she's writing, titled *The Other Side of the Pain*. "Everything became about what Motown wanted, not what the kids wanted," she says. "My kids were fighting like enemies."

But according to Bunny, it wasn't just label troubles that derailed the Debarges' dreams of glory. "We weren't able to sustain our success because of our childhood," she says. On the surface, they seemed like a model family. But the parents' relationship was troubled. "Interracial marriage was still controversial, and we were talked about everywhere," says Bunny. To make matters worse, Bunny says her father and mother were always fighting. "Mom came from a loving, church family. She wasn't used to people who were violent."

Even family friends sensed problems at home. "To put it simply," says Williams, who's known and worked with the DeBarges since they were all youngsters, "their father was psychotic."

Etterlene Abney was 17 when she met the 21-year-old Army soldier Robert DeBarge at a Detroit skating rink. "At first I didn't think he would like me because I was so dark," Etterlene recalls. "A white man with a black woman . . . we were a freak show." They were married in 1953, two weeks before he was shipped out overseas. Etterlene says she'd never known brutality in her life—until she wed. "Robert was very jealous," she says with a sigh, "and an extremely abusive father." They stayed together 21 years before divorcing in 1974.

"Bobby went through a lot of pain," says Chico DeBarge of his oldest brother. "My father sexually molested a lot of my brothers and sisters. You could hear that anguish in Bobby's music."

Robert DeBarge Sr. has a voice as dry as sandpaper. At 75, he's had three surgeries and breathes with the help of an oxygen tank. "She has the right to her opinion," he says of his wife's allegations of abuse. "I don't think that I was at all . . . I don't speak a lot against her because she's the mother of my children. There are a lot of things, for the sake of the children, some things are best for them not to even know." Now remarried, with one son who died in a car accident, he firmly denies abusing his children sexually or otherwise. "Ohh no, no, no," he says, sounding shocked at the idea.

"That may be our fault," says Bunny, unsurprised to hear her father's denials. "We never made daddy stand up. I don't hate my father, but he has a way of blocking things out of his mind."

Robert Sr. was a trucker after leaving the Army. A religious man, he sometimes found time to play the piano. "I was musically inclined," he says with a laugh, "so the children couldn't help but be talented." Although he had split with "the boys' mother" by the time his children moved to Los Angeles, he says he "wasn't tickled to death about it," preferring they further their education instead. He never thought Motown would treat them right. "I knew they would use them instead of being fair with them. Being in the limelight is a struggle," he says. "Here today, and gone tomorrow."

According to Bunny—who, like her mother, is working on a book, ominously titled *The Kept One*—the DeBarge siblings' experience with drugs started early. She tried sniffing coke after the group finished its second album and eventually became dependent on pills. "It was the '80s—doing drugs was the thing to do," says Bunny, stressing that she never went to sessions high. "If you weren't doing drugs, you weren't in."

By 1987, Bunny had left DeBarge and was in a free fall. "I had no drugs to help me cover, no fame to hide behind," she writes in her forthcoming book. (Bunny has since kicked her habit, crediting the turnaround to her relationship with God.) The following year, Bobby and Chico were convicted, along with two other accomplices, on drug conspiracy charges. Chico's self-titled debut album had been released just two years earlier, and he should have been enjoying the success of his single "Talk to Me" (Motown, 1986). Instead, both brothers found themselves in jail cells serving five-year sentences. But the most tragic fall of all was Bobby's.

"Bobby was always very sensitive and withdrawn," says Williams, "and there was a lot of abuse at the hands of Mr. DeBarge. Heroin became his main way to escape." Though he stayed clean for a while, after the success of Switch II, Bobby began slipping. "He was back on drugs, and his ego was out of control," Williams says. "Bobby was going around saying, 'I'm Switch.'"

But Etterlene believes her son had simply outgrown the group. "There was a lot of hating going on," she says. "People might have bought Switch records, but they were really buying Bobby's voice."

Maybe he didn't need the band to show off his musical talents, but Bobby did seek refuge at his former bandmate's California home after being released from prison in 1994 with the HIV virus ravaging his immune system. "Bobby's last years were hell," Williams says. "He was separated from his wife and kids and acting paranoid toward everybody. Bobby knew his life was basically over." He moved back to Grand Rapids the following year, and his family checked him into a hospice. After riding the heroin horse since his teens, Bobby died from complications of AIDS on August 16, 1995, at the age of 39. Taking his big brother's death to heart, El would never be the same.

Much was expected of Eldra. Like Bobby, El had "it." Aside from his vocal talents, El was also a keyboardist and producer who seemed destined to run in the same company as Michael Jackson and Prince. But at his core, El was more tortured balladeer than mammoth pop star.

"I've seen him get to a special place while performing, and he'd just start crying on stage," says his friend and collaborator David "DJ Quik" Blake from his Southern California home. "That's how powerful his music is."

Legendary producer Kenneth "Babyface" Edmonds, who did production work on El's *Heart, Mind & Soul,* remembers when his old group the Deele—which included drummer-turned-Island-Def-Jam-chairman Antonio "L.A." Reid—and DeBarge opened for Luther Vandross. "I was in awe of El back then," says Babyface, "and learned much about songwriting and performance from studying him."

El's solo track record is frustratingly short. Motown released his self-titled solo debut in 1986, featuring the lighthearted "Who's Johnny." A second solo album, *Gemini,* was received with moderate fanfare in 1989. In 1992, he laced Quincy Jones' majestic "The Secret Garden." El's first post-Motown disc, *In the Storm* (Warner Bros., 1992), featured underrated collaborations with Earth, Wind & Fire's Maurice White, a duet with Chanté Moore, and a chilling remake of Marvin Gaye's "After the Dance" with Fourplay. While that track was a hit on urban radio, the disc was a commercial disappointment. In 1995, Warner Bros. dropped El. With the exception of supplying keyboards and background vocals on Chico's classic post-prison disc, *Long Time No See* (1997), DJ Quik's 1999 *Rhythm-al-ism* (Arista), and Quincy Jones' 1999 *I'm Yours* (Warner Bros.), El hasn't recorded anything for public consumption in more than a decade.

So, what happened?

"Drugs happened," blurts Etterlene. "It's painful to talk about, but when El got into drugs, it just paralyzed him." As usual, the drug abuse masked deeper scars. "El was lonely without his brothers," his mother says. "He just couldn't deal with all the people in the music industry. Motown had taken all his publishing, and they're still making money from those songs." His own financial needs were just the tip of the iceberg. According to Bunny, El sired as many as 10 children, starting from the time he was 14. He could do little more than put all this stress and pain into his music, but then one day the music stopped.

"Is this going to be a cover story?" El asked in measured tones the one time *Vibe* spoke to him for this article, in April 2007. Chico, who was recording new material in a Times Square studio, had gotten him to the phone, if only for a minute.

"Not my decision," this writer replied.

"Well, call me on Monday," El said. "We can talk then."

After weeks of repeated phone calls that seemed to be ringing inside a black hole, it was obvious El had no intention of talking to anyone. But there may yet be another chapter to El's story. The reclusive soul man has recently been spending time in a California recording studio with Babyface. Williams holds out hope for El's redemption, but an interview is another matter. "Most of the time I can't even get a hold of him," says Williams, CEO of Switch Entertainment, who is also acting as El's manager. "But the voice is still there. El still has that gift."

Along with older brothers Bobby and El, the suffering "soul man" strain can be heard in Chico's music as well. While Switch, DeBarge, and El enjoy top billing in the DeBarge family's musical hierarchy, Chico's *Long Time No See* is a conceptual gem that recalls Marvin Gaye's 1978 *Here, My Dear* (Motown). When he signed to Kedar Entertainment, home of Erykah Badu, Chico wasn't aware that he was creating such a memorable project. "Coming out of prison," he says, sipping a Grey Goose and cranberry in a Brooklyn restaurant, "my goal was to make music that would get me to the other side of the pain."

After the release of Chico's 1999 follow-up, *The Game*, he and label founder Kedar Massenburg parted company. "We both have very strong opinions," says Massenburg. "His ideas for *The Game* were corny; Chico wanted to be more bling and mainstream. We did manage to make one classic album, but sometimes Chico can be his own worst enemy."

It's 2 a.m. one Saturday in Times Square, and perfectionist Chico has spent the night working at Quad Recording Studios. Dressed in a sweatsuit and sneakers, he's just recorded a new track called "Make You Feel Good," featuring rappers Jim Jones and Young Nic, which he plans to release on his own Innovator Entertainment label as part of his new album, *Lessons*.

The heartbreak in Bobby, El, and Chico's music has many sources, but part of it stems from having to constantly prove themselves worthy. The Jacksons are constantly namechecked as the first family of R&B. But when it comes to defining the canon, the artistry and rich contributions of the DeBarge family have been unfairly kicked to the curb.

Slightly buzzed from the vodka cocktail, Chico watches a taxi zoom down Broadway. "You know what us being in the studio tonight means?" he asks of no one in particular. "It means the DeBarge story is not over. What my brothers and sister gave me was a beautiful musical legacy that has already been written in stone," he says. "Nobody can change that history." And that's a story, no matter how painful, that Chico intends to carry on.

But his mother takes a different view. "If I had to do it again, I'd never allow my kids to be in the music industry," says a somber Etterlene DeBarge, who recently put a bunch of Chico's keyboards and recording equipment up for sale on eBay. "There are a lot of snakes out there," she says. "And they bite real hard."

SCIENCES, TECHNOLOGY, EDUCATION

None of the Above: What I.Q. Doesn't Tell You About Race

Malcolm Gladwell

One Saturday in November of 1984, James Flynn, a social scientist at the University of Otago, in New Zealand, received a large package in the mail. It was from a colleague in Utrecht, and it contained the results of I.Q. tests given to two generations of Dutch eighteen-year-olds. When Flynn looked through the data, he found something puzzling. The Dutch eighteen-year-olds from the nineteen-eighties scored better than those who took the same tests in the nineteen-fifties—and not just slightly better, much better.

Curious, Flynn sent out some letters. He collected intelligence-test results from Europe, from North America, from Asia, and from the developing world, until he had data for almost thirty countries. In every case, the story was pretty much the same. I.Q.s around the world appeared to be rising by 0.3 points per year, or three points per decade, for as far back as the tests have been administered. For some reason, human beings seemed to be getting smarter.

Flynn has been writing about the implications of his findings—now known as the Flynn effect—for almost twenty-five years. His books consist of a series of plainly stated statistical observations, in support of deceptively modest conclusions, and the evidence in support of his original observation is now so overwhelming that the Flynn effect has moved from theory to fact. What remains uncertain is how to make sense of the Flynn effect. If an American born in the nineteen-thirties has an I.Q. of 100, the Flynn effect says that his children will have I.Q.s of 108, and his grandchildren I.Q.s of close to 120—more than a standard deviation higher. If we work in the opposite direction, the typical teenager of today, with an I.Q. of 100, would have had grandparents with average I.Q.s of 82—seemingly below the threshold necessary to graduate from high school. And, if we go back even farther, the Flynn effect puts the average I.Q.s of the schoolchildren of 1900 at around 70, which is to suggest, bizarrely, that a century ago the United States was populated largely by people who today would be considered mentally retarded.

For almost as long as there have been I.Q. tests, there have been I.Q. fundamentalists. H. H. Goddard, in the early years of the past century, established the idea that intelligence could be measured along a single, linear scale. One of his particular contributions was to coin the word "moron." "The people who are doing the drudgery are, as a rule, in their proper places," he wrote. Goddard was followed by Lewis Terman, in the nineteen-twenties, who rounded up the California children with the highest I.Q.s, and confidently predicted that they would sit at the top of every profession. In 1969, the psychometrician Arthur Jensen argued that programs like Head Start, which tried to boost the academic performance of minority children, were doomed to failure, because I.Q. was so heavily genetic; and in 1994 Richard Herrnstein and Charles Murray, in *The Bell Curve*, notoriously proposed that Americans with the lowest I.Q.s be sequestered in a "high-tech" version of an Indian reservation, "while the rest of America tries to go about its business." To the I.Q. fundamentalist, two things are beyond dispute: first, that I.Q. tests measure some hard and identifiable trait that predicts the quality of our thinking; and, second, that this trait is stable—that is, it is determined by our genes and largely impervious to environmental influences.

This is what James Watson, the co-discoverer of DNA, meant when he told an English newspaper recently that he was "inherently gloomy" about the prospects for Africa. From the perspective of an

I.Q. fundamentalist, the fact that Africans score lower than Europeans on I.Q. tests suggests an ineradicable cognitive disability. In the controversy that followed, Watson was defended by the journalist William Saletan, in a three-part series for the online magazine *Slate*. Drawing heavily on the work of J. Philippe Rushton—a psychologist who specializes in comparing the circumference of what he calls the Negroid brain with the length of the Negroid penis—Saletan took the fundamentalist position to its logical conclusion. To erase the difference between blacks and whites, Saletan wrote, would probably require vigorous interbreeding between the races, or some kind of corrective genetic engineering aimed at upgrading African stock. "Economic and cultural theories have failed to explain most of the pattern," Saletan declared, claiming to have been "soaking [his] head in each side's computations and arguments." One argument that Saletan never soaked his head in, however, was Flynn's, because what Flynn discovered in his mailbox upsets the certainties upon which I.Q. fundamentalism rests. If whatever the thing is that I.Q. tests measure can jump so much in a generation, it can't be all that immutable and it doesn't look all that innate.

The very fact that average I.Q.s shift over time ought to create a "crisis of confidence," Flynn writes in *What Is Intelligence?* (Cambridge; $22), his latest attempt to puzzle through the implications of his discovery. "How could such huge gains be intelligence gains? Either the children of today were far brighter than their parents or, at least in some circumstances, I.Q. tests were not good measures of intelligence."

The best way to understand why I.Q.s rise, Flynn argues, is to look at one of the most widely used I.Q. tests, the so-called WISC (for Wechsler Intelligence Scale for Children). The WISC is composed of ten subtests, each of which measures a different aspect of I.Q. Flynn points out that scores in some of the categories—those measuring general knowledge, say, or vocabulary or the ability to do basic arithmetic—have risen only modestly over time. The big gains on the WISC are largely in the category known as "similarities," where you get questions such as "In what way are 'dogs' and 'rabbits' alike?" Today, we tend to give what, for the purposes of I.Q. tests, is the right answer: dogs and rabbits are both mammals. A nineteenth-century American would have said that "you use dogs to hunt rabbits."

"If the everyday world is your cognitive home, it is not natural to detach abstractions and logic and the hypothetical from their concrete referents," Flynn writes. Our great-grandparents may have been perfectly intelligent. But they would have done poorly on I.Q. tests because they did not participate in the twentieth century's great cognitive revolution, in which we learned to sort experience according to a new set of abstract categories. In Flynn's phrase, we have now had to put on "scientific spectacles," which enable us to make sense of the WISC questions about similarities. To say that Dutch I.Q. scores rose substantially between 1952 and 1982 was another way of saying that the Netherlands in 1982 was, in at least certain respects, much more cognitively demanding than the Netherlands in 1952. An I.Q., in other words, measures not so much how smart we are as how modern we are.

This is a critical distinction. When the children of Southern Italian immigrants were given I.Q. tests in the early part of the past century, for example, they recorded median scores in the high seventies and low eighties, a full standard deviation below their American and Western European counterparts. Southern Italians did as poorly on I.Q. tests as Hispanics and blacks did. As you can imagine, there was much concerned talk at the time about the genetic inferiority of Italian stock, of the inadvisability of letting so many second-class immigrants into the United States, and of the squalor that seemed endemic to Italian urban neighborhoods. Sound familiar? These days, when talk turns to the supposed genetic differences in the intelligence of certain races, Southern Italians have disappeared from the discussion. "Did their genes begin to mutate somewhere in the 1930s?" the psychologists Seymour Sarason and John Doris ask, in their account of the Italian experience. "Or is it possible that somewhere in the 1920s, if not earlier, the sociocultural history of Italo-Americans took a turn from the blacks and the Spanish Americans which permitted their assimilation into the general undifferentiated mass of Americans?"

The psychologist Michael Cole and some colleagues once gave members of the Kpelle tribe, in Liberia, a version of the WISC similarities test: they took a basket of food, tools, containers, and clothing and asked the tribesmen to sort them into appropriate categories. To the frustration of the researchers, the Kpelle chose functional pairings. They put a potato and a knife together because a knife is used to cut a potato. "A wise man could only do such-and-such," they explained.

Finally, the researchers asked, "How would a fool do it?" The tribesmen immediately re-sorted the items into the "right" categories. It can be argued that taxonomical categories are a developmental improvement—that is, that the Kpelle would be more likely to advance, technologically and scientifically, if they started to see the world that way. But to label them less intelligent than Westerners, on the basis of their performance on that test, is merely to state that they have different cognitive preferences and habits. And if I.Q. varies with habits of mind, which can be adopted or discarded in a generation, what, exactly, is all the fuss about?

When I was growing up, my family would sometimes play Twenty Questions on long car trips. My father was one of those people who insist that the standard categories of animal, vegetable, and mineral be supplemented with a fourth category: "abstract." Abstract could mean something like "whatever it was that was going through my mind when we drove past the water tower fifty miles back." That abstract category sounds absurdly difficult, but it wasn't: it merely required that we ask a slightly different set of questions and grasp a slightly different set of conventions, and, after two or three rounds of practice, guessing the contents of someone's mind fifty miles ago becomes as easy as guessing Winston Churchill. (There is one exception. That was the trip on which my old roommate Tom Connell chose, as an abstraction, "the Unknown Soldier"—which allowed him legitimately and gleefully to answer "I have no idea" to almost every question. There were four of us playing. We gave up after an hour.) Flynn would say that my father was teaching his three sons how to put on scientific spectacles, and that extra practice probably bumped up all of our I.Q.s a few notches. But let's be clear about what this means. There's a world of difference between an I.Q. advantage that's genetic and one that depends on extended car time with Graham Gladwell.

Flynn is a cautious and careful writer. Unlike many others in the I.Q. debates, he resists grand philosophizing. He comes back again and again to the fact that I.Q. scores are generated by paper-and-pencil tests—and making sense of those scores, he tells us, is a messy and complicated business that requires something closer to the skills of an accountant than to those of a philosopher.

For instance, Flynn shows what happens when we recognize that

I.Q. is not a freestanding number but a value attached to a specific time and a specific test. When an I.Q. test is created, he reminds us, it is calibrated or "normed" so that the test-takers in the fiftieth percentile—those exactly at the median—are assigned a score of 100. But since I.Q.s are always rising, the only way to keep that hundred-point benchmark is periodically to make the tests more difficult—to "renorm" them. The original WISC was normed in the late nineteen-forties. It was then renormed in the early nineteen-seventies, as the WISC-R; renormed a third time in the late eighties, as the WISC III; and renormed again a few years ago, as the WISC IV—with each version just a little harder than its predecessor. The notion that anyone "has" an I.Q. of a certain number, then, is meaningless unless you know which WISC he took, and when he took it, since there's a substantial difference between getting a 130 on the WISC IV and getting a 130 on the much easier WISC.

This is not a trivial issue. I.Q. tests are used to diagnose people as mentally retarded, with a score of 70 generally taken to be the cutoff. You can imagine how the Flynn effect plays havoc with that system. In the nineteen-seventies and eighties, most states used the WISC-R to make their mental-retardation diagnoses. But since kids—even kids with disabilities—score a little higher every year, the number of children whose scores fell below 70 declined steadily through the end of the eighties. Then, in 1991, the WISC III was introduced, and suddenly the percentage of kids labelled retarded went up. The psychologists Tomoe Kanaya, Matthew Scullin, and Stephen Ceci estimated that, if every state had switched to the WISC III right away, the number of Americans labelled mentally retarded should have doubled.

That is an extraordinary number. The diagnosis of mental disability is one of the most stigmatizing of all educational and occupational classifications—and yet, apparently, the chances of being burdened with that label are in no small degree a function of the point, in the life cycle of the WISC, at which a child happens to sit for his evaluation. "As far as I can determine, no clinical or school psychologists using the WISC over the relevant 25 years noticed that its criterion of mental retardation became more lenient over time," Flynn wrote, in a 2000 paper. "Yet no one drew the obvious moral about psychologists in the field: They simply were not making any systematic assessment of the I.Q. criterion for mental retardation."

Flynn brings a similar precision to the question of whether Asians have a genetic advantage in I.Q., a possibility that has led to great excitement among I.Q. fundamentalists in recent years. Data showing that the Japanese had higher I.Q.s than people of European descent, for example, prompted the British psychometrician and eugenicist Richard Lynn to concoct an elaborate evolutionary explanation involving the Himalayas, really cold weather, premodern hunting practices, brain size, and specialized vowel sounds. The fact that the I.Q.s of Chinese-Americans also seemed to be elevated has led I.Q. fundamentalists to posit the existence of an international I.Q. pyramid, with Asians at the top, European whites next, and Hispanics and blacks at the bottom.

Here was a question tailor-made for James Flynn's accounting skills. He looked first at Lynn's data, and realized that the comparison was skewed. Lynn was comparing American I.Q. estimates based on a representative sample of schoolchildren with Japanese estimates based on an upper-income, heavily urban sample. Recalculated, the Japanese average came in not at 106.6 but at 99.2. Then Flynn turned his attention to the Chinese-American estimates. They turned out to be based on a 1975 study in San Francisco's Chinatown using something called the Lorge-Thorndike Intelligence Test. But the Lorge-Thorndike test was normed in the nineteen-fifties. For children in the nineteen-seventies, it would have been a piece of cake. When the Chinese-American scores were reassessed using up-to-date intelligence metrics, Flynn found, they came in at 97 verbal and 100 nonverbal. Chinese-Americans had slightly lower I.Q.s than white Americans.

The Asian-American success story had suddenly been turned on its head. The numbers now suggested, Flynn said, that they had succeeded not because of their higher I.Q.s but despite their lower I.Q.s. Asians were overachievers. In a nifty piece of statistical analysis, Flynn then worked out just how great that overachievement was. Among whites, virtually everyone who joins the ranks of the managerial, professional, and technical occupations has an I.Q. of 97 or above. Among Chinese-Americans, that threshold is 90. A Chinese-American with an I.Q. of 90, it would appear, does as much with it as a white American with an I.Q. of 97.

There should be no great mystery about Asian achievement. It has to do with hard work and dedication to higher education, and belonging to a culture that stresses professional success. But Flynn makes one more observation. The children of that first successful wave of Asian-Americans really did have I.Q.s that were higher than everyone else's—coming in somewhere around 103. Having worked their way into the upper reaches of the occupational scale, and taken note of how much the professions value abstract thinking, Asian-American parents have evidently made sure that their own children wore scientific spectacles. "Chinese Americans are an ethnic group for whom high achievement preceded high I.Q. rather than the reverse," Flynn concludes, reminding us that in our discussions of the relationship between I.Q. and success we often confuse causes and effects. "It is not easy to view the history of their achievements without emotion," he writes. That is exactly right. To ascribe Asian success to some abstract number is to trivialize it.

Two weeks ago, Flynn came to Manhattan to debate Charles Murray at a forum sponsored by the Manhattan Institute. Their subject was the black-white I.Q. gap in America. During the twenty-five years after the Second World War, that gap closed considerably. The I.Q.s of white Americans rose, as part of the general worldwide Flynn effect, but the I.Q.s of black Americans rose faster. Then, for about a period of twenty-five years, that trend stalled—and the question was why.

Murray showed a series of PowerPoint slides, each representing different statistical formulations of the I.Q. gap. He appeared to be pessimistic that the racial difference would narrow in the future. "By the nineteen-seventies, you had gotten most of the juice out of the environment that you were going to get," he said. That gap, he seemed to think, reflected some inherent difference between the races. "Starting in the nineteen-seventies, to put it very crudely, you had a higher proportion of black kids being born to really dumb mothers," he said. When the debate's moderator, Jane Waldfogel, informed him that the most recent data showed that the race gap had begun to close again, Murray seemed unimpressed, as if the possibility that blacks could ever make further progress was inconceivable.

Flynn took a different approach. The black-white gap, he pointed out, differs dramatically by age. He noted that the tests we have for measuring the cognitive functioning of infants, though admittedly crude, show the races to be almost the same. By age four, the average black I.Q. is 95.4—only four and a half points behind the average white I.Q. Then the real gap emerges: from age four through twenty-four, blacks lose six-tenths of a point a year, until their scores settle at 83.4.

That steady decline, Flynn said, did not resemble the usual pattern of genetic influence. Instead, it was exactly what you would expect, given the disparate cognitive environments that whites and blacks encounter as they grow older. Black children are more likely to be raised in single-parent homes than are white children—and single-parent homes are less cognitively complex than two-parent homes. The average I.Q. of first-grade students in schools that blacks attend is 95, which means that "kids who want to be above average don't have to aim as high." There were possibly adverse differences between black teenage culture and white teenage culture, and an enormous number of young black men are in jail—which is hardly the kind of environment in which someone would learn to put on scientific spectacles.

Flynn then talked about what we've learned from studies of adoption and mixed-race children—and that evidence didn't fit a genetic model, either. If I.Q. is innate, it shouldn't make a difference whether it's a mixed-race child's mother or father who is black. But it does: children with a white mother and a black father have an eight-point I.Q. advantage over those with a black mother and a white father. And it shouldn't make much of a difference where a mixed-race child is born. But, again, it does: the children fathered by black American G.I.s in postwar Germany and brought up by their German mothers have the same I.Q.s as the children of white American G.I.s and German mothers. The difference, in that case, was not the fact of the children's blackness, as a fundamentalist would say. It was the fact of their Germanness—of their being brought up in a different culture, under different circumstances. "The mind is much more like a muscle than we've ever realized," Flynn said. "It needs to get cognitive exercise. It's not some piece of clay on which you put an indelible mark." The lesson to be drawn from black and white differences was the same as the lesson from the Netherlands years ago: I.Q. measures not just the quality of a person's mind but the quality of the world that person lives in.

DRIVING

~❦~

Kenneth A. McClane

I have put off writing this for some time, largely because it was too painful for me to write about my parents, and largely, too, because I was worried that my experience—which is purely that, *my* experience—might cause others undue consternation. In all honesty, the first reason is the most telling: Alzheimer's disease is a horrendous ailment—it takes someone away, before the body is gone, and it diminishes that person in very small but codifiable ways. First, the loved one loses some of her vocabulary or seems stuck in the interstices of life, as if the film of one's daily happenings were cut, and one was living in a few frames, with the rest of the narrative unfolding in the next theater, which, somehow, one can readily see. For a powerful second, the two theaters are showing the same frame, but then things devolve, the correspondences unhinge, and both theaters grow shadowy—the film is still playing, there's even a show of delight on the loved one's face, but it is a private, peculiar delight, as hard to imagine as the joy of a snake cut in halves, its two severed pieces struggling for a rapprochement.

The disease, most centrally, is about loss and love, both so tightly entwined, that I am reminded of a wonderful Chinese painting of a brilliant long-stemmed lily that I confronted a few years ago at the

Johnson Art Museum at Cornell. Initially, the overwhelming flower seemed merely vibrant, resplendent, and triumphant. Its color was vital; its presence, incontestable. But then if one was attentive, one noticed a slight sliver of decay, like a small finger, at the bottom of the stem—one realized, that is, that beauty and destruction share the same root, that one undergirds the other. Alzheimer's sadly, God knows, presents the decimation and even, at times, the possibility of a flower; but there is no balance, no artifice. There is no suitable metaphor.

Still, this is a far too romantic vision of Alzheimer's, though it does convey some of my experience, even as it suggests how I was able to cope with it, putting to good use my literary skills. My father and mother both died of Alzheimer's, and both of them, in different ways, confronted the disease. My mother succumbed first. Indeed, my mother was a *perfect* Alzheimer's patient, if one can say that, since she presented all the neurological signs of the illness. At the time of my mother's diagnosis in the 1980s, the disease could be confirmed only by an autopsy, which, of course, was of little help. There were, however, six warning signs—one was if the patient obsessively turned her thumbs in a counter-clockwise motion, another was if the patient splayed her feet outward, as if chronically pigeon-toed. As we used to joke, of the six indices, my mother exhibited seven. And please understand how important macabre humor became for my family, and for others with the illness, too. Before the disease we used to laugh a great deal: it was lifeblood to us; after the disease, we laughed less, but we still found moments of utter hilarity. When your father, who was usually a bit tight with money, suddenly throws all of his twenties out the window—which happened to a friend of mine—what else are you to do?

If this seems rather clinical, I am writing this after ten years. When my mother first entered the nursing home, after we had exhausted every in-home possibility, she was her usual elegant self. My mother was quite beautiful—she had lovely hair, an olive complexion, and was quite svelte for someone in her eighties. In her earlier years she had a 50s-movie-star figure—"full-figured" was the term then, I believe. In those days, my mother loved doughnuts and pies; she always had a sweet tooth, and I recall how she would always pester me to get her a jelly doughnut, especially if it came right out of the baker's oven. Her new slim weight was largely a response to the disease, and one could see her ribs, poking out like small tubers. She wouldn't eat, or she would forget to eat; and when she was told to eat, because she needed the caloric content, she couldn't understand the concept.

Interestingly, in temperament, my mother remained largely the person she had been throughout the ravages of the disease. When someone came to visit, she would immediately tell her how beautiful she looked and how happy she was that she had come to see her. This was her characteristic gentility—she had been born in Boston, she had attended the famous Boston Girl's Latin School, and she was, in truth, a Black Boston aristocrat. Where she evidenced a profound departure from her strict Yankee upbringing was in her love for outlandish clothes and color, which corresponded, ultimately, to her not small success as a painter. My mother would wear wild green pants and always wanted her husband and children to jazz up their sedate clothing palette—something that my father often did, God knows, to alarming effect. In her artwork, there was always a rhapsody of invention, involving boisterous, even hysterical, colors that would have astonished Hieronymus Bosch. If she was reserved in manner, her inner soul was irrepressible.

With her wonderful manners, my mother also evolved incredible coping skills. As she realized that her faculties were diminishing, she employed a brilliant ruse to keep up pretenses. When I came to visit her one day, I asked her, rather self-servingly, if she knew what my name was. Now, this is a question that almost all Alzheimer's family members employ as an essential calculus: if the loved ones remember your name, they are still present; they still share a reality to which you can attest. But this, sadly, involves a misspent logic. Why is your mother's inability to recall your name any more horrific than her inability to paint any longer? Or to open a carton of milk? It is all a great rupture from the previous: the person you knew before is not the person confronting you *now*. And yet all of us create these portentous lines of demarcation—once a person has crossed this threshold, say, well, things are truly bad. Well, *things are truly bad,* and there's no way around that.

And yet the need to create a personal graph of your loved one's dissolution is natural: if death is a problem for the living, since the dead one is clearly beyond all caring, the living-in-death aspect of Alzheimer's disease, which is how many people describe the illness, is clearly just a further embellishment of this truism. If one invests much of one's imaginative life in understanding others—if love is, as James Baldwin suggests, the difficult apprehension by one mind of the mysteries of another's life—then Alzheimer's clearly tests one's imaginative faculties. In some ways, the Alzheimer's loved one is the ideal subject to be modeled by one's graph; but just as one is about to make a truce with one's conception of the disease—just as the clay is about to set and hold the likeness, if you will—the disease irrefutably breaks the cast and leaves one dim-witted.

When I asked my mother my name, she quickly answered, "You *know* your name, why would you ask me that?" with that practiced New England refinement that showed both her mastery of the retort, and her ability, at least here, to keep the conversation rolling. My mother didn't have the foggiest notion who I was or what her connection was to me, of that I am certain. But she had outwitted me—and she had kept her own distress to a minimum.

As time passed, and she became more and more remote, my mother talked less and less, and my visits were more and more occupied with combing her hair and doing things for her. Others could talk to their loved one without a response; I, because I am terribly self-conscious, could only with great difficulty commune with the ether, something of which I am not very proud. It is sad when at the most intimate of times, one still feels as if one's response is never adequate, as if one is still being judged. In truth, where there had once been her towering presence, there seemed increasingly to be my own pitiful falterings.

Still, one day, after my mother had been silent for a very long period, barely evidencing even the slightest flicker of acknowledgement, I brought her a teddy bear that I had purchased from L.L. Bean. It was a big red bear—with a lovely bib—and I knew that the color would arouse her, if nothing else. When I presented it to her, my mother took it, ruffled the ears, and smiled; for a second, she was returned to me. And then I, suddenly empowered, asked her what she would name the bear, if she could call it anything.

In a shock of language, my mother replied, "I'd call the teddy bear Kenneth."

When she said this, I was near tears. Kenneth, of course, is my name and my father's name. For the last few months, my mother had shown no impulse to touch down with me; we had been together, but there had been no articulation on her part of our involvement; she had been as cut off from me as my brother's desire, many years ago, to become an astronaut. "*This* planet is strange enough for me," I remember telling him, rather cruelly.

Now, I pushed onward. "Mom, why do you call the bear Kenneth?" I asked her. Her eyes softened and she answered, "It's a name I know well, and it's a name that comforts me. Your name is Kenneth." And then she grew quiet. She would never speak an intelligible word again.

My mother died in 1995 and my father was diagnosed with Alzheimer's in 1994. For one year, they both shared a room in a well-run nursing home in Falmouth, Massachusetts, although their relationship was, at least to my father, completely mystifying. Although they had been married for fifty-three years, and had raised three children, my father couldn't understand why he was living with this woman, with the lovely face and the wild clothes. On one occasion he asked me, "Who is that woman; why is she always around?" And I had to stop myself from either laughing or crying. As I recall, I told him that she was his wife and that she and he had been together for many years, which I thought my father finally understood. But a few weeks later, in a rush of energy, my father informed me that he was going to marry someone, a friend of both my parents, and start a *new* family. And this was just the beginning of the story's complications.

My father had been a physician, and when he informed me that he was intending to marry Mary and begin a family, I was troubled, and not only because I had certain obligations to my mother, but because Mary was a good slice above sixty in age. Thus, her ability to have children was certainly a medical challenge, something that a younger Dr. McClane would have easily discerned. Interestingly, when confronted with the implication of having *two* wives, my father quickly told me that he had consulted a lawyer, and the lawyer had told him that as long as he kept my mother with him, it would be fine to marry again. This reasoning, however opportunistic, was vintage my father. He would always try to please everyone; and no one, in his world, was ever left bereft. As a doctor, with his office in Harlem, he had treated seventy-five percent of his patients gratis—they simply did not have the money to pay. And I well remember how his thankful patients would bring him pawn tickets, pies, and freshly caught fish—anything that might remotely be conceived as payment.

When I walked around my neighborhood, people would often comment on how my father had saved a life, often thrusting the bene-factor, if it were a child, into my hands; one woman, wearing a per-fume that almost suffocated me, told me, through the vapors, "Your father is a *big* man; we're little people. He's God's face on the earth." Now, that was heady stuff!

Still, my father was a *good* doctor, although he would never speak about his work. I recall one day when he came home mysteriously in the middle of the day, with blood covering his shirt, the stain resem-bling an errant Jackson Pollack painting. When I asked him what had happened, he told me it was "just work." I later learned that my father had literally held a man together with a towel. A number's runner had burst into my father's office, his guts tumbling out, and fell onto the re-ceptionist, ruining her taffeta dress. The man had been brutally stabbed in the stomach because he had failed to honor a bet; and my fa-ther, seeing that the man was perilously close to dying and beyond anything that he in his office might do, grabbed a bath towel and tied it around the man's mid-section, holding his innards in, until the ambu-lance came. The man survived, but two weeks later, he was shot in the head. These things *happened* in my father's office, and he kept them se-cret, honoring a code of medical ethics, as ancient as it is draconian.

In the nursing home, my father had started to write Mary, his in-tended, salacious notes—which, of course, embarrassed her. These notes, interestingly, were in my father's usual handwriting—one could barely decipher every third word. Yet Mary was right: my father was fantasizing about what he would like to do with her, even if it was, thank goodness, a fantasy of few connections. And so I was con-fronted with a very odd dilemma. In the first instance, I had never known my father to have a sexual fantasy life—which is as it should be. And in the second instance, my father never—and of this I am cer-tain—cheated on my mother, or wanted to. So I was on very shaky ground. And then, too, Mary was a close friend and she felt decidedly uncomfortable. That both of us realized that my father was sick was of little help: we could only calibrate our response in the language of our own lives, which tended, hopefully, toward the rational. And Mary, of course, was in a much more difficult position than I, since I had seen my father's progressive decline, and I did not have the same divided loyalty. Quintessentially, I was able to see my father as merely *other-bodied*; she, for her part, saw him as both her friend—which meant as he once was, in his verve and brilliance—and as the husband of someone whom she very much respected. She knew that *this* was not my father, but she couldn't figure out how to deal with the cipher before her.

My father's descent into the disease was horrible, in many ways, largely because he fought it so tenaciously. As he was losing his faculties, he, like my mother, learned to play to his strengths. As a doctor—and a very good one—he knew how to charm people. And, interestingly, his medical acumen was the last of his skills to leave him, with, just as tellingly, his ability to spin a good story. He might forget your name, but he would not forget how to diagnose a disease, or what to prescribe for a malady, which made his presence in the nursing home problematic. In short order, I made certain that my father had no access to prescription pads; Ms. Smith would not find an order for bursitis medicine, penned by Dr. Feelgood. And as luck would have it, just before my father became ill, he had co-authored an article on a rare form of hyperthyroidism, and it had received much notice in medical circles. When he talked to doctors—or anyone else who seemed interested—he would often mention the article, and they would be suitably impressed.

Indeed, early on, when I wanted a physician to diagnose my father's condition—I had seen signs of his mental impairment, which were worrisome to me—the doctor came to our house, began to talk to my father, and lo and behold, after my father held forth about his article and the fact that he had recently retired from Columbia Presbyterian Hospital (where he had served on the medical school faculty for forty years), the diagnostician was clearly in his hands. When I asked the consultant for his recommendation about my father's mental acuity, he replied, "Your *father*? Is there something wrong with your father?"

Here, of course, the physician was encountering a unique situation: first, my father knew how to keep the conversation anchored in a narrow channel that he had well learned to navigate, and my father was *truly* brilliant; even with a few synapses misfiring, he could astound and astonish; second, the doctor, understandably, was delighted to meet someone who knew more medicine than he did. Most doctors have not been exposed to the latest medical techniques; as my father used to tell me, "You're only as up-to-date as your last medical school class." Indisputably, my father had been at one of the premier medical schools in the world for the last umpteen years—he knew a great deal. And just as accurately, I do not believe that the consulting doctor could imagine that another doctor might be losing his faculties: it was simply too frightening a consequence to contemplate.

Getting my father to move to the nursing home was quite a feat, and I needed the help of my wife, my father's best friend, and a bold-faced lie. My father did not want to go to a nursing home: he loved his small house. For most members of his generation, your house—if you *owned* it—signified your achievement, even your personhood. Though a professional, my father had no stocks, bonds, or antiques: he simply had his home. To take it from him was, in truth, to remove something almost corporeal. At the time, my father was living on Martha's Vineyard Island, in a very efficient ranch home, with every-thing all on one floor, so he needn't struggle with stairs. But after he went missing for six hours on a very cold night, and was found by the police lying in a hedgerow a half-block from his house, it was clear that the sixteen-hour-a-day, live-in staffing was no longer adequate to keep him safe. With an uncanny ability, my father would somehow find the one "soft spot" in our preparations: if we wanted to protect him, to keep him alive, he could no longer live at home.

On the day I planned to convince my father to enter the nursing home, I deployed a rigor of persuasive techniques worthy of Homer's Sirens, although at the time I simply felt despicable. Time permits you perspective, but perspective can't alleviate the horror of metaphori-cally pelting someone who seems inert, who, in his suffering, can offer only the most inglorious of supplications.

At first, my father's best friend, Bill Preston, asked him a few gen-eral questions: what is the day of the week, who is the president, and in which city did my father once work? Of course, my father did not have a clue, although he did try to offer a number of inventive expla-nations, which was both enormously poignant and sad. To see this formerly luminous man take small tentative stabs at reality was heart-wrenching. At one point, my father began to talk about the New Deal with Rooseveltian fervor; and I almost believed that I was listening to a fireside chat when, like a whirlwind, my father migrated into a diatribe about John Kennedy's civil rights posture and then evolved into the small chapel where his father had once preached, which was a true remembrance, except that it suddenly found congress with an allusion to Tin Pan Alley. I tried to keep up, like a child chasing after an untethered kite, the trans-historicity was so spellbinding, and my father had just begun his peroration—details were colliding like seatossed stones: there was the FBI, Emmitt Till, my wife, John Betti at BU, Adolph Jones, Duke Ellington, Boston Blackie, May Fane, the Federation of Protestant Agencies, the Kentucky Derby, Paul Robeson, and World War II; there was Cornell University, Robert Scott, Elizabeth Taylor, Spinkie Alston (known as Charles), Dr. David Spain, Menemsha, clambakes, Block Island, Harvey Russell, Brigadoon (the house with the "big porch," he merrily added)—all congealing in a Whitmanic cumulus.

With a grim determinism that could only involve the warp and woof of love, Bill told my father how he had exhausted all our remedies, reminding him how he might have frozen to death had the police not been so zealous. Bill and my father had been inseparable for twenty years—they had shared countless fishing trips, suffered dreary near-football games (watching Columbia U. lose and lose and lose), and attended numberless civil rights benefits, where my father and Bill would often give brilliant exhortations, the money easily flowing, like curses at a juke joint. After his wife left him, Bill had lived in our home for a year, and he and my father were "spitting close," as my aunt would say. Bill, in fact, was the only man who could call my father an ass, and have my father learn from it. And my father did the same for Bill.

Bill's father had been the New York editor of the *International Herald Tribune,* but with seven children, it was often touch-and-go. Bill—who should have gone on to college, he read more deeply certainly than anyone I knew—worked so his siblings might have a better life. When the Second World War broke out, he enlisted. As a young boy, Bill had walked out of his parish after a "difficult confession" and never found use for God again. "Hard as a pool ball," he'd make it on his own, and the war, of course, just further cemented his detachment. "Ken," he told me, "no god could *permit* this carnage." If war would make everyone a believer, as is often said, it did not do so for this lonely, wounded traveler.

As a tank sergeant, Bill had landed in North Africa, participated in

D-day, and was waiting to go to Japan when the bomb dropped. When
Bill had a few drinks, he would always return to the same tragic story.
In Germany, his outfit had set up a perimeter around a fuel depot, near
a grove of trees. Bill's tank was the lead one, and should there be any
sound, it was his duty to ascertain what the commotion was. If it was
suspicious, it was he who was to spray the area with his machine guns.
One day, there was a slight ruffling in the trees, and Bill yelled, demanding to know who or what was present. There was no response.
Quickly, he pummeled the field with bullets, leaving chunks of bark
splayed on the ground like broken teeth. As he would always recount,
he jumped out of his tank, grabbed his carbine, ran into the woods,
and found a dead young girl, who had been scavenging for food. Bill
had been in the war for three years, he'd killed hundreds of men, and
had liberated two concentration camps: he'd seen the worst human beings could do to one another. But that child's face was always with
him, like a phantom limb. "She's only a child," he'd say, speaking un-
wittingly in the present tense; "Christ, she *is* only a child." When Bill
would get into his story, my mother and father would hug him, and he
would weep, hoping—inveterate atheist that he was—that the world
might someday offer him a godless absolution. "I *killed* her," he'd say,
over and over, the weight of it as heavy as a vat of mercury.

"Ken," Bill said to my father, "you can't do this any longer. You've
got to move. You can't do this to yourself, to your son and his wife."
When Bill finished talking, my father simply looked sullen, as if we
had beaten him with sticks. Bill was his great friend, but friends could
be wrong.

Then it was my wife, Rochelle's, turn. In her characteristically
generous way, she suggested how much we loved my father, and how
he would be able to have a better life, in a better situation, if he would
move to the nursing home: he'd be able to travel with others, see recent plays, and possibly even go fishing, things he had always loved.
Although my father was clearly listening to her, I couldn't tell if he
was simply being the good, attentive father-in-law; his face was totally
inscrutable.

After a time, Rochelle stopped talking, and my father smiled at
her. I realized that he was trying to balance his great care for her, as he
maintained his independence. Suddenly, I recalled how he would look
as he straddled the small centerboard of our seventeen-foot sailboat

when the boat would be coming about. At that magnificent moment when everything for a second stills and the sails luff, my father would hunker down, crumpling his big six-foot frame, waiting as the boom flew across, telling us in which direction we might proceed. Sailing, of course, is an art, and my father was very skilled at it. I never saw him frightened—the wind might be blowing, I often thought we might perish, but my father was simply engaged in the work.

Now, it was *my* turn to convince him, and I had one ploy, if only it might succeed. After recounting the dangers of my father's present situation, I reminded him of how he would wear his clothes all night long, so he wouldn't be found undressed when the senior citizen bus came. Since he couldn't tell time, my father would sport his jacket and trousers twenty-four hours a day, his clothes bedraggled, his shoes mismatched. My father was always prompt; he was never late; and he knew that the only way he could be ready for the bus—to look presentable—was to remain dressed all day. Seeing him struggling to measure up nearly stopped my heart: my father looked like a thin reed in a windstorm, his face so full of anticipation, his bearing so tentative. After I had piled every stone of oratory on him, I suggested that he try the nursing home for one week. If he did not like it, we would bring him back home. And that's a promise.

In truth, I hoped that my father would not call me on the agreement—for once I placed him into the nursing home, he was not going to return. It was a terrible lie, and I hated to lie to him. But he accepted the bargain.

I well recall that journey to the nursing home, from one life to another. As we had so many times before, we took my father on the ferry from Vineyard Haven to Woods Hole, slicing between the picturesque East Chop and West Chop lighthouses, where we had often sailed in our small boat, and he talked to everyone he could on the ferry, telling them about his life and his family. My father was enormously proud of my wife and me, and as he recounted our tribulations, I felt great ambivalence. As always, people enjoyed him: he could tell a riveting story, and he wore his age well. Now, he was a wizened old man, and people rallied at the Norman Rockwellian ideal of the octogenarian, which possesses great power, no matter how hackneyed it might first appear. If it is sentimental, so are we—and thank goodness, we are.

After the ferry docked, we took the four-mile drive to Falmouth, where we had a wonderful dinner—of shrimp, his favorite—and went shopping for everything he might need: toiletries, new shoes, a bathrobe, stamps, and clothes that could be easily laundered. As always, my father was a raconteur. He spoke to all the sales people, flattering them; he was in rare form, telling the sales girls—always the *pretty* ones, as he would remark—something about his travels that day. His stories were always full-bodied, if not a bit freewheeling with fact. Then we entered the nursing home, and hoped that he would make a life there. My mother was already a patient, so he knew the place well. It was poignant to see him give her a small, winsome kiss on the lips.

At the end of that first day, just before we had to take the ferry back to the Vineyard, my father thanked us. "Ken, I had a wonderful first day," he said. And then, in the most generous act of a parent, he told me: "Ken, you did the *right* thing." There he was, my parent of old—the one who would never place his wants before his child's smallest wish. I needed to hear that; I had felt, in truth, like Judas.

My father quickly made a life in the nursing home. Since he was a realist at heart, he knew that his faculties were deteriorating. He'd still charm the nursing staff, tell wonderful stories, and thrill any listeners with tales of Dr. Martin Luther King and other notables he knew. My father, here, was not fabricating: he and my mother had been directly involved in the civil rights movement on a national scale, and they had worked with the Southern Leadership Conference, the NAACP, and the Committee on Africa. At our home, one might see Roy Wilkins, William Kunstler, and Ralph Bunche; Sydney Poitier came to my tenth birthday party, although he was most interested, I must admit, in the beautiful divorced parent of one of my friends.

It was not that my parents were extraordinary, or at least not in the way one might think: they were simply doing what they had to do as black professionals, who lived at a certain time, and who shouldered their weighty responsibilities. That my father also rented his office from Congressman Adam Clayton Powell gave him tremendous entrée into the world of the doers; that Congressman Powell, at every chance, also touted my father's medical acumen provided him with much needed work, fellowship, and visibility. So my father's stories were rich with luminaries, historical ephemera, and wonderment. His listeners, probably, thought that much of it was balderdash; but, in truth, there was a great deal of bedrock under his embellishments.

Indeed, it was these stories that were his last connection to the world to vanish. As my father became more and more sick, he grew thinner and thinner, and his stories grew less historically accurate; and yet, interestingly, they never failed to have a consistent beginning, middle, and end. However bizarre their content, they were always narratively complete—that is, they were *good* narratives, and I'm speaking here as a teacher of writing.

In one of the most painful episodes I can recall, my father inquired about my brother Paul, who had died twelve years earlier of alcoholism. Paul was a tough, truculent kid, who was enormously talented, but he did not love himself; or, more accurately, he loved others more than he did himself. In fact, he so identified with others, that he almost chromosomally became them. Thus, if his friend was manic, Paul became manic. If his friend had a fight with his girlfriend, Paul's relationship with his sweetheart became perilous. In this odd transference, Paul's life seemed strangely to vanish, as if he existed only as a medium for others. "There was not enough of life left over to keep him around," a friend of his once said, and though I might quibble with the language, the sentiment was irrefutable.

When my father asked about Paul, I slowly explained that Paul had died a few years ago. Suddenly, my father began to wail, his once great shoulders slumped over. *Paul's dead, Paul's dead; I didn't know,* he murmured. Then he wailed again, his small ribs poking out like fish bones. *Paul's dead. Paul's dead,* as if this was the first time he had learned of his son's demise. I realized that this revelation might occur daily—that in my father's besotted mind, he might each day relive his son's death. Each day my brother would die; each day my father would confront life's utmost devastation. It was horrible: Kafka could not have anticipated a more terrible scenario.

Yet, miraculously, the next day, my father had completely forgotten about Paul and our conversation. And he never returned to the subject again.

Alzheimer's disease wends its way rather predictably (although no one who lives through it can intuit this, for good reason), and I think of the disease metaphorically, as mirroring how one sees a landmass from an airplane. From a great height, everything is viewed as large sinews and great gentle curves: there are no rough edges to the shore, or ragged, ill-shaped promontories. With Alzheimer's, a person first loses her memory; then she loses control of her body; then she stops eating; and then, finally, succumbs to an ultimate malady. One does not die of Alzheimer's: one dies of septicemia, pneumonia, or a heart attack. During this progression of diminishment, the person reacts in any number of ways—my mother, for example, when I brought her an easel and suggested that she might like to paint again, simply told me that she didn't need art anymore. When I asked her why, she told me that she "could see hundreds of trees and they were filled with dogs laughing." Now this vision, worthy of the best hallucinogens, aptly synthesized my mother's true enthusiasms: she loved dogs, and we always had a number of them, to the great distress of my father. And just as poignantly, my mother also cherished gardening. Her mind, therefore, whatever else it was doing, was providing her with much satisfaction. If she was not in the world I understood, she was not unhappy. And this for me was a great dispensation.

Near the end of my father's life, his stories became far more impressionistic, and yet they would always meet the demands of a sturdy narrative. When I brought a number of family members to see my father, realizing that this was probably the last time that he would be at all present, the family was ushered en masse into his room, talked with him for two hours, and made a wonderful fuss over him. His brother Warren was there—whom he hadn't seen in a year—and his niece, her son, my wife, and a few other people; it was a lively throng, and my father was holding court. At times, he would say things that were clearly appropriate: when he looked at his brother, he asked him, rather unfortunately, why he hadn't come to visit sooner. And I felt especially horrible for Warren, who, I knew, found confronting his brother in this state unbelievably painful. It had taken enormous courage for Warren to make the trip from New York City, and now he was being denounced. This, I think, in truth, was a brotherly confrontation, with a history that harkened back to Warren's birth placement as the youngest of three siblings, the baby of the family, who had always been beholden to my father, something that must have rankled Warren, too. In Alzheimer's, often a long-ago rift finds a bizarre idealization: the disease is no respecter of persons or truth, but it does providently mine the fault lines, and it mines for lode. In a more conciliatory vein, my father asked his niece about her life, and he seemed to enjoy her passion for her new job. After a great deal of ballyhoo, my father simply dozed off, and we all departed.

The next day, pleased with last night's happenings, I asked my father about the family gathering, and he could not recall a thing. But then, almost as an afterthought, he began to describe a magical excursion, where he had visited an "enormous party," with hundreds of boats "dancing" in the harbor; there was a "great table," he joyfully added, replete with omnipresent shrimp for everyone. Shrimp, here, of course, was an expression of both his greatest delicacy and extravagance—when there was abundant shrimp at a salad bar, it was a true feast for this child of the depression. What most impressed him, he said, was that "no one made him come in early." Clearly, something had pierced his isolation: it was not the true event; there was not one accurate detail. But my father had encountered something extraordinary, and it had brought him great pleasure.

I said at the outset of this memoir that I did not want my experience to be seen as representative of how Alzheimer's patients handle the disease or how families deal with their loved ones. Each family is different; the disease, I know, is horrific, and it can only bring unimaginable sorrow to a family, in ways that are specific, brutally intimate, and often disabling. Even the strongest family can flail apart under the enormous pressure of trying to conflate a wonderful past—or at least one where there was an assumed level of intimacy and identification—with an increasingly distraught present. It is the height of horror to confront someone who has the shape, the smell, and the aspect of a person with whom you have shared your most intimate moments, and yet that person is merely a shell. It's like confronting a simulacrum of your father or brother or mother; and still—and this is both a blessing and a curse—he or she can suddenly blurt out a sound, or give you a slight nod, or make a shrill whistle-like noise, and the world is returned to a moment of clarity, of identification, where you once shared a glass of wine, or tried to fix the toaster, or simply collapsed into a hearty laugh. As A. R. Ammons asks in his poem, "What destruction am I blessed by?"

Near the end of my father's life, as he was sitting in the nursing home, he suddenly looked up at me, his head almost jerking. "Ken," he said, "would you like to take a drive? We could drive down the West

Side Highway and go to the Village." I knew what he was suggesting. My father worked six days a week, from 8 A.M. until 9 P.M., seeing patients. On our wonderful, rare outings, we would often travel to the Village, where we might get a sausage sandwich; or go to O'Henry's, where we might purchase a hamburger and he, a planters punch; or, most wonderfully, have *paella* at La Saville—a marvelous Spanish restaurant on Charles Street, where my family was treated as royalty. These were among the best moments of my childhood, when Paul and I, the boys, would be with our father. Interestingly, my mother would only rarely join us on these sojourns. I think she wanted us to have our father on our own terms—it was she, doing what she always did best, effectuating something, even if it demanded her orchestrated absence. It was, in Coltrane's terms, "a love supreme," since I know how much she missed us, even for those few moments.

I thought for a second about my father's proposition. I could, of course, remind him that there was no automobile, that we were in a Massachusetts nursing home, and that he was near the end of his days—I could tell him that. But I was *driving* with my father, the car was slowly snaking from our Harlem brownstone, down Riverside Drive, and we'd soon cross over Seventy-second Street to get to the West Side Highway, we'd brush along the Hudson River until Twenty-third Street, and then we'd turn and go down Seventh Avenue, which would be full of people hawking wares—and possibly a street concert would provide us with congas, or violins, or a tender drift of Brahms; there might be a small art show near St. Mark's Place, and he'd comment on how much better my mother painted; but I could also sense, for the first time, my father's growing impatience with the transgressive jaywalkers—he was tight in the shoulders, his breath labored—and so I suggested, with great tenderness, "Dad. Let's swing by Central Park. It's lovely this time of year."

Part I: I Had a Dream

Bill Maxwell

The August sun beat down and the temperature already was approaching 80 degrees on Monday morning as I neared Stillman College. This would be my first day as a professor at this small historically black school in Tuscaloosa, an old Southern city of fewer than 80,000 residents where the University of Alabama and the Crimson Tide football team overshadow everything else.

As I drove through Stillman's black-iron main gate and approached Martin Luther King Jr. Hall, a three-story men's dormitory, I was on a mission to fulfill a promise to myself. The college was founded in 1876, sits on a tidy 106 acres and has an enrollment of fewer than 1,000 students. Many locals see the campus as an oasis, the only real symbol of hope in the most racially segregated, most economically depressed part of Tuscaloosa. The original front section of the campus, with its sprawling green lawn and red brick buildings, has some of the grand magnolias that greeted students at the turn of the 20th century.

Driving my 13-year-old, unairconditioned Chevy Blazer past the guard house, I became apprehensive when I noticed about a dozen male students wearing baggy pants, oversized white T-shirts, expensive sneakers and assorted bling standing around shooting the breeze.

At least two had "jailhouse tats" on their arms, crude tattoos suggesting that these young men had spent time behind bars. They carried no books or anything else to indicate they were on a college campus.

I got a good look at their faces. I wanted to remember these young men if any of them showed up in my classes.

Behind them, several others sat on a low brick wall near the dorm entrance. They, too, were clad like extras in a gangsta rap video. It was a scene straight out of "the hood"—young black men seemingly without direction or purpose, hanging out on the corner. In this case, they were hanging out on what is popularly known as "The Yard" on a college campus where they were supposed to be preparing for a more productive life.

I had expected a more collegiate scene on Aug. 9, 2004.

A year before coming to Stillman, I had written a commentary for the *St. Petersburg Times* arguing that Historically Black Colleges and Universities, or HBCUs, remain viable. I further argued that given the increasing reliance on standardized tests to determine college admission and given the nation's conservative turn, HBCUs are needed more than ever to provide an opportunity for many young blacks who otherwise never would be able to attend college because of factors such as low standardized test scores and criminal records.

There are 106 HBCUs in 24 states, and they are mostly in the South. They are public and relatively well-funded, such as Florida A&M University in Tallahassee; private and well-financed with solid academic reputations, such as Howard University in Washington, Spelman College and Morehouse College in Atlanta and Hampton University in Virginia. They are also tiny, poor and struggling, such as Stillman. They offer four-year and two-year degrees, liberal arts and technology paths. Some have graduate schools and schools of law and medicine.

Before the 1964 Civil Rights Act, these schools were the ticket to the good life for blacks. But integration gradually siphoned off many of their best kids, and HBCUs now enroll just 12 percent of all black college students.

Yet I still believed in these schools. So in 2004 I resigned from my job as a *St. Petersburg Times* columnist and editorial writer that paid more than $70,000 a year to teach at Stillman for $33,000 a year. I wanted to fulfill a long-ago promise I made with the professors who taught and nurtured me during the 1960s at two historically black colleges, Wiley College in Marshall, Texas, and Bethune-Cookman College in Daytona Beach.

When I began my first day at Stillman, I was channeling my experiences of long ago. I would be a professor who would inspire and guide the lives of young black women and men who wanted to become successful journalists.

As it turned out, I would last just two years before returning to the *Times*. I left the campus disheartened and disillusioned, and I regretted leaving behind a handful of dedicated students with real potential. Another graduating class has just left Stillman through the same gates I first entered in 2004, but I no longer feel welcome on campus.

I had chosen Stillman for several reasons. I had friends in Tuscaloosa, and I had a nostalgic connection dating back to 1964, when I helped register voters who had sought the safety of the campus.

I also liked Stillman president Ernest McNealey. An Alabama native, McNealey wanted Stillman to have a strong journalism program. He knew that newsrooms around the nation look for competent black reporters and editors, and he wanted me to re-establish the journalism major that had been discontinued in 1997. With an effective program, we could find good jobs for many of our graduates. He was the kind of man I wanted to work for.

With a $100,000 gift from a Tampa donor, my colleagues and I re-established the major during my first semester, and we set up a modest scholarship. After that, my main responsibilities were managing the program, teaching and recruiting students and co-advising the student newspaper.

"Take your seats and be quiet!"

At 8 on that first morning, I met my freshman English class. I had volunteered to teach it because I wanted to assess the writing skills of the students in general. Because the chairman of my department had promised me small classes, I had expected no more than 15 students. Instead, I faced 33. All were black; more than half were women. Four of the men had been in front of King Hall earlier.

The room was noisy, and two who had been in front of King Hall were horsing around. I put my books on the table and raised an arm for silence. When only a few students paid attention I raised my arm again, and this time I yelled.

"All right, knock it off! Take your seats and be quiet!"

I could not believe that I had to yell for college students to behave in a classroom. This is not going to be a good experience, I thought, unfolding the roster and preparing to call the roll. When I could not pronounce the second name on the list, I knew for sure I was in big trouble. As I fumbled with the strange combinations of alphabets and apostrophes, the class roared.

"He can't even read," a student said.

More laughter.

The air conditioner was down, and sweat dripped from my face as I struggled with the last name on the roll. After getting the room quiet, I instructed the students to "write an in-class essay of no more than 500 words describing at least three positive or negative things about your high school." I told them I would read the essays and return them the next time we met.

"This is a diagnostic essay," I said. "I won't grade it. I simply want to see how well you write. If you plan to major in journalism, I want to see you after class. I will hand out the syllabus next time."

After class, just two female students said they wanted to major in journalism. During office hours and lunch, I read the essays. I wondered what I had gotten myself into when only one paper demonstrated college-level writing. During my 18 years of previous college teaching, I had never seen such poor writing—sentence fragments, run-on sentences, misspellings, wrong words and illogical word order.

From one paper: "In my high school, prejudism were bad and people feel like nothing." From another essay: "Central High kids put there nose in other people concern."

I was surprised and disappointed that the two prospective journalism majors had as many mistakes in their copy as their classmates.

I shared the results with a colleague who had taught journalism and English at Stillman for three years. Her response was discouraging. The abysmal writing was par for the course, and I had better brace myself if I intended to keep my sanity.

"I AIN'T TAKING THIS CLASS"

That afternoon, I met my opinion writing and news writing/reporting classes. I had five students in one and seven in the other. Again, I called the roll and took writing samples. That night at home, I eagerly read the papers. These budding journalism majors were the reason I came to Stillman.

But after an hour of reading, I did not see how any of them would become reporters and editors without superhuman efforts on their part and mine. None had any sense of how a news article comes together. None knew how to write a compelling lead or how to use the active voice. Only one, a young woman in the opinion writing class, had written for a high school newspaper.

During the next class meetings, I returned the papers. I did not mark the work, but I explained the writing was disappointingly bad and that they would have to work overtime to learn to write at an acceptable level. All except the one student who had a decent essay were outraged.

"I thought this was going to be a real English class," a student said.

I asked her which high school she had attended and what she meant. The Selma High School graduate said her English teacher had let students spend most of their time discussing current events and writing short paragraphs. They wrote one essay all term. Most of the other students nodded approvingly. I did not tell the class that Selma High was considered to be academically inferior. I did tell them we would follow the syllabus, which required eight essays and four revisions. I also told them they would have to complete the grammar quizzes in the textbook. Everyone, except the competent writer, groaned.

"I ain't taking this class," one of the students who had been in front of King Hall said. He stood, nodded to his three friends and walked out of the room. One of them followed. The other two stared at me and scowled for the remainder of the period.

The journalism students in the other two classes accepted my criticism without grumbling. In fact, they were pleased with the prospect of learning how to write "like real reporters," said Kristin Heard, a freshman from Montgomery.

"THE ENDANGERED CHAIR"

Even as I attended my first faculty meeting in those first few days, I sensed I might not belong at Stillman. During a break, I went to the refreshment table for orange juice. I spoke to two black professors already there.

"You're Bill Maxwell, right?" one asked.

"Right," I said.

"The new endowed chair," he said slyly.

"The endangered chair," the other said.

They had a big laugh at my expense.

"It's scholar-in-residence," I said, trying to save face.

By the beginning of my second year, I would find myself alienated from most of the senior administrators and most of the longtime staff members who were responsible for the day-to-day operations of the institution.

My alienation, a colleague told me, was the result of a disease found at most HBCUs: professional jealousy. The college president hired me as the "scholar in residence" on a 10-month contract for a modest salary. Some professors resented the arrangement because they had been there for several years and were earning the same or less.

In addition to re-establishing the journalism major, my duties included teaching at least three courses and advising the student newspaper. Unofficially, I was expected to be the guest speaker at select campus functions and assist with public relations.

At least two colleagues publicly complained that the president had created a job for me and was spending money unnecessarily. Several colleagues called me "McNealey's boy."

Although I considered the whole affair to be childish and foolish, I was offended and embarrassed.

REFUSING TO BUY THE BOOK

After a week, I faced another problem that my seasoned colleagues knew well but failed to warn me about: Most Stillman students refuse to buy their required textbooks. I discovered the problem on a Friday when I met my English class to discuss the assigned essay in the text. They were to write an essay in response to the reading.

Only one student, the young man who wrote well, had read the essay. He had the text in front of him. The others had not purchased the text. I warned them that if they returned to class without their books, they would receive an F. But only five of 31 students brought their texts to the next class.

Most students had book vouchers as part of their financial aid, so I told those without books to walk with me to the bookstore, a distance of about three football fields. Some did not follow me, and I tried to remember who they were. At the store I watched students wander around, obviously trying to avoid buying the book. Only about eight wound up buying one.

I became angry that I had to deal with such a self-destructive, juvenile problem. I saw the refusal to buy the text as a collective act of defiance. I knew that if I lost this battle, I would not have any control in this class and no respect.

The next Monday, I went to class dreading a showdown. While calling the roll, I asked the students to show me their texts. Eighteen still did not have them. One said he had bought the book but left it in his dorm room "by mistake." I told him to go get it. He gathered his belongings and left. He never came to class again.

As promised, I recorded an F for all students who did not bring their texts. The last two young men from in front of King Hall walked out. I saw myself as having failed them as a professor, but I was relieved they were gone.

I also decided to take away students' excuses for not having access to the texts. I personally bought two copies of each book and put them on reserve in the library. From time to time, I would check to see who had used them. During the entire semester, the books were used only six times.

BELOW AVERAGE BY MOST MEASURES

As I settled into my routine at Stillman that first fall, I researched the backgrounds of the students in the English class. None had an SAT score above 1000. The average combined SAT score for the nation was 1026; the best possible score was 1600.

None of them had taken advanced placement courses in school. Of the 33 students, 21 came from single-parent, low-income families who lived mostly in Alabama. Some came from the state's Black Belt, one of the poorest areas in the nation with some of the worst public schools. The Black Belt's most famous town is Selma, home of the Edmund Pettus Bridge and the site of "Bloody Sunday," where state troopers and sheriff's deputies beat hundreds of civil rights marchers on March 7, 1965.

Of the nearly 1,000 students on campus, all but 100 or so received financial aid and loans. Nearly everyone qualified for federal Pell grants. I had come to campus having read studies showing that students in this demographic group tend to perform below average by most academic measures.

Instead of being disheartened, I remembered I was much like my students as a 17-year-old freshman at Wiley College not knowing what to expect. Unlike the majority of my students at Stillman, though, I was an avid reader. Even at age 13, I knew that I wanted to be a writer. I was determined to learn my first day at Wiley, which I attended from 1963 to 1965.

I played football my first semester. During the second semester, I gave up my football scholarship and got a federal student loan. I wanted to devote all of my time to my studies and to reading on my own. And I was not alone. Many of my schoolmates were similarly inspired after a few months on our tiny East Texas campus.

I also had caring professors who introduced the life of the mind to this kid reared as a migrant farm worker in labor camps up and down the eastern United States. My professors were intellectuals, and I wanted to be just like them. Our professors—whether we liked them or hated them—were gods, and we were to learn all we could from them.

For many of us, Wiley was the only opportunity to earn a four-year degree. Jim Crow barred us from most colleges and universities in the South, and our low ACT and SAT scores disqualified us from attending most other campuses nationwide. Wiley was our lifeline to professional success. And we knew it.

HIGHLY DEDICATED TEACHERS

While students at Stillman often had a lower assessment of their professors, there were some highly dedicated teachers who were not there for money or fame. Most earned doctorates from some of the nation's best universities. Of the college's 88 full-time professors during my time there, about 70 percent were white. Stillman was typical of the overwhelming majority of other HBCUs, where white professors outnumber black professors, a trend pejoratively referred to as the "whitening" of the HBCU faculty. A major reason for this phenomenon is that mainline universities seeking ethnic diversity on their faculties heavily recruit new black Ph.D.s and specialists. Another reason is that many black Ph.D.s see teaching at the HBCU as being "drudge work"—a step down, not a step up.

As far as I could tell, black and white professors were collegial to one another, and I never heard of any serious racial conflicts. I did hear several black students complain about having so many white professors in a historically black environment.

One student, Jillian Freeman, a freshman cheerleader, said: "I came here because I wanted black professors, but most of my professors are white. I don't like this."

Before coming to Stillman, I had heard and read about the so-called inferiority of the professors at HBCUs. Because Stillman was essentially a teaching institution, the "publish or perish" rule did not apply. But I was surprised that many of my colleagues still had impressive scholarly publications.

I have taught at several other colleges, and I must say that Stillman's faculty, despite the low salaries, is highly competent. I regularly sat in on lectures that were outstanding. Most are dedicated to the institution and to the students. On any given night, many professors return to campus to attend student events. Professors also routinely spent their own money for field trips and classroom supplies.

The college had precious few young professors because they could not support their families on the low salaries. Only older people who had spouses earning decent salaries or who had other sources of income could teach at Stillman without struggling financially. I supplemented my much-envied salary with two small pensions and money from freelance writing.

AN ALLY AT MY SIDE

Lucinda Coulter was one of the bright lights at Stillman and an ally in the mission to groom young journalists. The professor, who is white, had a doctorate in American literature and had written for several magazines. She was a journalism instructor at the University of Alabama until she was hired at Stillman for a tenure-track position in 2000.

It wasn't an easy transition.

"During my first semester, I was overwhelmed with the work-load," she told me during one of our gripe sessions. "I taught five classes and revitalized the student newspaper. The president had shut it down. It had become unprofessional. It looked like a yearbook instead of a newspaper.

"I was discouraged by the end of the year because of the workload. I returned the next year only because the faculty members in the English department were so supportive. We became close friends. We felt a common bond because we had a handful of genuinely wonderful kids."

We quickly developed a similar bond as we each taught about a dozen journalism students my first semester. Together we urged the students to read the *Tuscaloosa News,* which cost 50 cents, so we could discuss the news and how the newspaper approached it. But the newspaper had long ago removed its lone paper rack from Stillman's campus because of theft and vandalism. The nearest racks were several blocks away at two gas stations. None of our students would walk that far to buy the newspaper, and only a few would go online to read it.

"If you want to be a piano player," I often said in class, "you have to practice playing the piano. If you want to be a reporter, you have to read newspapers."

Hardly any students brought the newspaper to class. So Lucinda and I used our own money to buy each student a copy of the *Tuscaloosa News* every morning. The students repaid us for about three weeks, but when they stopped we kept buying it anyway. We knew some of them were living from hand to mouth. We also bought enough copies of the *New York Times,* the *Birmingham News* and *USA Today* for the students to share each day.

Newspapers weren't all we bought. Students at other college newspapers have plenty of camera equipment. We bought dozens of disposable cameras for students to take photographs to go along with their stories for the student newspaper, the *Tiger's Paw.* We changed the name to *The Advance,* a more mature-sounding name, during my second semester.

While many college newspapers are printed daily or weekly, we struggled to publish one edition each semester. Of the 12 students on the newspaper staff when I arrived, eight were English majors and only three had journalism experience in high school.

Few efforts in academia are tougher than trying to teach English majors how to write like journalists. English majors tend to believe that complicated prose and obfuscation are smart. Clear prose—the bread and butter of journalism—is considered unsophisticated and incapable of conveying deep thought and important ideas.

I had a hard time getting students to use short words instead of long ones: "ended" instead of "terminated"; "use" instead of "utilization"; "aim" instead of "objective."

Constance Bayne, a freshman from Tennessee, was an immediate exception. After I graded three of her stories, she had an epiphany during an individual grading session.

"I see what you mean," she said, studying my revision of one of her attempts at pomposity. "Yours is better. It's real easy to read."

"That's what we always want," I said. "Simplicity is elegant."

She smiled and read the rest of my revisions.

THE MESSAGES WERE LOST

I tried my best to cultivate a love of language and reading. Two sayings were on my office door. One was a Chinese proverb: "It is only through daily reading that you refresh your mind sufficiently to speak wisely." The other came from me: "Being Smart Is Acting Black."

But the messages were lost on students who had read so little growing up and had never acquired basic academic skills. I was not surprised to learn that only two of my students had read more than three of the books most high school students have read, books such as *Moby Dick, The Sun Also Rises, The Color Purple* and *Invisible Man*.

Those of us who were teaching the required general education courses—all of us from the nation's respected universities, such as the University of Chicago, Indiana University, the University of Florida and Princeton—had to face a harsh reality. We primarily were practicing remediation.

Every day in my classes, I reviewed basic grammar and showed students how to use the dictionary effectively, lessons normally taught in elementary and middle school.

Homework was another major problem. Writing courses, especially journalism courses, are labor intensive for students and the professors. Reporting—going into the field, interviewing sources, finding official records and verifying information for accuracy—is essential. After most of my students continued to hand in articles that had only one interview, I began requiring at least four interviews, with the sources' telephone numbers, for each story. Most of the students balked and continued to hand in work with an insufficient number of interviews.

Meeting deadlines, a must in journalism, was yet another problem. Few of my students regularly met the Monday deadline. I would deduct a letter grade for each day the copy was late. Some students received F's on all of their work. To avoid flunking them, I let them write in class.

But that required them to show up, and I seldom had all students present. Attending class seemed to be an inconvenience. The college had an official attendance policy, but few professors followed it strictly because most of our students would have flunked out before midterm. On most days, I did not call the roll. I simply tried to remember who was present.

I recall the afternoon I sat alone in my room waiting for the seven students in the reporting class to show up. At 20 minutes past the hour, a white colleague peeked in and saw me in the otherwise empty room.

"You must've had a serious assignment due?" he said.

We had a big laugh. But it was a painful laugh.

"It's the Stillman way," he said. "A lot of these kids won't attend class, and, when they do, they walk in late. They're on CPT (Colored People's Time)."

Although I laughed with my colleague, I was ashamed that a white person so easily joked about CPT.

"They don't have intellectual curiosity," I said. "We weren't like that at Wiley or Bethune-Cookman."

"I know what you mean."

This time, we did not laugh. I gathered my books and newspapers, turned out the lights and left.

I hardly ever saw anyone take notes during lectures in the English class. Instead, I had to regularly chastise students for text messaging their friends and relatives and for going online to read messages and send messages. The college issued free laptops to all students who maintained a passing grade-point average.

When I confronted students about text messaging, I was met with hostility. I even had a few students leave class to make calls or send text messages. Two male students threatened to physically attack Lucinda and another female professor because they demanded that the students put away their laptops in class.

Each time, I would leave the English class exhausted, angry and sad. I would go home on many evenings during my first month wanting to cry, and things didn't get much better as the year progressed.

I had come to Stillman on the mission of my life: I wanted to be of use, to help "uplift the race" as my professors had taught me. But as my first school year ended in the spring, instead of feeling useful and as if I were helping to uplift the race, I was feeling helpless and irrelevant.

PART II: A DREAM LAY DYING

Bill Maxwell

After spending the summer trying to shake off the disappointment over my first year as a professor at Stillman College, I began the 2005 fall semester looking for even the smallest signs that I could make a difference in the lives of black students by setting high standards and inspiring them to rise to the challenge.

The first ray of hope that August morning came as I unlocked my office door and was greeted by Constance Bayne, my most diligent journalism student. The mere fact that she had bought her textbooks made me feel some degree of success. My first year, many students had refused to get the textbooks even when they had vouchers to cover the cost. Constance's enthusiasm was reassuring, and I remember thinking that if I had 10 students like her I could transform the college into a place that attracted other high achievers from throughout Alabama.

I became even more hopeful that afternoon when I met with Stillman president Ernest McNealey. He had invited me in 2004 to leave the *St. Petersburg Times* editorial board, revive the journalism major at the small historically black college in Tuscaloosa and fulfill a promise I had made to myself years ago. Now McNealey agreed it was time to order new computers and other supplies to open a newsroom for the student newspaper and for editing and design classes.

During those first few weeks of school, the new equipment began arriving and my hopes continued to rise. My first year at Stillman, which had fewer than 1,000 students, had not been as smooth or as fulfilling as I had hoped. My students' academic performance had been generally disappointing, and I could not persuade most students to even attend class regularly.

Still, I believed that with a real newsroom we were ready to make significant progress. Before my arrival at Stillman, my colleague Lucinda Coulter had produced the student newspaper on her home computer without charging the college a dime. With a campus newsroom, we assumed that our students would begin to take the profession seriously and would love hanging out in their own space.

We soon learned that we had been naive. Nothing changed. Students rarely came to the newsroom except for classes. The majority preferred to socialize with their friends during their spare time, and others knew that one way to avoid an assignment for the newspaper was to avoid the newsroom where story leads and tips were posted on the bulletin board.

My colleagues and I were witnessing the result of low admission standards. Were we expecting too much of young people who scored poorly on the SAT, who were rarely challenged to excel in high school, who were not motivated to take advantage of opportunities to learn, who could not imagine where a sound education could take them?

An unfortunate truth was that most of my colleagues and I never got an opportunity to teach the breadth of our knowledge. I had great difficulty, for example, teaching something as simple as the distinction between "historic" and "historical" or between "infer" and "imply," distinctions that careful writers, especially journalists, want to know.

I wasn't the only one. A white professor labored to get her students to critically read the assignments. She could not discuss the major themes and literary conventions when her students did not read. When she got nowhere with Zora Neale Hurston's novel *Their Eyes Were Watching God*, she asked me to speak to the class. Perhaps a black professor would have more success talking about one of the best-known black authors.

A few minutes into my exchange with the class, I realized the white professor was not the problem. The students simply did not—or could not—read closely. My colleagues and I could not teach what we had been trained to teach.

"My students don't use me," an English professor said. "At most, I may run into two or three a year who make me work. Talking over your students' heads is a waste of everybody's time."

TREAT STUDENTS AS YOUR OWN CHILDREN

Nonetheless, President McNealey and his administration wanted us to nurture our students. During faculty meetings, we regularly were encouraged to treat our students as if they were our own children. We were responsible for saving them all. This was familiar terrain; a generation earlier my professors had nurtured me at two historically black colleges, Wiley in Marshall, Texas, and Bethune-Cookman in Daytona Beach. Some of them even had given me a few breaks I may not have deserved.

Many of my Stillman colleagues regularly invited their students to their homes for dinner. The discussions often were about personal matters involving romantic relationships, family crises and money problems. Professors were the first confidants many students ever had. Indeed, they often became surrogate parents.

As a single man living in a small apartment, I did not feel comfortable inviting students over. I did go to my colleagues' homes whenever I was invited to have dinner with students, and faculty members often attended student-sponsored events on and off campus. Some professors even showed up at their students' churches on Sundays. I am not a churchgoer, but I rarely missed a football or basketball game.

The bottom line was the same as it is at most HBCUs. Professors who had the best success connecting with students, especially below-average male students, emphasized friendly, personal and supportive involvement in their lives. For example, Stephen Jackson, who taught sports writing, was an effective professor because he understood the importance of winning students' trust. He even ate lunch in the cafeteria with students each day.

This style of teaching, which I grudgingly adopted, was unlike anything I had used during my previous 18 years of teaching on traditional campuses such as those of the University of Illinois at Chicago and Northern Illinois University. On those campuses, professors were respected for their achievements and position. Subject matter usually was taught without developing strong personal relationships between students and professors, and professors may not have cared if students liked them.

At Stillman, being professional but impersonal created frustration for the student and the professor. Students, especially males, liked and respected the flexible professor, and they learned when they respected the professor.

The flexible professor encouraged lively exchanges of subject matter, ideas, beliefs and opinions during class discussions. The flexible professor often did not require written responses or exams. The flexible professor let students keep pace by retaking exams, completing take-home exams or giving classroom presentations.

I had difficulty becoming flexible. The majority of my students in the English class failed to complete most of the assigned readings. Most of their essays were unacceptable, and attendance was low. I had a choice: Abandon my syllabus or flunk more than half of the class.

I abandoned the syllabus. Instead, I lectured and made assignments based on the problems and errors in the students' writing. I went over the same material, such as writing the topic sentence, again and again because some students could not master it.

"We're crippling these kids by mothering them," I told a colleague over a drink one evening.

"We're loving them to death," he replied.

"SOME OF THEM DON'T BELONG HERE"
During the fall semester, I would try to make eye contact with students and speak to them as we passed in the halls and on The Yard, the grassy campus gathering spot. Very few of them would return my greetings. Most were sullen. But I also saw something more disturbing in their faces: Many of these young people were sad and unhappy. Very few smiled.

A colleague who had taught at Stillman for more than 10 years confirmed my observations. "Our kids haven't had many good things in their lives," she said. "Many of them are angry and negative and rude. They've had hard lives. Some of them don't belong here."

She was right. A number of students had criminal records, and others were awaiting trial on criminal charges. Stillman accepted them because they could not attend college anywhere else.

Terry Lee Brock, a 41-year-old freshman, was shot several times by a woman around 2 one morning in early February in front of the Night Stalker's Lounge. He died a short time later at the hospital. His trial for rape had been scheduled to begin the following week.

I did not learn until after his death that many of our female students were afraid of Terry. At least two told me they had complained to college officials that an alleged rapist was allowed on campus.

While we had students such as Terry who had no business being on a college campus, we went out of our way to help others who faced adversity and worked to overcome it.

"A lot of my students reared themselves and their sisters and brothers," Lucinda said. "They're adults before they're ready to be adults."

One of my students, a 25-year-old senior journalism major, grew up in several foster homes in different states. At Stillman, she had a part-time job, carried a full academic load and wrote for the student newspaper. She was an inspiration. When she graduated, I wrote a letter of recommendation that helped her land a public relations job in Atlanta. Her boss e-mailed me a few months later to say that my student was doing well and could stay with the firm as long as she wanted.

The college did not keep an accurate count, but we knew many young women on campus were mothers. One of my students was a 20-year-old mother of two, pressed for time and money. But she had good attendance and turned in passable homework.

I met several students who had legally adopted their siblings. For one reason or another, their parents were temporarily or permanently absent. Some of my colleagues and I empathized and gave these students breaks, such as giving them take-home quizzes and exams and sometimes excusing them from class if they had written excuses from their employers.

We also had a handful of exemplary students. Leonard Merriman IV, who wrote for the student newspaper, was from New Orleans and did not know the whereabouts of his mother for several weeks after Hurricane Katrina. He was an inspiration to students and professors because he was intellectually curious, read voraciously and dared to be a nerd in an environment that celebrated everything hip-hop and categorized students by their fraternities or sororities.

After I had assigned a paper on the 2004 presidential election and required students to quote at least three political experts, a football player raised his hand one day and asked if he could use Leonard as an expert. The class cracked up, but I had to think about the question. Leonard claimed to have read all of George W. Bush's campaign speeches, and he easily rattled off statistics and summarized Bush's positions.

I decided Leonard was an expert and the football player could quote him. But we did not have many students like him. Instead of taking pride in being exemplary students, many were devotees of hip-hop culture. They were anti-intellectual, rude and profane.

I always was amazed that so many of the women tolerated the crude way the men spoke to them. One afternoon in my English class, a male student called a young woman "a big-assed ugly bitch." I expected her to slap him, and I would not have intervened. Instead, she dismissed the whole thing with a wave of her hand and turned to chat with her roommate. After class, I asked her about the insult.

"That fool don't mean nothing to me," she said. "He ain't nothing but a stupid brother from Anniston or somewhere."

The lesson was clear and disheartening: Personal insult, crude language and threatening behavior were a way of life for many students. I saw this kind of exchange repeated dozens of times in the classroom and on The Yard. I had no doubt that the influences of hip-hop contributed greatly to this ugly reality and other deleterious trends.

"Have you noticed that our students never have a sense of urgency?" a colleague asked one afternoon as we walked to a faculty meeting. "They don't seem to be going anywhere in particular. They just stand around or mosey along. Frivolity."

He was right. Greek organization activities such as step shows— the rhythmical, patterned dance movements favored by fraternities and sororities—and any excuse to party and play music were the most important events on campus.

When a professor brought a special lecturer to campus, the rest of us would require our students to attend the event. But more often than not only a handful would show up, a great source of embarrassment for the professors. I never invited any of my fellow journalists to campus. Besides the stinging embarrassment of low attendance, I resented the hassle of rounding up students for their own enlightenment.

"I'M GOING TO BE A NURSE"

The effects of poverty made teaching and learning arduous. I asked a student why she always fell asleep in my reporting and news writing class.

"I work full-time at Target at night," she said. "I can't get enough sleep."

I asked the obligatory questions: Why did she work so many hours? Did her family help her? What was she spending her money on? Did she have financial aid? Did she have a scholarship? Did she live on campus?

Her life's story was heartbreaking and yet typical of so many others. Born and reared in Selma, she was 19 years old. She had met her father once when she was 10. Her mother had been in and out of jail until her death in 1996 at age 34. Her then-64-year-old grandmother had assumed responsibility for her and her three siblings.

Although she had a student loan to help pay tuition, she had to pay for everything else and needed a car to get to work and to drive back to Selma. She also had to send money to her grandmother, who was living on Social Security and money from a part-time job as a caretaker for a disabled woman. Everyone except her grandmother said this teenager had no business attending college. Her place was in Selma with the rest of the family.

"Everybody told me I was just going to be a hoochie mama," she said. "I'm going to be a nurse."

I had no doubt she would become a nurse. Although she had a C average, she was one of my hardest-working students and had one of the best attendance records.

As we talked, I noticed her stealing glances at the basket of cosmetics and toiletries (soap, toothpaste, shampoo, conditioner, lotion) I had placed on my desk for the first time the day before. These were items I had collected when I traveled and stayed in hotels.

Trying to ease her embarrassment, I said: "If you want some of that stuff, take it. I need to get rid of it."

She hesitated. Faking nonchalance, she studied the items without touching anything.

"Go ahead and take what you want," I said.

She picked up bottles of shampoo, lotion and conditioner.

"Take some toothpaste, too," I said.

She took a tube of toothpaste, smiled and thanked me. I told her any time she needed something to feel free to take it. Embarrassed, she thanked me again and left.

Word got around about the basket. A few days later, several other students dropped in to inspect the items. A week later, the basket was empty.

Each week after that, I went to Kmart and CVS and shopped for travel-size cosmetics and toiletries to replenish the basket. I learned that several other professors also found acceptable ways to make personal items available to students free of charge.

We treated the students, even those who disappointed us, as if they were our children. I often wondered if we were doing more harm than good with our generosity.

ONE TAKER FOR A BIG TRIP

In early October, Lucinda and I planned a field trip to Washington for the 10th anniversary celebration of the Million Man March. Learning often takes place outside the classroom, and we thought our students would benefit from being around thousands of other black Americans who would travel from across the country to the National Mall. They also would see how professional journalists cover a national news story.

We reserved a college van for the 800-mile drive from Tuscaloosa. Six students agreed to come, and Lucinda and I reserved several Washington hotel rooms on our personal credit cards. But the day before we were to leave, all but one student backed out and we canceled the trip. Once again, I was angry and disappointed.

This wasn't the first nor the last time many students would pass up an opportunity to escape the campus and learn something.

We took only four students on a three-day trip to the University of Georgia and its student newspaper because eight others refused to go.

One didn't want to spend four hours in a van. Two others said they had quizzes on the morning that we were to leave, even though they would have been excused from class. When it was time to go, they simply did not show up.

They missed a great experience. At the University of Georgia, our four students attended lectures and spent two evenings at the office of the *Red & Black,* the student newspaper. They had never seen the newsroom of a daily publication. They attended a budget meeting, where the staff members decided which stories to publish in the next issue. Each Stillman student shadowed an editor and a reporter, and each worked on a real story in real time.

Since the college would not give us an advance for expenses, Lucinda and I paid more than $1,200 for the trip. We never were reimbursed.

We also personally paid for several in-state field trips to places important to the civil rights movement, such as the Safe House Black History Museum in Greensboro. That is where a handful of local residents hid the Rev. Martin Luther King Jr. overnight from a white mob. We took students to other civil rights landmarks in Anniston, Birmingham, Selma and Montgomery.

Lucinda bought two digital cameras, one that she and I used to shoot photographs for the student newspaper and one for our students to use. I regularly bought disposable cameras for our students without seeking reimbursement.

Campus-wide, professors bought many of their classroom and office supplies. In my building, for example, we rarely had an ample supply of paper for our copy machine. I learned early to buy my own paper and keep it in my desk.

Chalk? Forget about it.

THE MEAN WOMEN BEHIND THE COUNTER

Early in the spring semester, I realized I had never received an official roster for one of my classes. I went to the appropriate office to find out what had happened.

The woman who waited on me sharply responded that famous newspaper people would be treated no differently than anyone else.

"Why are you being so rude?" I asked.

"Rude?" she responded. "You just have to wait like everybody else."

That episode reflected my ongoing difficulties with the staff, the majority of whom were middle-aged to older black women with local roots. Instead of feeling like a professor, someone of relative importance and value, I felt insignificant. Even worse, students routinely experienced similar problems.

In an essay, a female student wrote: "Each time I go to the financial aid office, I get my feelings hurt. The ladies behind the counter talk to you like you're dirt. I hate to go in there. They don't know how to treat people, and they don't try to help you. They make everything so hard. My mother said they're just a bunch of sadiddy niggers, and I shouldn't worry about it. But I have to worry. They give me my check or they don't give me my check. You better not make them mad."

Many of my colleagues agreed. They told me that much of our students' hostility was the result of the constant rudeness and humiliation they experienced while trying to do something as routine and essential as completing the right forms for a loan or a grant.

I tried to conduct all of my affairs by e-mail. Unfortunately, I had to go to the business office to deduct funds from the $100,000 that a Tampa donor provided for me to establish the journalism major. The woman in charge was routinely arrogant and uncooperative.

Another example: The *Tuscaloosa News* printed our student newspaper for $1,500 and billed the college. One of the *News'* designers, Danny Dejarnette, did our layout for each issue for the bargain price of $500. On more than one occasion, the college did not pay the *News* or Dejarnette in a timely manner.

Embarrassed by such a lack of professionalism, Lucinda would pay the printing bill out of her pocket and I would pay for the layout. We would submit our receipts and proper forms to the business office. After several months and regular reminders, the college would reimburse us.

SETTING FIRES IN THE DORM

While disagreeable staff members and financial red tape were constant irritants, nothing was more appalling than the students' disregard for college property.

During the spring semester, the Tuscaloosa Fire Department put out trash can fires in King Hall. I was angry and embarrassed to see a team of white firefighters trying to save a dormitory named for the Rev. Martin Luther King Jr. that black students had trashed.

"Why do they do this to their own buildings?" a white firefighter asked me.

I went inside the dorm to see the damage. Students had stuffed trash cans with paper and fabric and set them on fire. The smoke damage was enormous. The walls were blackened, the windows were smudged and the pungent smell of smoke lingered and stuck to everything.

Even without the fire damage, the place would have looked like a war zone. Holes had been kicked and punched in the walls. Windows were broken, floors were scarred and most of the furniture was damaged. The two dorms routinely underwent major repairs after each semester.

Two of my students, both journalism majors, were desperate to move out of King Hall. The last time I saw them, one had found an apartment and the other was looking for a place he could afford.

I'VE WASTED TWO YEARS

By the end of the spring semester, I knew that I could not remain at Stillman another year. I had a few good students, but a few were not enough. One morning as I dressed for work, I accepted the reality that too much of my time was being wasted on students who did not care. I felt guilty about wanting to leave. But enough was enough.

A week before I left Stillman as a professor, I drove through the main gate en route to a final exam. As always, I saw a group of male students hanging out in front of King Hall.

The same four I had seen when I drove onto campus nearly two years earlier were milling about on the lawn. I parked my car and walked over to the group.

"Why don't you all hang out somewhere else?" I asked.

"Who you talking to, old nigger?" one said.

"You give the school a bad image out here," I said.

They laughed.

"Hang out somewhere else or at least go to the library and read a book," I said.

They laughed and dismissed me with stylized waves of the arm.

I walked back to my old Chevy Blazer, sad but relieved that I would be leaving.

In my office, I sat at my desk staring at a stack of papers to be graded. I'm wasting my time, I thought. I've wasted two years of my professional life. I don't belong here.

I put the papers in a drawer. I did not read them. Why read them?

TWO YEARS AT STILLMAN

May 13: The first year: Trying to make a difference.

Today: The second year: A bad situation gets worse.

May 27: The epilogue: Should historically black colleges be saved?

PART III: THE ONCE AND FUTURE PROMISE

❧

Bill Maxwell

The conflict between my head and my heart over the future of Historically Black Colleges and Universities is reflected in enduring scenes from my two years of teaching at Alabama's Stillman College.

There were the young men who hung out at the entrance gates of the small Tuscaloosa school and had no interest in learning. They represented my frustration with too many students who arrived on campus unprepared for college, who failed to attend class or buy the textbooks, who refused to complete the assignments and who forced professors to coddle them.

Then there were those few dedicated students who saw Stillman as their only path to a brighter future. There was the young single mother who worked full-time at night and struggled to stay awake in class, the unpolished journalist eager to improve and find work at a newspaper, the young man who turned himself into an expert on President Bush's campaign speeches and dared to stand out from the hip-hop culture around him.

One group leads me to question whether historically black colleges are worth saving. The other is an inspiration and symbolizes why these institutions still are vital for many young people struggling to build productive lives.

Nearly a year after leaving the campus, I am only now resolving the conflict in my own mind.

GLORY YEARS ARE GONE, BUT . . .

Undeniably, the picture is bleak for many historically black colleges. There are more options for high-achieving black students, and integration has left these schools with diminished but more difficult roles in higher education.

The situation was different before the 1964 Civil Rights Act, when a degree from one of these schools was the primary route to respectability, success and the good life for black Americans. Back then, they enrolled most black college students and were responsible for the bulk of the black middle class.

The glory years are long gone, especially at the smallest of the 39 private schools that receive money and other support from the United Negro College Fund. Majority white campuses seeking ethnically diverse student populations are enrolling many of the nation's best black students.

Now only 1 in 5 black students earn bachelor's degrees from historically black schools, which have increasingly become dependent upon marginal students from poor families. Two-thirds of HBCU students receive federally funded Pell Grants, aimed at families earning less than $40,000 annually. More than half of the students receive those grants at every HBCU except at 13 of the best schools, such as Spelman, Howard and Morehouse.

Studies show schools with a high number of Pell recipients tend to have low admission standards, and the reasons for their low graduation rates are well-documented. Most low-income students have parents who did not attend college, which often signals that their homes have few books or other reading materials. Many of the students never develop a love of learning, and they tend to perform poorly in class and on standardized tests.

The statistics reflect my experience as a professor between 2004 and 2006 at Stillman, which had fewer than 1,000 students. Most of my students would not study, regularly turn in their homework on time or read the assigned material. I walked grumbling students to the bookstore to try to force them to buy their required textbooks.

These students lacked the intellectual vigor taken for granted on traditional campuses. They did not know what or whom to respect. For many, the rappers Bow Wow and 50 Cent were at least as important to black achievement as the late Ralph Bunche, the first black to win a Nobel Peace Prize, and Zora Neale Hurston, the great novelist.

In time, I realized that my standards were too high for the quality of student I had to teach. Most simply were not prepared for college-level work, and I was not professionally trained for the intense remediation they needed and deserved.

Many HBCUs, including Stillman, lack the resources and money to assist these students with effective remediation. These students naturally find friends on campus who share their streetwise, anti-intellectual views and behavior. They lose interest in education or become so overwhelmed they leave school altogether.

Only a handful of HBCUs, including Fisk University in Tennessee, Spelman College in Atlanta, Claflin University in South Carolina and Miles College in Birmingham, graduate more than half their students (the graduation rate at Florida A&M is 33 percent). These schools funnel large sums of money into remediation, advising and counseling. They also offer small classes so students have easy access to their professors.

Others, such as Southern University in New Orleans, Allen University in South Carolina and Stillman, graduate less than 30 percent of their students.

As the number and quality of students drop, historically black colleges cannot depend as they once did on the financial generosity of their alumni. The problem is compounded by the reality that many corporations and foundations scaled back their philanthropic efforts following the 2000 economic downturn. Many donors still are not as generous as they once were, and struggling HBCUs have been hit especially hard.

Stillman president Ernest McNealey regularly told this joke: "I have a very large tin cup . . . and I'm constantly running through airports with my tin cup, and wherever the plane lands; I will go to the tallest building and work my way from the penthouse on down to the garbage unit with my tin cup. And whether it's the CEO or the janitor, I will hear this long story about the declining stock market."

It does not help that too many black colleges have serious management issues. The media has regularly reported academic, financial or administrative problems at schools such as Morris Brown in Georgia, Lemoyne-Owen College in Memphis, Grambling State in Louisiana, Edward Waters in Jacksonville and Florida A&M in Tallahassee.

The numbers for many historically black colleges are not encouraging. Declining enrollments, loose admission standards and low graduation rates produce ever-tighter budgets, less reliable alumni networks and grimmer futures.

EXCELLENCE BY THE HANDFUL

Yet I cannot turn my back on these schools. I cannot forget what they did for me many years ago, and I cannot forget the handful of dedicated students at Stillman who were determined to succeed even in the face of the school's considerable shortcomings.

All of my public school teachers were HBCU alumni, and I admired them. My sisters graduated from HBCUs, Bethune-Cookman in Daytona Beach and Florida Memorial in Miami. Bernard Irving, my high school football coach, graduated from Wiley College in Texas and was responsible for my attending that school. I went there from 1963 to 1966, when I joined the U.S. Marine Corps. After I was discharged from the Corps in 1969, I went to Bethune-Cookman, where I graduated with a double major in English and history in 1971.

Just as those schools provided me with an opportunity, I tried to create the same chances for my most engaged students at Stillman. I had a few successes, but I mostly fell short.

A researcher for the Education Trust, an independent policy group, said in 2005: "Instead of a certain kind of student dragging down some institutions, we could just as easily argue that some institutions are dragging down a certain kind of student."

I found that to be true. I had a handful of excellent journalism students at Stillman who all had SAT scores below 1,000. Ebony Horton, for example, was a natural-born reporter. She had an eye for a good story, knew how to find the right sources and was a better-than-average writer. She did not, however, have classmates who shared her enthusiasm and gift for reporting. As a result, she bowed to peer pressure: She often cut corners, handed in flawed copy and missed deadlines more times than I liked.

Because she had natural skills, Ebony interned at the *Tuscaloosa News* and after graduation landed a full-time job with the *Dothan Eagle* as a general assignment reporter. Although Ebony found a good job, I am certain that we ill-served her at Stillman because we lacked a critical mass of motivated, competent students and the right facilities that would have enhanced her skills.

The same was true of Cedric Baker. Even before he graduated, the *Tuscaloosa News* hired him as a part-time sports reporter, where he had a byline, sometimes two, each week. Ironically, he is on Stillman's public relations staff today. I regret that we did not have an environment that could inspire Cedric to produce his best work.

Three of my other promising students withdrew after only one semester. One of them, a young man from Mississippi who was a talented reporter and photographer, said: "I can't stand it here, Mr. Maxwell. Nobody's serious. The students don't study. They just bullshit all the time, and the administration doesn't care. It's all messed up."

He gave up on an HBCU and transferred to Millsaps College in Mississippi. I pleaded with him and the others to stay. I did not want to lose such potential. Although they came to Stillman with low standardized test scores, they were smart and highly motivated. They were precisely the kind of students most HBCUs were meant to serve: those who otherwise would not see a college campus.

These were young people who needed the second chance the HBCU can provide. As I watched these students languish, I knew I was not delivering a quality college experience to young people who deserved better.

Because of our lack of money, inadequate services and incompetent leadership, we were not giving these bright young people the same quality of education they would have received 2 miles away at the University of Alabama—which would not have accepted most of them because of their low test scores.

MAKE SOME HARD CHOICES
In the end, the numbers signaling the decline of historically black colleges cannot trump my affection for these schools. I appreciate what

they did for me, and I appreciate the good they are doing today for their most dedicated students. Despite my disappointment at Stillman and the crises at many HBCUs, these schools still have an important role to play in society.

But to continue to play that important role, they must show huge improvement and make some hard choices.

The top-tier schools will continue to attract good students and remain vibrant, financially viable institutions. Among those familiar names are Spelman College and Morehouse College in Atlanta and Howard University in Washington, D.C., each a member of the so-called "Black Ivy League."

But some schools are so academically inferior and so poorly serving their students they should be shut down. Others, such as Lemoyne-Owen, which is millions of dollars in debt, are in such financial trouble that the operations should be handed over to independent agencies.

A few black colleges should merge into regional campuses. In Alabama, Stillman College and Talladega College are notable examples. Together, they could create a well-funded regional campus to serve thousands of students.

Because of students such as Ebony Horton, Cedric Baker and others, most historically black institutions still serve a valuable role. Although these students are intelligent, motivated, ambitious and morally decent, their low standardized test scores and low family incomes prevent them from attending most traditional schools. But they deserve a chance to discover their self-worth and mature into responsible adults, just as I did.

At Stillman, there were not enough of these dedicated students to overcome my own frustrations. Yet despite my personal disappointments, I am not willing to write off historically black colleges.

For the good they still do and the opportunities they still provide for deserving students with few other options, the majority of HBCUs are worth saving. It will take a lot of effort, but it is too important not to try.

GAY

GET OUT OF MY CLOSET

CAN YOU BE WHITE AND "ON THE DOWN LOW"?

⧼⧽

Benoit Denizet-Lewis

On *Aug. 27, 2007,* Roll Call *newspaper reported that in June an undercover police officer arrested U.S. Sen. Larry Craig outside a Minneapolis airport bathroom on a misdemeanor charge of disorderly conduct. The officer was investigating complaints of "lewd conduct" in the public bathroom, and the police report says the Idaho senator gave a series of signals—fidgeting with his hands, tapping his foot in the stall next to the police officer, and ultimately running his hand under the stall divider— that the plainclothes officer interpreted as sexual advances. On Aug. 8, Craig pleaded guilty to the charges. Subsequent discussion of the arrest has involved questions about the closeted gay subculture of anonymous sexual encounters in public locations. In August 2006, Benoit Denizet-Lewis wrote in* Slate *about "down low," the expression black men use to describe their underground homosexual activities, and closeted white men's growing appropriation of that phrase. The article is reproduced below.*

Three years ago, I wrote a story about black men who have sex with men but don't identify as gay—or even, in many cases, as bisexual. Instead, they adopted the label Down Low and formed a vibrant but secretive subculture of DL parties, DL Internet chat rooms (Thugs4Thugs, DLBrothas), and DL sex cruising areas (parks, bath-houses). Some of the Down Low guys I met were married but had covert sex with men, while others who claimed the label only had sex with men but considered themselves much too masculine to be *gay*. Most equated gayness with effeminacy—and, to a lesser extent, white-ness. From their perspective, to be an effeminate black man (a "punk," a "faggot") is to not really be a black man at all.

The Down Low was a relatively new response to a very old behav-ior. Men of all races have long had secret sexual and romantic male re-lationships, complete with the usual accessories of a double life: lies, deception, and shame. But the Down Low was a uniquely African-American creation. If the closet is a stifling, lonely place for white guys who realize they're gay but aren't ready to admit it publicly, the Down Low is a VIP party for "masculine" black men who will never admit to being homosexual—because they don't see themselves that way. And while men on the DL certainly have their share of shame, among themselves it masquerades as bravado and sexual freedom: They're the ultimate pimps and players, man enough to do their girl-friend on Thursday and do their best friend, Mike, on Friday. And un-til 2003, most black women didn't have a clue.

But then I wrote my story, J.L. King published his memoir (*On the Down Low*), Oprah turned King's book into a best seller, and *Law & Order* devoted an episode to the subculture. The Down Low quickly ceased to be, well, on the down low. And now, in a sure sign of the DL's cultural currency, white boys—apparently unsatisfied with hav-ing co-opted hip-hop—are claiming to be on the "Down Low," too.

I knew nothing of this until two months ago, when I met my first white guy who claimed to be "on the DL." He was 24, tall, masculine, attractive, and said "bro" a lot. I met him at a New York City gay club (he had made the trek from Long Island), and I'm embarrassed to say that we sort of hit it off. On the first of a few dates, I asked him where he worked—and whether people there knew he was gay.

"Bro," he said, "I'm on the Down Low."

"Dude," I said, "you're white. You can't be on the Down Low!"

"Bro," he said. "All kinds of white people are saying they're on the Down Low now."

"That's ridiculous," I protested. "Why don't you just say you're in the closet?"

"Because the closet sounds stupid," he said.

I wasn't sure I believed him, so a few days later I went searching on Craigslist, and, sure enough, I found dozens of ads from white men claiming to be on the Down Low. In Boston, where I live, I saw an ad for a 38-year-old "slightly stocky, hairy and kinky bi married white guy on the down low." In New York City, a 29-year-old Italian looking to "take care of a nice guy" who is "kool and looking for some fun" wrote that he needed someone discreet because he's on the Down Low. In the San Francisco Bay Area, a 25-year-old "white boy on the down low" posted that he was looking to "chill with the same."

(Interestingly, white guys also use the expression as an adjective—as in "I have a down-low place" to hook up, or "I need Down-Low Head." By far the most common usage, though, is some variation of "We need to keep this on the Down Low," meaning that if you happen to bump into your hookup around town, you won't bear hug him and shriek, "Bro, last night was awesome!")

Keith Boykin, the author of *Beyond the Down Low: Sex, Lies, and Denial in Black America,* told me he isn't surprised that white men are co-opting the expression. "It's become trendy to be on the DL," he says. "It has always had an appeal because it refers less to sexuality than it does to masculinity. It's an alluring term for men who identify as butch or masculine. The closet has a certain shame and weakness attached to it. The Down Low sounds more powerful, more empowering. It also sounds like a secret group, or club."

Maybe so, but white guys claiming to be on the DL is a little like two straight roommates pretending to be domestic partners so they can save on health insurance. While white guys want the perceived benefits of being on the Down Low (being seen as cool, tough, and masculine), they certainly don't want the unenviable choices facing many black men attracted to other men. For all their supposed freedom and masculine power and independence, black men on Down Low are stuck: "Come out" as anything other than heterosexual and suddenly they're a double minority, likely to be ostracized by their friends, family, and church. (Black men still have less economic mobility than whites, making their community connections all the more

critical.) Don't come out and live a secretive, dishonest, compartmen-
talized—but, in some ways, safer—life on the DL.

"We know there are black gay rappers, black gay athletes, but
they're all on the DL," Rakeem, a black gay man from Atlanta, told
me three years ago when I interviewed him for my Down Low story.
"If you're white, you can come out as an openly gay skier or actor or
whatever. It might hurt you some, but it's not like if you're black and
gay, because then it's like you've let down the whole black community,
black women, black history, black pride."

I called Rakeem recently to ask him what he thought about white
guys claiming to be on the Down Low. "Are you really asking me to
explain the behavior of white dudes?" he said, laughing. "I'm not even
going to try." Next I called Jimmy Hester, a white former music executive and an expert on the Down Low. "What haven't white people
stolen from black culture?" he said. "But seriously, it's incredibly sad
that there are still millions of men of every color living in the closet,
or on the Down Low, or whatever they want to call it. I say, let's retire
the Down Low. It should be extinct, like a dinosaur. It's 2006, and people need to free themselves."

GIRLS TO MEN

YOUNG LESBIANS IN BROOKLYN FIND THAT
A THUG'S LIFE GETS THEM MORE WOMEN

Chloé A. Hilliard

At the Lab, a Brooklyn nightclub and rental hall, a petite Hispanic bartender sporting braids down the middle of her back and a baseball cap is taking a break on a recent Friday night. Then she spots something in the crowd and leaps onto the bar. She sees another woman dressed in boyish hip-hop gear hitting on her femme girlfriend on the crowded dance floor. The bartender jumps to the floor, pushes her way past dancers, and grabs her woman by the arms. After giving her a rough, disapproving shake, she drags her quarry back to the bar, where the girlfriend will remain standing in silence the rest of the night.

"It's a property thing," explains Siya, who, like the bartender, looks like she's walked out of a rap video. Among the 15 tattoos that adorn her beige complexion are a large *Bed-Stuy* on her forearm and *Brooklyn* on the back of one hand. She's 20. "You can be holding your femme girlfriend's hand in the club, and she could be looking around, searching for a flyer AG. She's going to want to stray, slip her a number. All lesbians are sneaky," Siya says.

At the weekly 18-and-over females-only hip-hop party going on, about half of the black and Hispanic crowd is femme, the other half "AGs," or "aggressives," who also refer to themselves as "studs," whether they're fly or not.

Later, when two AGs get into a pushing match over a femme, one shouts, "Suck my dick, nigga! I'll fuck your whole shit up!" Friends break it up, pulling one outside the club to get the story. One of the women had tried to talk to the other's girlfriend while her back was turned. But it's a common occurrence. No femme, committed or not, is really off-limits.

"When you go to the club and you're an AG, your mission that entire night is to find the baddest femme in the club and make her your girl," says another woman, who calls herself Don Vito Corleone. "Just like every rapper wants the baddest video chick on his arm, so do AGs."

Rap videos have long provided men of color with milestones on their journeys to manhood. From being a successful street businessman (Notorious B.I.G.'s "Ten Crack Commandments"), to learning how to treat a woman (Dr. Dre's "Bitches Ain't Shit") and protecting their manhood (50 Cent's "What Up Gangsta?"), guys are told how to be indestructible, sexually assertive, and in general, badasses. The misogyny and homophobia implicit in that message has long raised the hackles of critics. Oprah Winfrey and columnist Leonard Pitts Jr. made news recently for saying "enough" to the influence of rap's rougher edges on black culture.

But for increasing numbers of very young black and Hispanic lesbians, the bitches-and-'hos lyrics of their musical heroes are the soundtrack for a thug's life they pursue with almost as much passion as they do the hottest femme in the club.

"These AGs have a disrespectful mentality, and they get it from men, hoodlums, dudes that are in the 'hood all day," says Kysharece Young, an AG, rapper ("Ky Fresh"), and freshman at Monroe College. "They act like a bunch of little damn boys that ain't got no sense."

In 2005, filmmaker Daniel Peddle chronicled the lives of AGs in his documentary *The Aggressives,* following six women who went to lengths like binding their breasts to pass as men. But Peddle says that today, very young lesbians of color in New York are creating a new, insular scene that's largely cut off from the rest of the gay and lesbian community. "A lot of it has to do with this kind of pressure to articulate and express your masculinity within the confines of the hip-hop paradigm," he tells the *Voice*.

As rap songs boom through the Lab's speakers on a Friday night, AGs dominate the place, shouting lyrics that objectify women as playthings. They point their fingers in the air to simulate gunfire, and throw down lyrics at other AGs like they were calling out rival gang members.

Like most men in the culture, young lesbians respect Jay-Z's business sense, consider themselves to be hustlers like Jeezy, and take the no-holds-barred approach of Lil Wayne. For these women, there seem to be few older lesbians they can look up to, or organizations that mean much to them, other than the crews they create themselves.

Among the older women who do make the scene, Kimmeee and Madison, lovingly called "Uncle" or "Father" by the younger women, promote the parties at the Lab and run girlzparty.com, the nexus for the black lesbian club scene. They say they've watched the change in younger women in the last few years.

"It gets rougher each year, and it has a lot to do with who their idol is and who they want to image themselves after, like these thug rappers," says Madison, who launched girlzparty.com 12 years ago.

"I wouldn't say there are too many [female] role models," says Kimmeee. "We get a lot of girls that come out and their idols are men and they feel like they have to be men."

After a previous location closed, the women moved their weekly dance party to the Lab after a five-week hiatus. "When we had our grand opening, almost two years ago, the fashion trend had changed dramatically. Our grand opening night we had 650 females. Half the crowd had on 'do-rags and the whole thug look going on."

Kimmeee and Madison call their weekly party at the Lab Friday Night SinSations. The DJ, playing a mix of old-school hip-hop and reggae, jumps on the mic to incite the crowd.

"If you came in here to steal another chick's bitch, let me see your hands in the air!" The dance floor turns into a sea of five-finger flags. "If you want to fuck tonight, let me hear some noise!" The hands are replaced by whooping yells and screams.

"Look at these so-called aggressive girls and how they act and carry themselves," says Rutgers adjunct professor Stacey Patton. "You see the hyper-masculinity that's been adopted by them. I don't know if it's conscious or not, but I think hip-hop has its influence."

The day after a Friday night at the Lab, Siya is contemplating whether to check out LoverGirls, a Saturday night party at the Millionaire's Club in the Financial District that caters to an older crowd. The elevator in her Bed-Stuy apartment building is broken and the hike up and down 13 flights of stairs has put a damper on her mood.

She lives in a three-bedroom apartment with her grandmother, who has raised her since she was 11. Siya was born Michelle Sherman in California. Her father is black and was a military man. Her mother is Hispanic and was addicted to drugs. Her father left when she was young, but after hearing what horrible conditions his daughter was living in, packed her up and sent her to live with his mother in Bed-Stuy's Eleanor Roosevelt Projects. Two years later she came out of the closet.

"My aunt was doing my hair and she was trying to put it in a girly hairstyle," says Siya, who is sitting on top of a dresser in her meticulously organized bedroom. Behind her hangs a photomontage of her in Times Square with girlfriends. "I got upset and flipped. 'I hate this. I want to wear my hair braided. I like girls!'" Her family took the news well. "My grandmother is real cool, and I think in a way my being gay meant she didn't have to worry about me going out and getting pregnant and bringing home more kids for her to take care of."

But school officials weren't so thrilled, she claims. She says that she and her friends were made to feel that they were a gang. "They kinda forced me to drop out," she says. "I left high school in junior year."

At 16, she began rapping about being a lesbian. It's won her a small following, but also held her singing career back, she believes.

Ky, the Monroe College freshman, is also nursing a budding rap career. Majoring in criminal law, she says that she's often mistaken for a guy. But she doesn't mind.

She attended an all-girls Catholic high school and played basketball on the school team. For several years, she had a "cover-up boyfriend" while seeing girls. But a girlfriend outed her at 14. "My boyfriend tried to commit suicide after he found out," she says.

Ky kept her secret at school until her team traveled out of state for a weekend basketball tournament. "Girls were running around the hotel pulling off towels, throwing around basketball shorts," says the 18-year-old. "It was just mad gay, and it was open. I was having fun, and I thought when I got back I could talk about it, and relive the experience, because it was open for me. This was the first time I could actually touch a girl and she laughed and liked it, and everybody else knew." But when she returned to school and began telling her classmates about the team's lesbian romps, she was shunned by teachers and her teammates.

Both Siya and Ky, after difficult starts, are trying to manage an existence as rappers and party promoters. AGs have had only limited success in music marketing. Ruin, a rapper from Richmond, Virginia, managed to chart on *Billboard* in 2005 with her maxi-single "Be Me/Stop Trying." But masculine lesbians have a tough path to success, says Erik Parker, director of content for hip-hop news site sohh.com.

"Female rappers are marketed to sell sex, and their target audience is largely men. And the males in hip-hop, or outside of hip-hop for that matter, find femme lesbians appealing, rather than a more masculine female who challenges their personal ideals of masculinity."

Ruin is touring clubs, but larger success eludes her. "Every executive that I sat down with has said the same thing: 'You hot, you got something different. We want to work with you here, we want to do this and do that, but is there any way we can put you in tighter clothes? Can we put you in a skirt; can we put you in heels?' "

Datwon Thomas, the editorial director of urban lifestyle and music magazines *King, Rides,* and *Hip-Hop Soul,* says that hip-hop's resistance toward gay women can shift. "It's hard for them to be taken seriously because their sexuality is so dominant. However, when it comes to them being rappers, the line becomes blurred. The good thing about hip-hop is that you are judged by your skills first and foremost, and if a gay rapper comes out and she's dope, most people will look past her being gay."

Siya dreams of success in the music market, but she's already a steady presence at the Lab. And one thing she has in common with some of her musical idols: a rap sheet.

"It's hard for me to find a legit job because of my criminal record." At 16, she ran away from home with her then girlfriend. The two became engaged and moved to Albany, where money got tight and Siya, like many AGs, took to hustling.

It's a pressure many young AGs feel as the dominant figure in their relationship. If you have the sand to knock down another woman in order to grab the hottest femme in the club, you don't want to admit that you have little cash to keep your prize happy.

Siya served four months for grand larceny, first degree assault, and attempted assault, and was placed on three years' probation. "Hustling is the next best thing if you can't find a legit job. There are a lot of females that boost or sell drugs," she says. "I wouldn't say it's hard for all aggressives to find jobs because there are some that are sacrificing: putting on tight clothes, female suits, or business suits to go to work. Then there are a lot of us who wouldn't feel comfortable like that. I could apply for a whole bunch of jobs and if I don't come in looking like the girly girl or because of my tattoos or just by me being gay raises a red flag."

Ky has also been around hustling most of her life. Her older brother was a drug dealer and is serving time in prison. Siya's father is serving 125 years for the GHB* raping of eight women. And one older woman they both look up to was delivering drugs for her uncles when she was only seven years old. But Don Vito, 35, is out of that now, and she has plans to keep the young women of her "house" out of more trouble.

––––––––

During the day Don Vito (she's reluctant to give up her real name) works on Wall Street in the IT department of a prestigious law firm. Her co-workers don't know that she's gay, but some of her female co-workers wonder why she never talks about a boyfriend.

"I've never been with a man," she says. "That's gross. But I'll tell you what's funny: I did have to go to prom when I was in high school,

*The date rape drug.

and what made it worse was that I was a debutante." She laughs at the thought of herself in a dress and heels. Sitting in the back corner of a café on Sixth Avenue in the West Village, Vito wears an oversized hoodie with skulls, a baseball cap, shoulder-length hair (which she pulls back in a ponytail for work or wears braided when she's in the club), and baggy jeans. She stands around five foot eight, and though an AG, doesn't deepen her voice or bind her breasts. She walks with a light bop and likes wearing a bandanna over her face when she's in the club. It gives her mystique.

Two years ago, Vito moved to New York with her then girlfriend to attend film school. After the program ended she got the job in IT but writes screenplays in her spare time.

She's the "father" and creator of House of Corleone, a tightly knit group of young black and Hispanic lesbians. Modeled on the extended-families structure used by previous generations of New York gays and lesbians, a number of hip-hop houses have sprouted up recently with names like the Da Vincis, House of Mecca, and the Bossalenos and Belladonnas. Vito's crew has attracted young AGs like Chick Murda, a/k/a Aisha Sampson.

"I joined House of Corleone four or five months ago," Sampson tells the *Voice* during a photo shoot held at the Lab. "I was on downelink.com and Vito hit me up. She told me to look into it. I didn't know gay women had houses. As time went by, I saw the house's progress. I like to meet new people, and met a lot of people in this house. It's a lot of exposure."

Vito says she was motivated to start her house as a result of the self-destruction she saw many young lesbians headed toward. "There are a lot of AGs that are going down the wrong path," she says. "A lot of them are selling drugs. I used to sell drugs and almost went to jail for a long time. A lot of these AGs do it because the girls think it's cute. They are so serious about keeping up appearances that they'll either hustle or take a fast-food job so they can wear their low haircut or gold teeth."

Life as a young lesbian of color, of course, has its risks. In 2003, a young AG named Sakia Gunn engaged in a shouting match with a man named Richard McCullough at Newark's Penn Station after Gunn had returned from an evening of partying in the West Village. The altercation turned violent, and McCullough stabbed and killed Gunn. He's serving 20 years in prison. Last August, Patreese Johnson and six other women got into another shouting match with a man named Dwayne Buckle, a street vendor outside the IFC Center. Buckle was stabbed, and identified Johnson as his attacker, telling the press that he was the victim of a hate crime against straight men. Johnson has pled not guilty to charges of attempted murder and gang assault.

Well aware of such incidents, Don Vito has recruited 50 women— a mix of femmes and AGs—including Siya, from across the country and even overseas into the family just since January. But a rash of other groups are giving houses like Don Vito's a bad name.

"Those gangs or crews are the really young kids. Some of them rob and steal; others just want to fight in the club over petty stuff. In my house I require my members to partake in at least two charity events a year. I want a family bond and I don't want it to be about drama."

Growing up in Atlanta with a preacher for a father, Don Vito wasn't able to talk about her feelings or her sexuality. "To this day I can't say to my parents, 'I'm gay.' I didn't come out to anyone until I was 26. I don't want my 'sons' to have to go through that."

The VIP lounge at the Lab on a recent Friday is filled with the members of the House of Corleone, who are all wearing their colors— red, black, and white. Siya and her friend Pretty Milly Corleone are standing on one of the balconies over the dance floor checking for cute femmes. The two have been friends for years, and next year Milly, an army reserve specialist, is expecting to head over to Iraq. Don Vito pulls out a camera and calls all her "sons" over to take a picture. They throw up their hand signals, flash their jewels, and clench their jaws. Siya crouches down in front.

Ky is sitting nearby with her new girlfriend, Lite Brite, on her lap. She whispers something into her ear; the two laugh. They stand up and Ky gently guides her by the hand down to the dance floor.

Behind these brick walls, the girls are free to be badass rap stars and their girly dates. They're free to grab their crotches, kick it to a pretty girl, or dance in a tight embrace. It's a life you might not imagine when you see one of them on the street, look at her face, and think to yourself, "She looks like a boy."

INTERNATIONALLY
BLACK

A SLOW EMANCIPATION

⁓⁂⊙

Kwame Anthony Appiah

Once, when I was a child in Kumasi, Ghana, I asked my father, in a room full of people, if one of the women there was really my aunt. She lived in one of the family houses, and I'd always called her auntie. In memory, I see her lowering her eyes as my father brushed the question aside, angrily. Later, when we were alone, he told me that one must never inquire after people's ancestry in public. There are many Ashanti proverbs about this. One says simply, Too much revealing of origins spoils a town. And here's why my father changed the subject: my "auntie" was, as everyone else in the room would have known, the descendant of a family slave.

My father was trying to avoid embarrassing her, although I don't think he regarded her ancestry as an embarrassment himself. Unlike her ancestors, she could not be sold; she could not be separated against her will from her children; she was free to work wherever she could. Yet in the eyes of the community—and in her own eyes—she was of lower status than the rest of us. If she could not find a husband to provide for her (and a prosperous husband was unlikely to marry a woman of her status), the safest place for her was with the family to which her ancestors had belonged. So she stayed.

Beginning around 1700, Kumasi was the capital of the Ashanti empire as it rose and fell. At some point in my education, I was taught that the empire had been the center of a great trading system, with roads radiating from Kumasi in every direction, connecting us with the Atlantic trading system along the coast and with the trans-Saharan trade to the north. Gold, everyone knew, was one of the commodities we exported: the empire of Ashanti covered most of what was once called the Gold Coast.

What I don't remember hearing much about was the role of the slave trade in the growth of Ashanti. More than a million slaves were sent to the Americas through the British, Danish and Dutch forts along the Gold Coast, mostly in the course of the 18th century. Next Sunday marks the 200th anniversary of the British Parliament's vote to ban the empire's North Atlantic slave trade. Following that vote, the Ashanti had to rethink the whole basis of their economy. But while the export of slaves had helped Ashanti consolidate power, it was arguably the importation of slaves from farther east—sold to the Gold Coast states by the Portuguese, starting in the 15th century—that made the empire possible in the first place. The rise of settled states in West Africa, as in much of the New World, seems often to have depended on the rise of plantation agriculture, and plantation agriculture depended on involuntary labor. Just as in the New World, moreover, the legacy of slavery has proved curiously durable. Indeed, to understand the nature of that legacy here, it helps to look at the experience of slavery on the African side of the middle passage.

When I was growing up, people used to visit us regularly from a village called Nyaduom, in the forest to the south of Kumasi. The village had belonged, I was told, to my father's family, and he inherited responsibility for it when he became the head of the family. He had the right to appoint chiefs and queen mothers for the village, and had some vague dominion over its land. A couple of hundred years ago, it turns out, an ancestor of my father's, an illustrious Ashanti general named Akroma-Ampim, had, with the permission of the king, settled the area with war captives and set up a plantation. In the slaving empire of Ashanti, as the Ghanaian historian Akosua Perbi tells us, there were different designations for different kinds of forced laborers—war captives (who could, if they were lucky, be redeemed by the payment of ransom), people held as security for their families' debts, people bought at the slave markets elsewhere and family servants with a status akin to feudal serfs—and each had a distinct status. Not all slaves were created equal. Still, to use our generalizing term, the inhabitants of Nyaduom had been slaves for generations.

And these days? Slavery hasn't been legal in Ashanti for roughly a century. (The final rules for abolition were made in 1908: they allowed slaves to be redeemed for a fixed fee, required men to emancipate female slaves with whom they had children, made cruelty a basis for emancipation and declared that children born to slaves after a certain date would no longer be slaves themselves.) The people of Nyaduom are now "ethnically" Ashanti if they are anything. Their ancestors were not, however, and their status as the descendants of captives was one of hereditary inferiority to free Ashanti. For the villagers, these customs outweighed anything on the statute books. They regularly brought us fruits and coffee that they had grown, as well as the occasional chicken, turkey or sheep. And they acted as if my father had duties that gave him authority over them.

That wasn't exactly his view. Though he met and talked to them, he always tried to persuade them that they had to settle their disputes for themselves. He was willing to help, he told them, but they no longer belonged to him. They shrugged off his protests. They were the descendants of Chief Akroma-Ampim's captives; my father was the descendant of Chief Akroma-Ampim. What could change that?

They weren't the only ones to see themselves that way. Whenever I visit Kumasi, I get to chat with a man who worked for my father's predecessor as head of the family and who'd had, as a result, many dealings with Nyaduom. Last year, I asked him about Nyaduom and he answered me only after reminding me that it was not his hometown. Only recently has it occurred to me why he has always been so emphatic about this point: his family, unlike most of those in the village, never belonged to anyone. Generations after slavery has gone, the lowly status of these slave ancestors still matters. It matters that he is not one of them.

When I think about how the world of the Ashanti remains etched and scored by slavery, an odd question arises: What is it about slavery that makes it morally objectionable? European and American abolitionists in the 19th century tended to focus, reasonably enough, on its cruelty: on the horrors that began with capture and separation from one's family, continued in the cramped and putrid quarters below the decks of the middle passage and went on in plantations ruled by the lash. William Wilberforce, the evangelist and Tory member of Parliament who was as responsible as anyone for the passage of the 1807 Abolition of the Slave Trade Act, was not an enthusiast for democracy when it came to expanding the franchise, and he railed against the "mad-headed professors of liberty and equality." It was the torments of slavery's victims that moved him so. (He was also a founding member of the Royal Society for the Prevention of Cruelty to Animals.) Once freed slaves had been properly Christianized, he believed, "they will sustain with patience the sufferings of their actual lot." In the United States, abolitionists mainly shared his perspective, naturally emphasizing the abundant horrors of plantation slavery.

Slavery's more sophisticated defenders had a response. They agreed that cruelty was wrong, but, they maintained, these horrors were abuses of the slavery system, not inherent features of it.

What if their paternalist fantasies had come true, and a world of kindly slave masters had developed? Would slavery be acceptable? Of course not. Even a well-treated slave is diminished by his status. As a social or legal institution, slavery has built into it a denial of the social basis of self-respect: it defines the slave as lower in status by denying that she could have personal aims worthy of consideration and rejecting the enslaved person's right to manage his or her own affairs. When you're a slave, someone else is in charge of your life. What keeps the wound from healing is that this subordination is something you inherited from your parents and will pass along to your children.

And to their children, and their children's children. Although the sale of slaves is now illegal, and demands for unpaid work are officially unenforceable, there are still slave descendants who work in the households of prosperous Ashanti without remuneration. (There are also some people who are sent by families that cannot afford to feed them, people who are properly servants, though their compensation is not monetary, and the families to which they go tend to treat them like the poor relation in a Victorian novel.) The status of these home workers, it seems to me, is like that of children. They are in the care of the families they work for, which have obligations to maintain and support them, but their labor and their lives are pretty much governed by the people in whose households they live. In principle, they are free to leave whenever they choose. In practice, they often have nowhere to go. Never having been paid, they have no savings. Often they have a very basic education, so their only skill is domestic work, a market in which there is a great deal of competition. Even without the legal apparatus of Jim Crow, liberated slaves can find themselves effectively recaptured.

None of this is peculiar to Africa, of course. The etymology of the English word "slave" reflects the large-scale forced servitude of Slavs into the Middle Ages; in modern Arabic, the word "abd," a classical designation for a slave, is used to refer to dark-skinned people. Because people almost always think of slaves as belonging to a kind— a race, a tribe, a class, a family—that is suited to enslavement, the slave status tends to survive the abandonment of the formal institutions of slavery.

This isn't to diminish the achievements of abolition. The bicentennial of the Slave Trade Act is eminently worth celebrating, and it's reassuring to know that slavery is officially forbidden in every country on the planet. (The word may yet prove father to the deed.) The United States National Slavery Museum is scheduled to open in Fredericksburg, Va., next year, while in Ghana, the remaining coastal slaving forts do a brisk trade in moralized tourism. Meanwhile, human rights campaigners have taken aim at nonchattel forms of slavery, like the millions of bonded laborers in South Asia whose employers force them to work in order to pay off a debt, or "peshgi." Groups like Christian Solidarity International continue to support slave-redemption programs in Sudan. The International Labor Organization of the United Nations monitors trafficking networks that bring an estimated 1.2 million children into forced servitude, from the cocoa fields of Ivory Coast to the brothels of Thailand. Various intergovernmental groups have helped secure the release of some of them.

But the politics of abolition and redemption, now as then, go only so far. You can legislate against the peshgi system, pass laws regulating working conditions and, in a dozen ways, deny legal recognition to the slaveholder's claim to manage the lives of his slaves. You cannot thereby command respect for them or grant them self-respect, because these things are not within the power of the market or a legislature. Nor can you guarantee that someone who has experienced only slavery will be prepared to manage a life alone, even if he had the money to do so. There's no neat toggle switch between slave and free.

The woman I asked my father about is not a slave. But she carries on something crucial to the enslavement of her ancestors. Beyond the possibility of being sold away and the impossibility of making your own decisions, slavery meant that certain people were hereditarily inferior. You can abandon the slave markets and demand that all who work are paid for their labor and free to leave it, but even if you succeed, the stigma and the status won't give way so easily. That's why I haven't told you her name. Emancipation is only the beginning of freedom.

Searching for Zion

Emily Raboteau

The security personnel of El Al Airlines descended upon me at Newark International Airport like a flock of vultures. There were five of them, in uniform, blockading the check-in counter. They looked old enough to have finished their obligatory service in the Israel Defense Forces but not old enough to have finished college, which put them beneath me in age. I was prepared for their initial question, "What are you?" which I've been asked my entire life, and, though it chafed me, I knew the canned answer that would satisfy: "I look the way I do because my mother is white and my father is black." This time the usual reply wasn't good enough. This time the interrogation was tribal.

"What do you mean black? Where are you from?"

"New Jersey."

"Why are you going to Israel?"

"To visit a friend."

"What is your friend?"

"She's a Cancer."

"She has cancer?"

"No, no. I'm kidding. She's healthy."

"She's Jewish?"

"Yes."

"How do you know her?"

"We grew up together."

"Do you speak Hebrew?"

"*Shalom,*" I began. "*Barukh atah Adonai . . .*" I couldn't remember the rest, so I finished with a word I remembered for its perfect onomatopoetic rendering of the sound of liquid being poured from the narrow neck of a vessel: "*Bakbuk.*"

It means bottle. I must have sounded to them like a babbling idiot.

"That's all I know," I said. I felt ashamed somehow, but also pissed off at them for making me feel that way.

"Where is your father from?"

"Mississippi."

"No." By now they were exasperated. "Where are your people from?"

"The United States."

"Before that. Your ancestors. Where did they come from?"

"Ireland."

They looked doubtful. "What kind of name is this?" They pointed at my opened passport.

"A surname," I joked.

"How do you say it?"

"Don't ask me. It's French."

"You're French?"

"No, I told you. I'm American."

"This!" They stabbed at my middle name, which is Ishem. "What is the meaning of this name?"

"I don't know," I answered, honestly. I was named after my father's great-aunt, Emily Ishem, who died of cancer long before I was born. I have no idea where the name came from. Possibly it's a slave name.

"It sounds Arabic."

"Thank you."

"Do you speak Arabic?"

"I know better than to try."

"What do you mean?"

"No, I don't speak Arabic."

"What are your origins?"

I felt caught in a loop of that Abbott and Costello routine, "Who's on first?" There was no place for me inside their rhetoric. I didn't have the right vocabulary. I didn't have the right pedigree. This is what my mixed race has made me: a perpetual unanswered question. This is what the Atlantic slave trade has made me: a mongrel and a threat.

"Ms. Raboteau. Do you want to get on that plane?"

I was beginning to wonder.

"Do you?"

"Yes."

"Answer the question then! What are your origins?"

What else was I supposed to say?

"A sperm and an egg," I snapped.

That's when they grabbed my luggage, whisked me to the basement, stripped off my clothes and probed every orifice of my body for explosives. When they didn't find any, they focused on my tattoo, a Japanese character which means different, precious, unique. I was completely naked, and the room was cold. My nipples were hard. I tried to cover myself with my hands. I remember feeling incredibly thirsty. One of them flicked my left shoulder with a latex glove. "What does it mean?" he asked. This was the first time I'd ever been racially profiled, not that the experience would have been any less humiliating had it been my five hundredth. "It means Fuck you," I wanted to say, not because they'd stripped me of my dignity, but because they'd shoved my face into my own rootlessness. I have never felt more black in my life than I did when I was mistaken for an Arab.

———

I was going to visit Tamar Cohen, my best friend from childhood. We loved each other with the fierce infatuation particular to friendships between preadolescent girls—a love that found its form in bike rides along the towpath, notes written in lemon juice, and pantomimed tea parties at the bottom of swimming pools. Looking back on the years we spent growing up in the privileged, picturesque, and predominantly white town of Princeton, New Jersey, where both of our fathers were history professors, I can see that what grounded our friendship was a shared sense of being different. She was Jewish. I was black. Well, I was half black, but in a land where one must be one thing or the other, that was enough to set me apart.

Being different was, for both of us, a source of pride and, I'm ashamed to say, enabled us to hold everyone else in slight disdain (especially if they happened to play field hockey or football). Tamar and I were a unified front against conformity. We stood next to each other in navy blue robes in the first row of the soprano section of the high school choir like two petite soldiers, sharing a folder of sheet music between us with a synchronicity of spirit that could trick a listener into believing that we possessed a single voice. When I received my confirmation in Christ, I wore Tamar's bat mitzvah dress.

We were bookish girls, intense and watchful. Our afternoons were spent sprawled out on my living room rug doing algebra homework while listening to my dad's old Aretha Franklin records. Our Friday nights were spent eating *Shabbat* dinner at her house around the corner on Murray Place. I felt proud being able to recite the Hebrew blessing with her family after the sun went down and the candles were lit: *"Barukh atah Adonai, Eloheinu melech ha'olam . . ."* The solemn ritual made me feel as though I belonged to something larger than myself.

Perhaps stemming from that warm feeling, much to my father's chagrin, I started to keep kosher, daintily picking the shrimp and crab legs out of his Mississippi jambalaya until all that remained on my plate was a muck of soupy rice. It was her father's turn to be chagrinned when we turned eighteen and got matching tattoos on our left shoulder blades. The Torah forbids tattooing (Leviticus 19:28). Tamar's might someday disqualify her from burial in a Jewish cemetery, but we relished the idea that, no matter where in the world we might end up, no matter how much time might pass, even when we were old and ugly and gray, we would always be able to recognize each other.

Tamar's father was an expert in medieval Jewish history, while mine specialized in antebellum African American Christianity. Both men made careers of retrieving and reconstructing the rich histories of ingloriously interrupted peoples. Both were quietly angry men, and

Tamar and I were sensitive to their anger, which was at once historical and personal. I was acutely aware of the grandfather I had lost to a racially motivated hate crime under Jim Crow, though my father didn't discuss the murder with me. He didn't need to give words to my grandfather's absence any more than Tamar's father had to give words to the Holocaust. There were ghosts in our houses.

Both of us knew at a relatively young age what the word *diaspora* meant—though to this day that word makes me visualize the white Afro-puff of a dandelion spore being blown by my lips into a series of wishes across our old backyard: to be known, to be loved, to belong. I didn't fit in. I looked different from the white kids, though I didn't exactly look black. Tamar didn't fit in either. In her case, the "otherness" was cultural: her summers were spent in Israel; her Saturdays at synagogue; and, up until the seventh grade, she attended a Jewish day school. I didn't see Tamar as white any more than I did my own mother. Consequently, it didn't confuse or surprise me when Tamar suddenly turned to me in choir practice one snowy morning and proclaimed, *"I'm not white."*

We had been rehearsing the French composer Jean L'Héritier's sonorous, sacred motet, *"Nigra sum sed formosa,"* whose Latin text is taken from the Song of Songs, and reads:

Nigra sum sed formosa filiae Jherusalem
I am black but comely, daughters of Jerusalem

Ideo dilexit me rex
Therefore have I pleased the Lord

Et introduxit me in cubiculum suum.
And he hath brought me into his chamber.

I thought I understood why she made her proclamation at that particular moment in choir practice. *"Nigra sum sed formosa"* is a heartbreakingly succulent song, one that brought tears to my father's eyes when we sang it a few weeks later at the winter concert. It was a song you wanted to be about yourself.

Tamar felt the same way about the freedom songs being broadcast at an exhibit held by the Jewish Museum in New York in collaboration with the NAACP, an exhibit linking Jewish and African American experience. My father brought the two of us there a few years after the Crown Heights Riot, during what must have been Passover, because I can remember nibbling on matzoh bread and leaving a trail of unleavened crumbs. Klezmer music played in a room showcasing a silver candlestick bent by a bullet in a Russian pogrom. The adjacent room displayed photographs of lynched black men. In each of those men's tortured faces I saw my grandfather, and I found myself on the verge of tears, more from anger than from sadness. "Go Down Moses (Let My People Go!)" issued from the speakers:

> *When Israel was in Egypt's land,*
> *Let My people go!*
> *Oppressed so hard they could not stand,*
> *Let My people go!*
> *Go down, Moses,*
> *Way down in Egypt's land;*
> *Tell old Pharaoh*
> *To let My people go!*

"I like this music better than klezmer," Tamar admitted. I trained my ears on the lyrics I knew so well, and they soothed me in my anger, just as they are meant to do.

"This is a liberation song," my father explained. "Do you girls know where Canaan is?"

"Israel," Tamar answered.

"In a sense. But that's not the place this song is about. Look." He pointed to a picture of Frederick Douglass with an attending quotation which read: "We meant to reach the North, and the North was our Canaan." My father continued talking to us that afternoon about how pivotal the Old Testament story of Exodus and the Promised Land was for African slaves in America, whose early involvement with the Christian tradition was born out of a feeling of kinship with the Hebrew slaves. They found redemptive hope in the scripture about Moses, the trials and tribulations of the Israelites, and their journey from bondage into Canaan. "I'll meet you in de mornin', when you reach de promised land: On de oder side of Jordan, For I'm boun' for de promised land . . ."

"Maybe that's why you like this music, Tamar," my father finished. "When we sang freedom songs about the ancient Israelites, we linked ourselves to you. Our people have a lot in common."

———

Tamar and I had promised to stay in touch when we parted ways for college. But while I was busy reading Hurston, Ellison, Wright, and Fanon, she was busy writing her thesis on Jewish history and practicing her Hebrew with foreign students from Israel. We called each other less and less. Shortly after we graduated, she moved to Israel and became a citizen under the Law of Return. I hadn't heard from her in months when she phoned at the start of the Second Intifada to ask me to visit. The desperation in her voice surprised me—it nearly had the quality of begging. I decided to go.

I fell in love with Jerusalem. How could I not? I was expecting to land in a desert place, hostile and khaki and hard as a tank, because that's what I'd seen on TV, and that's how El Al's security had behaved at Newark International Airport—hostile and hard. But when Tamar led me through that ancient city of soft hills and olive trees, its white stone going rosy in the sunset, when we entered the mouth of Lion's Gate and walked along the Via Dolorosa, when I smelled the peach tobacco smoke from a narghile pipe, when I saw the red wool of the Bedouin rugs on display in the Old City, when I heard the calls to prayer from a hundred mosques at dusk, my heart swelled round as the Dome of the Rock with a sense of holy longing, and I halfway understood why men would fight rock over stick, hand over fist, bomb over gun, in order to call this place their home. There is no real word in the Hebrew language for *home*. Yet Tamar had chosen to expatriate and make this place hers. As problematic as that choice was, no matter at whose expense, I felt enormously jealous of her ability to make it, and not a little rejected that she had.

As a consequence of growing up half black in a nation divided along unhealthy racial lines, I had never felt at home in the United States. I identified with the line James Baldwin wrote in *The Fire Next Time* about the experience of black GIs returning from war only to discover the democracy they'd risked their lives to defend abroad continued to elude them at home: *"Home! The very word begins to have a despairing and diabolical ring."*

Tamar, on the other hand, now had a divine Promised Land, a place to belong, and a people who embraced her. Here she was in Zion. It was a real place: a providential, politically sanctioned place, with roots and dirt she could hold in her hand. This wasn't the imagined heaven that black slaves (and their descendents) had to look forward to in the afterlife once they had reached the North, realized its spiritual bankruptcy, rubbed their eyes, and asked each other, "Where's de milk an' honey at? An' de streets all paved wit gold?" No, this was the real deal. Jerusalem seemed to me a place where the very *air* was gold—I swear the light had that imperial quality against my skin. It was a place I could lust after and visit, where my price of admission was a slight degradation, and where Tamar could have a physical address. Her beautiful old Arab house had tile floors, arched doorways, and room enough for a piano. It was situated in a dusty alley in the German Colony off Emek Refaim, a street name meaning "valley of the ghosts."

One of the ghosts was a woman named Hala Sakanini. She once lived a few doors down at no. 10 Emek Refaim, but left her home along with her family to escape mortar attacks during the Arab-Israeli War. That was in 1948, the year the State of Israel was proclaimed. Over 700,000 Palestinian refugees fled at that time. Their houses were quickly expropriated by Holocaust survivors and Jewish immigrants from Arab lands. Many Palestinians, including Hala Sakanini, expected to return. They refer to their exodus as the *Nakba,* or "cataclysm." In her memoir, *Jerusalem and I* (1987), there is a photo of Hala Sakanini in her living room, shortly before *Nakba*. She sits in an armchair before a large ornate radio, in the light of a gooseneck floor lamp, unsmiling, with a hard set to her jaw. She describes the painful experience of revisiting her occupied home years later:

> We knocked on the door. Two ladies appeared. . . . We tried to explain: "this is our house. We used to live here before 1948 . . ." The elderly lady was apparently moved but she immediately began telling us that she too had lost a house in Poland, as though we personally or the Arabs in general were

to blame for that. We saw it was no use arguing with her. We went through all the house room by room—our parents' bedroom, our bedroom, Aunt Melia's bedroom, the sitting room and the library . . . the dining room, the kitchen . . . everything was so different. It was no more home . . . we stood there as in a daze looking across the street and the square at our neighbours' houses. . . . It is people that make up a neighbourhood and when they are gone it will never be the same again. We left . . . with a sense of emptiness, with a feeling of deep disappointment and frustration.

Reconciliation over property ownership remains a controversy between Israel and Palestine.

Who used to own the house Tamar had usurped? Where was that displaced person now? What kind of Zion was this, superimposed on top of another nation? What kind of screwed-up Canaan has an *intifada*? I was pondering these kinds of questions when Tamar's boyfriend, Yonatan, laid *Lady Sings the Blues* on the turntable, told me he loved Billie Holiday with all his might and asked me in earnest if I thought he understood her as well as I did. "Of course you don't," I scoffed, because my broken, darling Billie was singing "God Bless the Child" in her ripped-satin voice, and what could he possibly be thinking? He could have his Canaan land, but Lady Day belonged to me.

Once upon a time, Tamar had been a part of my tribe, but a shadow wall had crept up between us. I couldn't shake the uneasy feeling that, in spite of her leftist stance—which was about as far left as she could stand without falling off the edge into the unknown—she was complicit in an unjust occupation. It didn't matter that the State of Israel was declared, in large part, in reparation for the Holocaust. Palestine was under its colonial thumb. It didn't matter that Tamar didn't live in a settlement, or that she participated in peace protests and rallies, or that she rolled her eyes at the slogans in her neighbors' windows (*"Golan Heights Is Ours!"*). They were still her neighbors, and she'd chosen to leave me in order to live among them. It didn't matter that she wasn't the one who shined a flashlight between my legs to look for a bomb. I couldn't shake the feeling that her choice to be Israeli had turned my best friend white.

We were floating. Our twin tattoos were on display, but there were no living fish in the Dead Sea to look up at our naked backs and notice. It was nighttime at the nadir, literally the lowest point on the planet. Home was halfway around the world, and we were floating in the still, still water, whose salt lifted us up like hands. The lights of Jordan twinkled on the distant shore, and above us wheeled a soup of stars thick enough to stir with a spoon.

"It's so good to see you again," she whispered.

"You too. I'm glad I came here," I answered, "but I miss black people."

I was surprised to hear myself say it, but I realized it was true. With the exception of Maine, I'd never traveled to a place without black people.

"There are black people here, silly," Tamar said. "You're not the only one."

"Where are they?"

"All over."

"Really?" Where were they hiding? I hadn't seen them.

"Sure. The Falashas."

"Who?"

"Beta Israel. The Ethiopian Jews. And there's a bunch of black Americans squatting in the desert—the Black Hebrews. I think they're from Chicago."

"What are they doing here?"

"Why don't you ask them? They're not far away. Israel's only the size of New Jersey, remember?" She splashed me. "If you really want to see 'your people' that badly, we can find them."

"I'd like to, but I'm leaving in two days."

Tamar sighed. "I wish you didn't have to go."

There is such a thing as a black Jew. I rotated the thought in my mind. I'd always considered the two groups to be mutually exclusive. A light wind rippled the water. I shivered. I closed my eyes and perceived the imperceptible tilt of the earth on its axis. The pigeonholes I knew were collapsing. It was a delightful feeling.

Six months later, from my rooftop in Brooklyn, I witnessed the Twin Towers collapse. Two weeks after that, Tamar was in the States for Rosh Hashanah. We walked across the Brooklyn Bridge and found ourselves in the quiet ash at the foot of a twisted twenty-foot waffle of metal at Ground Zero. I gagged on the smell of burnt wire and flesh. Sickened and stunned, I said what we all said then: "It feels like a movie." Tamar looked at me sideways. "You know," she said, "in most of the world, this kind of thing goes on all the time."

She was right, of course. How could I have been so quick to judge her status as an Israeli without judging my own status as an American? She, at least, lived with the daily consequences of her nation's bullying; lived with the ruptures, the bombs, the protests. She had to confront this strife and examine her place within it.

I had to do the same. I began to see how globally hated my government was and, by extension, the citizens of my country. It didn't matter that my black friends and I hated our government too, or that we didn't support it. In my travels, I began to feel ashamed. If someone asked me where I was from, I said "New York" rather than "the United States."

When Hurricane Katrina set her wrath upon the Gulf of Mexico, I sat glued to the TV screen in a state of near paralysis, scanning the black bodies abandoned in the Superdome and marooned on the rooftops of those spoiled houses for the faces of my relatives, who lived in Bay Saint Louis, Mississippi, a beach town sixty miles from New Orleans now under fifteen feet of water. My grief didn't protect my cousins from the deluge, nor did it bring them to dry land. My outrage at the infrastructure that had failed my family didn't serve them either. Even in this age of information, it took months for us to locate them in their great dispersal. This was another diaspora. But what did my sense of loss matter to my homeless Mississippi aunties as I sat in a yoga class or walked my dog?

I published a book and was made a professor, like my father. I moved to Harlem to be closer to the university that employed me. Harlem was shifting. It didn't matter that I belonged halfway to the race being slowly squeezed out of Manhattan's final frontier of affordable real estate. As much as I hated to watch the sad, slow effects of gentrification spill over the stately brownstones of Sugar Hill and Strivers' Row, home of Madam C. J. Walker and Langston Hughes and all those wild jazzmen I loved so much, I couldn't pretend, with my Ivy League degree, that I wasn't a member of the gentry. I myself was not disinherited. Recognizing this, I began to feel my terrible whiteness, and I was ashamed. Avoiding my reflection in storefront windows, I meandered through Harlem and beyond: northward to the Cloisters of Fort Tryon Park, eastward to the movable Macombs Dam Bridge and into the Bronx, westward over the Washington Bridge across the dirty Hudson, southward down the long finger of Manhattan. On one of these rambles, in the shadow of the elevated subway tracks off 125th Street, I stumbled upon a short stretch of alleyway, *Old Broadway*. And there, in the middle of the alley, stood a small, sweet shul with a dirty façade and bricked-up windows. Here was Harlem's last remaining synagogue, a remnant from the neighborhood's former days of Yiddish theaters and crowded Jewish tenements. I stopped in front of it and cocked my head. Why did I feel I'd been there before? It was Friday night and the sun was setting. Slowly I pushed open the heavy wooden door.

"Welcome!" cried an old black man in a *kippah*. "Good Shabbos." He adjusted the *tallit* on his shoulders and took my hands in his. "This is wonderful," he smiled, revealing the whitest teeth. "Another wandering Jew has found their way home." Home! Either as a result of his kindness or as a result of his mistake, I was afraid I might begin to weep.

———

Somehow six years went by. Tamar had settled down with an Argentinian Jew who shared her last name, and together they bore a daughter. I returned to Israel in order to visit them and also to find those black folks. Did they think they were home? Did Tamar?

On the flight, I worked on the patchwork quilt I was nearly done sewing for Tamar's baby, Nina, who had just celebrated her first birthday, and whose first steps I was hoping to witness. I labored over this quilt. It was hand stitched in strips, chromatically schemed like a rainbow. The last step was to finish the border, now fastened by forty little pins, ten on each side. I was worried that security would mistake the pins for tiny explosive devices. I was worried that they wouldn't let me bring my gift into their country. But they didn't take the baby's quilt.

They didn't strip search me in the basement. Instead, they brought me behind a heavy black curtain, rifled through my luggage, and confiscated my iPod.

Without my music to comfort me, I grew restless on the long flight to Tel Aviv. The plane was almost empty. Israel was in its sixth day of war with Lebanon, exchanging escalating fire with the Hezbollah militia. It was a grossly lopsided exchange—Beirut was being steadily, smolderingly, mercilessly destroyed—but northern Israel was not a safe place either. My mother had begged me to postpone my trip. I was flying headlong into a war zone.

The first place I went looking for black folks was a reggae club on Tel Aviv's Harakevet Street. *The rasta* was painted in block letters on a pan-African green, gold, and red sign hanging above a chain-locked doorway being guarded by a stocky Russian Jew in a leather jacket.

"You don't want to go in there," he warned me.

A fighter plane roared above us, and then another, flying north.

"Oh, yes I do."

"No." He crossed his arms.

"Isn't there a show tonight?" I looked at my watch. A band called "Tony Ray and the Amjah" was supposed to play at ten. It was now rounding midnight.

"It's not for you. Karaoke is next door."

"But I came for this."

"You won't like it. Believe me. They get drunk and fight like animals. It's messy."

"Look," I said. "I came all the way from New York for this."

"It's not safe."

"Are you going to let me in or not?"

The guard sighed with annoyance, got down from his stool, unlocked the door, and called for the club owner—none other than Tony Ray himself—a tall man in his early fifties from Jamaica by way of England. He had a head of graying beaded dreadlocks, a gold tooth, and an easy manner.

"Don't pay that bald-head guard no mind. You're just early, little daughter. We on colored-people time," he said, leading me to the bar and pouring me a liberal shot of cheap rum. Behind the bar hung an embossed picture of Haile Selassie, a small felt banner of the Lion of Judah, and a poster of Bob Marley. On the shelf with all the liquor bottles sat a glow-in-the-dark plastic alien smoking ganja.

As a Rastafarian, Tony Ray believes that he is ancestrally tied to Ethiopia; that his captive forebears originated from that homeland; that the messiah has come and gone in the form of Ethiopia's last emperor, the Conquering Lion of Judah—formerly known as Ras Tafari/Haile Selassie (who claimed to descend directly from King Solomon and the Queen of Sheba); and that Ethiopia is the Promised Land.

"How'd you wind up here instead of Addis Ababa?" I asked him, thinking of Marcus Garvey's nationalist "Back to Africa" repatriation platform.

He explained that he'd come for a three-month tour with his band as a young man, "And I tell you, I din like it one bit. Israeli folk are rude and out of order. Yuh see me?"

I nodded.

"Then I return to London, where they act so civilized, but underneath their smile they want to kick their boot inside I and I mouth. I start miss Israel. My gut was craving for figs! So I came back, and now it's thirty years gone. I and I is a natty Nazarite now. Is my place this." He spanked the bar with a wet rag for emphasis, and began wiping it down.

The door burst open and a young man sauntered in with an electric bass. "Jamaican-boy!" he cried.

"Etiopian-bwoy!" Tony Ray answered, embracing him. "You ready to make music, my brethren?"

By three in the morning, in my beer-soaked haze, I thought I may as well have been in Addis Ababa. The Rasta was packed shoulder to shoulder with Ethiopians stirring it up to the reggae of Tony Ray, backed by the Amjah on trombone, bass, drums, and krar. Hardly anyone in the crowd spoke English, but they all knew the lyrics of the Bob Marley covers: "Redemption Song," "Buffalo Soldier," and the rest. So we danced and sang "I'm gonna be Iron like a Lion in Zion" until somebody opened the door allowing a shock of July sunlight to land in a trapezoidal wedge on the edge of the dance floor, and I realized it was morning. The guard was snoring on his stool in the entryway, slumped like an overstuffed rag doll. Out on the sidewalk of Harakevet Street, it took me a full minute to remember where I was. I blinked. The fighter jets were still droning overhead.

———————

The second place I went looking for black folks was an absorption center in the northern port city of Haifa, roughly thirty miles from the Lebanese border.

"What exactly is an *absorption center*?" I asked Tamar's friend Yitzhak on the taxi drive from Tel Aviv up the coastal highway. I couldn't help noticing that all the cars were traveling in the opposite direction. I would rather have put my question to Yitzhak's friend Abate, who actually lived in an absorption center when he made *aliyah* from Ethiopia in 1999, but Abate's English was limited. He sat in the front seat, cradling the beat-up case of his soprano saxophone as if it were a baby. I watched his face in the rearview mirror. He had a pencil-thin mustache, a slightly receding hairline, and preternaturally large eyes—Louis Armstrong eyes—through which he looked out at the passing road signs in studied silence.

Abate's integration into Israel was a painful one. While he'd enjoyed a successful jazz career in Addis Ababa and had toured Europe several times over, he wasn't recognized as a musician in Israel, he didn't speak Hebrew, and he had to work several menial jobs in order to support his family. One was washing dishes in a restaurant; another was at a chemical factory. He worked nights as a security guard. A grant from the Ethiopian Jewry Heritage organization eventually enabled him to quit all but the night job, leaving him enough time to practice his instrument during the day, but not before the chemicals and dishwater had damaged his hands. He had to wait a long, long time for his fingers to heal.

Tamar had introduced me to Yitzhak, a serious, bespectacled composer in his thirties who described his sound as "third-stream jazz." Yitzhak had two things on his lap in the backseat of the taxicab that day: an electric keyboard and a rolled-up marriage license that had just been rejected by the Rabbinate Council on the grounds that it didn't conform to their standards.

"What did you say?" he asked me. He seemed distracted.

"An *absorption center*," I repeated, "what is it?"

Before he could answer, his cell phone rang. It was his fiancée.

"Don't go to Haifa!" she screamed, loud enough for me to hear.

Yitzhak pacified her in Hebrew. I'm guessing he told her the same thing he'd told me in English, which was that, as an army reservist, it was his civic duty to go. It was the will of *ha-Sokhnut*, the Jewish Agency. This bureaucratic arm of Israeli government facilitates immigrant absorption into Israel. Tamar later described it to me as "floundering" and "inept." The Jewish Agency had ordered Yitzhak to play music for the Falashas. A USO sort of thing.

In the ancient ecclesiastical language Ge'ez, the word *falasha* means "landless one" and, by association, "wanderer," "exile," "stranger." It is used to describe the Beta Israel, Ethiopian Jews whose tradition holds that they descend from the line of Moses himself—specifically from the lost tribe of Dan—though the origin of their Judaism remains contested by scholars (unlike the Lemba, a South African tribe of black Jews whose DNA has linked them to ancient Judea). Many scholars theorize that Ethiopian Jews converted from the Christian faith during the thirteenth and fourteenth centuries. Ethiopisant Ephraim Isaac, on the other hand, believes that the Jewish presence in Ethiopia dates back to the period of the First Temple. He points out that the Bible mentions Ethiopia more than fifty times, "but Poland, not once." One thing is certain: the Beta Israel have longed for Jerusalem for centuries. Maybe for millennia.

The Israeli Rabbinate recognized the status of Ethiopian Jewry in the mid-seventies and, in so doing, paved the way for a mass exodus under the Law of Return. Coming mostly from the mountainous northern Gondar region, where they made up only a small minority of Ethiopia's population and were denied the right to inherit land unless they converted to Christianity, their number in the State of Israel is now approaching one hundred thousand. This is thanks in large part to two massive, highly publicized "rescue" efforts, Operation Moses (1984) and Operation Solomon (1991), which airlifted the Beta Israel by the planeload from Africa. *Falasha* is decreasingly used in Israel to describe Ethiopian Jews like Abate, because they themselves prefer that the term not be used. It has a pejorative tinge, like the Hebrew word *kushi* (darkie) but is not as strong a word as *nigger* in the United States.

As Yitzhak finished placating his fiancée, Oz, the taxi driver, directed my attention to a sprawl of modest white houses around Hadera. Oz was in his early fifties and looked like he spent the better part of his time lifting barbells in a gym. "Look at their ugly houses!" He spat. "They're not like us. They have ten, twelve children, and they don't take care of them. They're like cockroaches." He was speaking, of course, about a community of Palestinians. I wondered if Abate could understand Oz's speech and, if so, whether it made him as uncomfortable as it made me. I wondered if his allegiance was torn, if the return to the Promised Land, whose government had "saved" him from the Dark Continent, was worth the harsh decline in his status as a musician. I wanted to ask him if this was home.

"Are you American?" Oz asked me.

"I'm from New York," I said.

"Israel is the America of the Middle East!" He meant modernity.

"I know." I meant the malignancy of Manifest Destiny.

"Do you have children?" Oz asked me.

"No," I replied as coldly as possible, having summarily dismissed him as a racist. I was trying to figure out how to discourage further conversation when he tightened his greasy ponytail and started talking again.

"Me? I have four children. Two of them are mine, and two of them I adopted from my best buddy. He was killed when we were soldiers in Lebanon, so this war is nothing new to me. Maybe you heard about the missile that hit a car in Haifa yesterday? Don't worry, Miss. You can be comfortable in my cab because I know what to do. If we hear a siren, I will park, and we will find a safe place."

Oz offered me a piece of hard candy, which I refused. Then he fisted his right hand to flex a muscle in his forearm, which was marred by an ugly keloid scar. "You see that? I got that in '82 from the bullet that went into my buddy's face."

I was horrified.

"These people are animals," he reasoned. "They want to kill us."

"What a coincidence!" said Yitzhak, who had shut off his phone by this point. "Abate! Show them *your* scar."

Abate rolled up the long sleeve of his button-down shirt.

"He got that in an Ethiopian war."

The scar on Abate's left arm looked just like the one on Oz's right.

The two of them clasped hands in the front seat in a gesture of solidarity. I'd seen this symbol before, a white hand holding a black one. In my lexicon, it was supposed to mean *Peace*.

Yitzhak gave me a loaded look over the top of his spectacles. "You see?" he asked. "We have a lot in common."

Abate lowered his sleeve.

"We have a lot to learn from the Ethiopians in this country," Yitzhak continued. "Do you know the word *chutzpah*? We have a lot of chutzpah in our personality. It makes us prickly. But the Ethiopians are a gentle people."

I'd heard the Beta Israel characterized as gentle before. In my experience, they tend to be talked about in two contradictory, yet equally patronizing, ways by the Alphas of the greater society: either in terms of docility—*humble, peaceful, quiet, soft*—or with regard to their inability to hold their liquor—*drunk, messy, sloppy, loud*.

"I wasn't interested in playing music with Abate at first," Yitzhak revealed. "I don't like world music, but I've really learned a lot from him. He's an amazing musician. Do you want to hear a song he wrote for the Ethiopian radio station? Put on that CD, Abate. . . . That's Abate singing. You'll hear him sing later today, too. It's in Amharic. I don't know what he's saying. Hey, Abate, what do the words mean?"

Abate carefully translated the lyrics into Hebrew. Oz laughed and slapped his thigh. Then he corrected Abate's pronunciation. Yitzhak translated into English for my benefit: "Abate is singing, 'The fool who tries to crush the State of Israel will himself be crushed.' "

Haifa was a ghost town. The beach was empty. The streets were empty. The stores were closed. The absorption center was an ugly four-story building complex with a Star of David and the Lion of Judah painted on the wall next to the front door. Almost all immigrants from Ethiopia move through way stations like this on their path to Israeli citizenship.

This particular center housed three hundred Beta Israel, some of whom had immigrated as recently as two weeks before—others who had already lived there for as long as eight months—in overcrowded rooms crammed with bunk beds and fold-up cots. In the kitchen, foil-wrapped trays of unappetizing food (anemic-looking vegetables and congealing globs of macaroni and cheese) were rationed out to the head of each household. There was no *berbere* spice in the kitchen. There were not enough bathrooms in the building. In a classroom furnished with child-sized desks, both adults and children were given lessons in dietary laws, Hebrew, and hygiene. A picture of Theodor Herzl, the founding father of Zionism, hung on the wall.

In such rooms, the Beta Israel are halfheartedly assimilated before being shunted to the ghettos of Netanya, Rehovot, and Ashdod. They are not given proper job-skills training nor oriented to the shock of Western society. Instead, they are given Orthodox lessons in how to pray and eat. While some of the Beta Israel express gratitude for these lessons, others find them humiliating. They can't be granted full Jewish status or marry religiously unless they undergo formal conversion by immersion in a *mikveh*. People like the *Kessim* (Jewish priests) who led the spiritual community back in Ethiopia don't want their brand of Judaism converted to mainline Israeli Rabbinate standards. The Kessim's status in the community has dropped precipitously as a consequence of the conversion efforts made in classrooms like these. This is where they begin to lose institutional power.

In a concrete lot behind the absorption center, two uniformed female Israeli soldiers corralled dozens of Ethiopian kids into a moon-bounce, one of those air-inflated nylon pleasure-houses you might find at a carnival. A third soldier, with a rifle strapped to his chest, was busily spinning cotton candy onto cardboard wands and distributing them to the kids, who stuffed the sugar into their mouths with sticky fingers. These kids looked dirty, like they hadn't had a bath in a good long while.

I wondered if they would grow up and join "the lost generation." Israeli schools make few allowances for cultural difference. As a result, twenty thousand Ethiopian teenagers have fallen behind, grown disaffected, and dropped out, with no plans to join the army or go to college. This generation identifies less with Ethiopian or Israeli culture than with the black pride, oppositional politics, and the message of self-reliance found in the music of rap artists like Tupac Shakur and in reggae clubs like The Rasta. This is a weird circularity. The Jamaican searches for Ethiopia. The Ethiopian searches for Israel, arrives, then searches for Jamaica. And me, the African American searching for

what, exactly? The Promised Land seems always out of reach, some-
where on the other side of the planet. Maybe Jamaica will turn into the
Promised Land for those bouncing doe-eyed children someday.
Maybe America will.

In the meantime, these children were walking on the moon. Their
parents looked afraid. A rocket had ripped into the building across the
street the day before. This was the landscape of their new home. I suspected that today's concert and candy were meant to keep the
Ethiopians quiet.

"You don't see this on the news," said Oz, "but you should. You
see what we do for these people, because we are Jews? *This,*" he indi-
cated the bright moonbounce, "is Israel."

Assuming he was right, I wondered what the hell those children
were doing there. Everyone else in the city with the means to leave had
left. Why *wasn't* this in the news? Tamar had shown me an article in
the *Haaretz Daily* newspaper about the pets that got left behind by
evacuees:

> More than 8,000 dogs and cats have been abandoned in the
> north by owners who have fled south. These include street cats
> who lost their food supply. . . . "Numerous abandoned dogs
> are roaming the streets in the Galilee," says veterinarian Gil
> Shavit of Yesod Hama'ala. . . . "There is no excuse to aban-
> don a dog. This is a very sensitive creature that is adversely af-
> fected by being deserted."

Where was the article about the Ethiopians? Where does one even
find a cotton candy machine in the middle of a war? I thought of
Katrina—the dispossessed being left behind in the face of disaster.
Then I tried to put things in perspective. It seemed an Ethiopian Jew in
Israel had less value than a dog—but not too much less, since the
Ethiopian was being taught Hebrew and fed candy. Still, an Ethiopian
was worth far more than an Arab, whose value was only that of a
cockroach.

Of course, it was ridiculous for me to identify Ethiopian Jews as
my kinsmen just because their skin appeared to be black, and for me to
think they were black just because they appeared to be second-class
citizens. Actually, several groups in Israel can lay claim to "blackness"

as far as marginalization, disenfranchisement, and second-class citizenship are concerned.

When Sephardic Jews began immigrating to Israel in the 1950s from the Arab nations of North Africa and the Middle East, they met with poverty, low-paying jobs, life in the slums, and widespread discrimination by the European Ashkenazi Jews who preceded them. In 1970, an anti-establishment group of Sephardic youth organized to struggle for their civil rights. What did they call themselves? The Black Panthers. Later waves of *aliyot* brought Mizrahi and Russian Jews who met with a similar fate.

One of the overtaxed workers at the absorption center in Haifa told me, "We have never dealt well with immigrants. Maybe it's worse for the Falashas because they're black, but it's always been hard for immigrants here. We haven't learned from our mistakes." She shut her eyes and pinched the bridge of her nose between her forefingers, as if trying to relieve herself of a migraine headache. Then she said, "You have to realize how hard this is. Imagine if the United States had to absorb all of Mexico. Can you imagine? Where would you put all those people?"

I'm not sure that she intended this as a rhetorical question, but I'm afraid I treated it as one. "These people don't like to be called *Falashas*," I said, somewhat possessively, still clinging to my association, as if it mattered at all.

The Beta Israel don't even think of themselves as black—at least they didn't while they were in Africa. They thought of themselves as *queyy*—red or brown, a harmonious shade that God finally got right after botching his palette on white and black people. Furthermore, they distinguished themselves racially from their black African slaves. Like non-Jewish Ethiopians, Beta Israel are separated into a master caste, the *chewa*, and a slave caste, the *barya*. This hierarchical relationship has not been dismantled through the process of immigration because the *chewa* have had the good sense to keep quiet about their slaves in Israel. The *chewa* justify their slave ownership by maintaining that the *barya* have different bones and descend from the cursed line of Ham. It was a slap in the face for the *chewa* to arrive in Israel along with their chattel and be referred to as *kushis*, or blacks.

As for their participation in the Israel Defense Forces, the Beta Israel soldiers are known for being fearless, for fighting as though they

have something to prove—which they probably do. They often vol-
unteer for the most dangerous posts, like border patrol, where their
duty is to frisk and humiliate Arabs, while letting Israelis pass. They
might be "black" to white Israelis, and the object of some race preju-
dice, but the most consistently profiled racial group in Israel is the
Arabs—the truest niggers of the Holy Land.

Before I could peel my notion of blackness off of Beta Israel and
paste it onto Palestine, Yitzhak yanked me away from the moon-
bounce by the elbow and told me a story.

"I don't agree with everything Oz said in the cab. I don't think all
Arabs are inhuman. I even went to protest the building of the separation wall. It's true. I marched on their side because it was too much like
apartheid for my taste. The Israeli soldiers came to stop us. One of
them pointed an M16 at my chest. He was Ethiopian. I thought, 'He
could kill me. I might die today. What am I dying for? Which side am
I on?' Do you know what the Palestinian standing next to me said?
'Look at that filthy *kushi* who wants to shoot us. I can't believe it's
come to this. My homeland is being run by monkeys.' I was scared the
Arab would yell 'Go back to Africa!' and the soldier would open fire. It
gets so confusing here sometimes."

"I see what you mean," I said.

Then a siren wailed and the whole lot of us—children, soldiers,
masters, slaves, black, white, and *queyy*—flew down into the basement. The basement was set up for the concert with folding chairs.
The soldiers walked around the dank periphery, spraying bottles of
perfume, presumably to mask the fetid odor of sweat. Something
cracked outside. It sounded like the scratch of a needle on a record followed by a low boom. "Was that a *katuba* rocket?" I asked.

"No," said Yitzhak, laughing at my poor Hebrew. He held up his
marriage license like a baton. "*This* is a *katuba*. *That* was a *katyusha*." I
didn't think it was a funny joke, but right on cue to spike the punch
line, a second explosion sounded. I had to pee suddenly, but there was
nowhere to go. Instead, I helped Yitzhak set up his keyboard while
Abate warmed up the crowd. I wondered what he was telling them. I
wondered what I was doing there. And then they began to play the
blues.

Let me be precise. It was unbearably hot. The women sat on the left. They wore colorful head wraps and Jewish-star necklaces, seemingly at odds with the Coptic crosses tattooed on their foreheads, though these are less a symbol of Christianity than a phylactery protective charm against evil. The men sat on the right. They wore *kippahs*. The children sat on the floor, holding hands. The room reeked of perfume. Everyone was very still. Everyone was watching Abate. Abate had his saxophone strapped around his neck. When he closed his eyes and opened his mouth, the basement widened into a vast space. He sang in Amharic, backed by Yitzhak on stride piano, and when his voice grew jagged, he wet the reed of his horn and transformed the line of the Ethiopian song into indefinable flights of improvised jazz. Then Abate circled back to the plaintive root of his own voice.

The two-man band played in a minor pentatonic scale, one mode of which is called *tezeta*. The word means nostalgia. I looked at the delicate faces of the women, some of whom were nursing babies. Some of the women were beginning to smile. I could sense that they recognized Abate's song. *Tezeta* is the mode in which the Jews in Ethiopia express their longing for Jerusalem, but that's not what Abate was singing about. This song expressed his longing for *Ethiopia*. I recognized it as the mode of the blues—a sound that goes straight to the heart, the sound of the Negro spirituals, the sound of "Amazing Grace." It didn't matter that I didn't understand the words. Everyone in that basement understood the song, including me. It was a sorrow song about homesickness, and it soothed us in our fear, just as it was meant to do. While it was being sung, the war outside went away. I realized then that I had done Billie Holiday a great disservice when I told Yonatan that he couldn't comprehend her depth.

Tezeta was also the name of the woman I talked to at the Israeli Association for Ethiopian Jews. The IAEJ office was inside a Jerusalem shopping mall and decorated with children's artwork that portrayed the dramatic exodus of the Beta Israel from Africa in sequential order, like the Stations of the Cross. I was particularly taken by a tempera painting of a fat blue propeller plane with white stars on its wings. It flew above several brown-faced figures in a yellow desert landscape. All but one of these figures held the Torah in their upraised hands. The one who didn't belong stood in the lower right-hand corner holding a red umbrella, as if she knew it was going to rain.

"Why are you interested in us?" Tezeta asked with suspicion. She was a fiercely determined and articulate woman in her late twenties with a wild, natural hairdo, kohl-rimmed eyes, and a direct stare. She had recently quit her job as anchorwoman on the Ethiopian cable access channel in favor of championing basic civil rights for Beta Israel. Her organization is primarily sponsored by American Jews, as are the majority of Ethiopian causes in Israel. In fact, Jews in America financially support Ethiopians above all other Israeli immigrant groups. What is behind this charitable giving? I don't mean to diminish their acts of much-needed generosity, but I do believe that guilt is a factor—guilt over race relations in America and fear that such relations might take hold in Zion. Tezeta herself had an American sponsor for a while. This benefactor sent her five hundred shekels a month, but abruptly withdrew funding when Tezeta went backpacking through Europe and forgot to send him the personal letters he'd come to expect about how grateful she was for his money. Understandably, she was suspicious of me.

A postcard of Martin Luther King, Jr., was tacked to the wall by Tezeta's desk. I pointed at his picture. "I'm interested in you because his dream is important to me," I said.

And then, because I was still thinking about the meaning of her name and the transformative power of Abate's music, I asked Tezeta what she thought of Idan Raichel. Raichel is a white Israeli musician whose eponymous debut album, *Idan Raichel Project,* went triple platinum when it was released in 2002, and won him such national accolades as "artist of the year," "album of the year," and "song of the year." His success was due in large part to the Ethiopian folk music sampled in his songs. Idan Raichel has toured the United States during Black History Month and has been described as the "Israeli Bob Marley." Since he doesn't play reggae, I can only assume he's called this on account of his waist-length dreadlocks. He is widely lauded for exposing Israel to both Amharic music and the gift of diversity that Beta Israel has delivered.

"I know Idan Raichel," said Tezeta. "You want to talk to him?"

"I'm more interested in talking to one of the Ethiopians he exploited by neglecting to pay them for his success," I said.

Tezeta laughed and leaned toward me conspiratorially. "My best friend sings in one of the hit songs—'Bo'i.' She's really mad. He doesn't give her any money, and do you know how much money he has from her voice? His pockets are fat from our music. Ever since Idan Raichel made it big, I want to run and see what kind of car he drives because I can remember when he drove a jalopy."

"Maybe he's a necessary evil," I suggested. I told her about how much Abate's music moved me. Then I told her about The Rasta, how its door had been guarded, effectively segregating the club. "Maybe it takes someone like Idan Raichel to get Israel to open its ears to what you have to offer. Maybe he's a cultural bridge."

"I don't think so," she said. "Ethiopian music can only make it in Israel if it has white in the middle. If you take away the white, they don't want it. I know Abate. He is saying something deep. For Israeli listeners, they will be amazed to hear him play the sax. He will give them something rich they don't know. But they are deaf and blind to him. We all hear Idan Raichel on the radio. He sounds like cheap popcorn. He doesn't have anything new to give to an Ethiopian."

I tried to extend the implied metaphor about unfair trade to her own experience by asking Tezeta what she'd given Israel and what Israel had given her in return, but she was reluctant to talk about her service in the army and dismissive about her journey from Ethiopia during Operation Solomon fifteen years before. Maybe these personal topics were too painful to discuss.

"I'm supposed to be grateful to Israel for saving me," was all she would say.

This is the image the world has, that a fleet of planes swooped down like a flock of angels, scooped up the endangered black Jews in the knick of time, and delivered them from starvation into Israel's bosom. It's true that Operation Solomon rescued the Beta Israel from violence in Addis Ababa during a civil war, but their journey to Jerusalem began long before that. At the start of their journey, they weren't at risk, they weren't starving, and they weren't particularly impoverished. Jerusalem was a magnet, and the force of its pull was stronger than the force of Ethiopia's push. What prompted tens of thousands of the Beta Israel to abandon their relatively safe and comfortable lives to risk everything by migrating to the point where those planes would pick them up? Perhaps opportunism was a factor, but more than that, the pull was their longing for Zion.

I pointed again at Dr. King's picture. "He said he went to the mountaintop and saw the Promised Land. I'm guessing this isn't it?"

Tezeta snorted. "I'm not a Zionist. Zionism was a bad idea. Israel wants to be a melting pot for all the world's Jews to make them one thing. She is very sexy. She has what every strong nation wants—a stable economy and an atom bomb. But we don't have any tolerance."

"Are you saying multiculturalism can't exist here?"

"I am saying this does not exist in Israel."

"And absorption is the price of Zionism? Everybody must conform?"

"Yes. You are right. Maybe we embrace Ethiopian music when a white man brings it on a plate, but they cannot see them as a full human. They want them to be white."

I pointed out Tezeta's pronoun confusion. She alternated between *we, they, us, them, ours,* and *theirs* to talk about both Israelis and Ethiopians, and I didn't think it was because English was her third language. Which did she feel she was: Israeli or Ethiopian?

"I don't know. I have my feet in two lands. I don't know what I am."

"I understand what that's like," I said. "Tezeta, are you black?"

"There is a lot of blacks here. The Mizrahi is black, the Bedouin is black, the Yemenite is black, the Moroccan is black, and the Ethiopian is the most black, because we came to Israel last. The next to come will be more black than us. It doesn't matter the color of their skin."

"Are the Palestinians black?"

"No. They are not playing in the game. We don't absorb them."

The next day, Tezeta and her boyfriend, Tsuri, brought me and Tamar to Mt. Herzl National Memorial Park. Tamar described the park as "the heart of the Zionist commemoration machine." The Holocaust memorial complex, Yad Vashem, is there, as are the military cemetery, the burial sites of Golda Meir and Yitzhak Rabin, and the construction site of a brand new memorial whose design Tsuri consulted on. It is being erected to commemorate the thousands of Beta Israel who died trying to reach Israel. Tsuri showed me the architectural design for the memorial, which included four round thatch-roofed huts. Tamar served as translator: "He says those are what their houses looked like in Gondar."

Tsuri pointed to a part of the construction site where a backhoe was lazily kicking up yellow dust. Tamar tried to keep up with his torrent of words. "He says the huts will go there in a diamond. One, two, three, four. . . . The idea was for each house to have text on the walls, a monologue about the exodus by four different Ethiopian characters . . . a mother, a child, a father who leads the family, and a holy man. He wanted visitors to be able to go inside their houses and read their stories."

Tsuri seemed angry.

"What's he saying?" I asked. Tamar struggled to keep up with his tirade. "He's saying that the Jewish Agency didn't approve the design."

"Why not?"

"He says they were afraid the Falashas would go in there to drink and do drugs. . . . Sorry, he's talking really fast. They're allowed to have the structures, but they have to be closed."

"So nobody can go inside," I clarified.

"That's right," Tamar translated. "No doors. You can only see the huts from the outside."

"But that's ridiculous," I said. "If the story remains hidden, then this is a memorial with no memory."

"I *told* you," Tezeta interrupted, gesticulating wildly. "They do not want what is in our heart. They only want what is in *her* heart." She meant Tamar. "For us they only want to pat themselves on their backs. Do you think they asked Tsuri to work for this memorial?"

She turned to her boyfriend and spoke animatedly at him. It took me a moment to realize her torrent of words was Amharic. Amharic is a softer-sounding language than Hebrew, but she was speaking it hard.

Tsuri sighed and tucked the blueprints into his bag. Then he said something brief and looked with resignation at the backhoe. "He says they didn't ask him," Tamar translated. "He heard they were building the memorial, and he fought to be included on the steering committee."

"He is the only Ethiopian making this. They think they know better than us how to make it," Tezeta hissed.

On our way through the cypress trees down the mountain, Tamar
admitted that when she'd come to Israel for summer camp in her
youth, she'd felt the land belonged to her, and she to it. "The coun-
selors instilled a sense of ownership in us," she said. "I thought the
Falashas were foreigners, but I didn't think of myself as a foreigner.
It's ironic, isn't it? They were living here. I was only visiting."

"It is not ironic," said Tezeta. *Chutzpah*. That is the word for how
she said this: "Israel does belong to you. Not to us."

"Do you guys think of this place as your homeland?" I asked the
young couple.

Tsuri was tight-lipped. Tezeta was fed up. "I have told you! I'm
not a Zionist! The Ethiopians dream of Zion as a place that our grand-
fathers dreamed. But they need to wake up from that dream and see
how this Zion treats us. That dream is not real. The day we say our
dream is just a dream is the day we will stand up for our rights. But the
Ethiopians want to stay asleep. They say, 'I dreamed to be here. I am a
Zionist and I belong to Zion.' Israel doesn't want them. She only
wants them if they play the game by her rules, pray the way she tells
us, think the way she tells us, be the Jew she wants. It was not my
dream to be a citizen of Israel. If you want to listen to that kind of talk,
you should go and see my boss."

Dany Admasu was a chain-smoking, poetic man in his early thirties
who looked like he hadn't slept in months. He had been airlifted in
from Sudan during Operation Moses in 1984, an era I remember for
Live-Aid, Hands-Across-America, the hit song "We Are the World,"
and starving Ethiopians on the cover of *Time* magazine. Having been
in Israel longer than Tezeta, Dany's English was more assured.

"I wrote this," he said, pulling a yellowed clipping of an article
from the *Jerusalem Post* off the bulletin board in his office. "It gives
you an idea of my politics." The headline read: "Which Way for
Ethiopian Israelis?" The article focused on discrimination against the
Beta Israel in the school system, the civil service, the private sector,

and the housing market, as well as their lack of representation in government and all other centers of power.

"What about the Ethiopian on *The Ambassador*?" I teased, referring to the reality show that pitted fourteen young Israelis against each other in tasks designed to boost Israel's disintegrating world image. "And wasn't there an Ethiopian singer represented on *Israeli Idol*?"

"They didn't win," he said. "They were just window dressing to complete Israel's cultural menagerie."

"What about Addisu Messele?" I asked about the former lone Ethiopian-born member of the one hundred and twenty person Knesset. "Window dressing?"

"More or less."

"I bet your article got you in trouble," I guessed. "You called the Ministry of Absorption a *disgrace*. That's pretty bold."

"I am bold—I'm an Israeli. We know how to shout to get our point across. But you're right. The government doesn't like me because I'm speaking the truth. My goal is to change their idea that we're not worthy. They don't understand. They think Jewish means white."

He offered me a cigarette, which I declined.

"They want you to think they love us because we're all Jews, but they don't think we have the same bones and blood."

"I heard about how they dumped all the Beta Israel blood out of the blood bank because they thought it was infected with AIDS."

"How did you hear about that?"

"I read about it."

"Are you American?"

"I'm from New York."

"Americans have a tendency to talk about the ethos of the community, and not of the individual. You think this war is between Israel and Lebanon, for example. You think about who is right and wrong, but you don't think about the experience of the soldier."

I thought about what he said, and how quickly I'd written Oz off. He was a man who had seen his best friend's face blown away. Who would I have turned against, if I had witnessed the same thing done to Tamar?

"I will tell you my individual story," Dany offered. "Imagine you are me. You are a little Jewish boy in Gondar, where you shepherd goats. Every morning you drink fresh milk from the goats you tend. But the real food in your life as you grow up is the dream of Jerusalem. This dream is in everything you do—the way you pray, the blessing, all the Jewish ceremonies. In every sentence the word *Jerusalem* comes up."

He stopped to ash his cigarette.

"One day, your father says to you, 'We're going to Jerusalem.' Imagine your surprise. You didn't know it was a real place. You thought it was a dream as far away as the moon. Your father has sold your goats and everything else but the donkey to carry the food. You begin walking with everyone else from your village. You're doing what Moses did to get to Israel. Every father in the village is a Moses.

"They knew there would be sacrifice. Somebody was going to die along the way. They were willing to pay whatever it cost to get to Jerusalem. Looking back, it was crazy. The government regime did not allow emigration. They arrested us along the way and sent us back to the village. So we began again. We walked at night and hid in the day. My sister was arrested three times, and she bore a kid in jail.

"Imagine you are walking. You walk from Ethiopia to Sudan. It takes two months. The weak ones didn't make it this far. You made it, but you have to stop walking because you ran out of food and water. You are so thirsty you would gladly drink your own urine, only you are too dehydrated to urinate.

"You live in a refugee camp, and it is hell. Sometimes the Red Cross brings medicine, but forty to sixty people die there every day from starvation and snakebites. Israel finally hears about you, but they don't think you're a Jew because you're black. You yourself didn't know there were white Jews. You have never seen a white person before.

"America is putting pressure on Israel to save you. A big safari truck comes to pick you up and drives you for three hours with your father to a big airplane. You have never seen an airplane, so you don't know it's strange that they ripped out the seats to fit more of you inside. On the airplane they feed you bananas. You eat so many you get sick. When you arrive in Israel your father is crying because he thinks he's in heaven. You made it. You know you are home.

"That is my story. The story the world knows is how Israel endangered herself to bring poor people from Africa. That's a big lie. I started my way to this land that I knew from the stomach of my mother without their help. My father put me in danger for this dream. He made it come true. I don't need permission from anyone to prove I'm Jewish. Israel doesn't need to feed me lies to turn me into an Orthodox Jew. I was Jewish before I was born."

Dany lit another cigarette, leaned back, took a long drag, and exhaled a slow rhapsodic haze of smoke. I noticed that he finished the narrative of his amazing journey homeward at the exact spot where spiritual Zion butts heads with political Zion. I am sure the euphoria of his arrival must have worn away painfully fast, perhaps beginning right when he stepped off the plane onto the tarmac and, along with everyone else on board, was bestowed a Hebrew name. Or did he like to be called Daniel? I wondered what his name used to be, the one his father gave him. I wondered when exactly the word *home* began to take on a "diabolical ring" for him and his father, but I didn't ask Dany about the second half of his journey. I understood that, along with his activism, the dream was what kept him alive. It didn't matter if home was a myth he was still walking toward. Maybe it mattered that he was walking on other people's backs to get there, but I don't think Dany thought about that. It only mattered to him that he hadn't stopped walking.

We were quiet for a while. Then I asked, "Do you know who James Baldwin is?"

He didn't.

"You'd like him. He's a black American writer. He said, 'I criticize my home because I love it.' Or something like that. This paragraph in your article made me think of him." I read it aloud:

> More than two decades have passed since the first significant wave of Jewish immigration from Ethiopia to the promised "Land of Milk and Honey" began. While coming on aliyah and being physically present in Israel fulfilled half of the dream, the intolerance towards their language, culture and color, which they have encountered in every aspect of life since their arrival in Israel, has buried the other half of Ethiopian Jewry's dream. Today we can speak more aptly in terms of the crushed dream.

Dany nodded. "I love Jerusalem. I am speaking the truth."

"I am speaking the truth," said the priest. I was at a Sabbath service in the multipurpose room at the Kingdom of Yah, home of the African Hebrew Israelites of Jerusalem, and I was wearing a white head wrap and a loose black dress that came down to my sandaled feet. The room was lit by a dozen *menorahs*. I sat between my hosts, Crowned Dr. Khazriel, head of the School of the Prophets, and one of his many wives, Sister Aturah. She had lent me the dress because the clothes I showed up in were immodest.

The priest was reading from the book of their prophet, Ben Ammi Ben-Israel, a former foundry worker from Chicago, born Ben Carter, whom the African Hebrew Israelites call "Abba" and believe to be the messiah. In 1966, he claims to have had a forty-five second vision from an angel who told him it was time for him and the rest of his lost tribe to return to Jerusalem. Their tradition holds that they were exiled from the Holy Land during the Roman Invasion nearly two thousand years ago, migrated southward, down the Nile, through the centuries, and westward to the coast of Africa, where a great number of them were captured and shipped into modern Babylon as a curse for sinning against God's law. They distinguish their progenitor from Judah, the Jewish father. Their father is Adam, the original man. They distinguish their curse (referred to in Leviticus and Deuteronomy as a great dispersal and a voyage into captivity by boat) from the eternal curse of Ham, which was used by white slave owners to justify slavery. While Ham's curse cannot be redressed, the African Hebrew Israelites believe their curse can be, by living according to certain principles, including a vegan diet.

This is a seductive idea for people who have grown up in inner-city slums, who can only reach four hundred years into their history and then bump against a wall. Being a charismatic leader, Ben Ammi convinced thirty black folks of his angelic vision. First, they traveled to Liberia to cleanse themselves of their slave mentality. In 1969, they showed up in Israel and were told by the Rabbinate that they were not Jews. But the African Hebrew Israelites saw themselves as the original Jews. They refused to convert, calling the Israelis "heathens" and publicly threatening to run them into the sea.

The priest read some more scripture from Ben Ammi's holy

book—*God, The Black Man and Truth*—and then launched into a sermon, much of which I agreed with. Up to a point.

"You can't get to freedom on an airplane."

"Tell it!"

"An airplane won't take you there. Brothers and sisters, I'm here to tell you, freedom is a place in your *mind*."

"That's right!"

"Back there we were sick."

"I was dying!"

"Sickness, perversion, and death abound in the land of Great Captivity, but our greatest sickness there was of our *spirit*. We didn't choose to live there."

"No!"

"They took us in chains! That place of wickedness was not our home. Theirs was not our way. Why would you want a house for your car when your brother was homeless? Because you were sick. You were thinking like them. Why would you poison your body with cigarettes, knowing they would kill you?"

"Because I was sick!"

"You were thinking like them. Why would you believe the earth moves around the sun? Does that make sense?"

"No!"

"No. The earth is the center of the universe. Jerusalem is the center of the earth. If the earth moved around the sun, then how could the sun rise and set every day? You didn't use your *mind*. You listened to their lies. You let them tell you Jesus was white, Adam was white. Jesus wasn't white. Neither was Adam. They were black men with wooly hair."

"That's right!"

"Why would you let your child play with a toy gun? If you let your child shoot water, he will grow up and think it's a game to shoot a bullet! Why would you allow him to shoot a brother over a pair of hundred-dollar sneakers or a vial of crack? Because you were sick. Our bodies weren't in shackles, but our minds were. They told us we were nothing, and we believed them, but we're not at the bottom of their boat no more. They told us we couldn't do it, but we did. We built the boat. We drive the boat."

"Amen!"

"They want you to believe we're a cult. Say the whole word!"

"Culture!"

I started to feel a little uneasy. I wasn't sure if it was the sermon or the head scarf—Sister Aturah had wrapped mine too tight, and I was afraid I might pass out.

"You don't go to Japan and say, 'That's a cult.' That's a *culture*. We're a *culture*. They say we're a weird sect. Say the whole word. We're a *section* of the Hebrew Israelite nation living in Dimona, Israel, Northeast Africa. If you conform to our vision, you will not be sick. You will not need a medicine chest. Diabetes—what's that? Cancer—what's that? Depression—what's that? Can I get a witness?"

"I haven't been sick since I came to the Kingdom nineteen years ago—not once!"

"The Torah speaks of people who lived nine hundred years, so why can't we? This is possible, people. Nine hundred years is a blink of Yah's eye and we are his chosen people. We don't have to die. Heaven is possible in the mind and body, and we are living proof. We don't use the word death around our children. Our children don't know the meaning of that word. We are making new people, with new minds, befitting of this new world."

"Hallelujah!"

After the service was over, Dr. Khazriel and Sister Aturah walked me through the Village of Peace to the guesthouse where I was staying in a room decorated with generic Afrocentric prints, a tall wooden giraffe and a two-by-three-foot poster of Ben Ammi's benevolent face. Aturah was quiet in her husband's presence. I learned that they'd been married only a few weeks before, and that none of his fourteen children was hers. I imagine that being middle-aged and childless was hard for her in a community that forbids birth control and puts a high premium on a woman's ability to bear children.

All of the women I met in the Village of Peace introduced themselves to me in terms of their motherhood, as in, "I'm Sister Zehorah, mother of eight." They told me that a man's wife is a piece of him just as Adam's rib is a piece of him, and that while Man keeps his hands in the hands of Yah, Woman keeps her hands in the hands of Man.

Aturah walked a few steps behind her new husband and me, her head bowed. I turned to ask her if the priest was using a metaphor when he spoke about immortality.

"Oh, no," she said.

"You don't believe in death?"

"We call it *transitioning*," she said softly.

I thought it would be gauche to ask where they put their dead people. "Do you celebrate funerals?" I asked.

Dr. Khazriel gave her a look.

"Everything we do promotes life and healing," she said. "What we put in our bodies, what we put into the earth, how we sing. We don't sing the blues anymore."

Dr. Khazriel had a slight lisp. He waved at the crooked little tar-papered shacks that make up the Kingdom of Yah with his cane. "None of this was here when I came," he said, fingering his gray beard. Although he is not one of the founders of the kingdom, Dr. Khazriel arrived a few short years after its inception. He was seventeen years old when he came to join his aunt and the swelling number of other African Americans who'd settled in the Negev Desert near a nuclear reactor, where the State of Israel had allowed them to squat. Now there are an estimated 2,500 members of their community living in Israel, where they have recently gained permanent residency status. Their population has grown thanks to the practice of polygamy and to widespread proselytizing efforts in "the provinces," which include Baltimore, Houston, Detroit, Atlanta, and New York. In fact, the African Hebrew Israelites make up the largest community of African Americans living outside the United States and, Dr. Khazriel told me, "the only progressive one—a historic fact in itself. We built this nation with our own hands."

At first, the sprawling shantytown didn't look like much to me, but then I considered the amazing accomplishment. My hosts pointed out their school, their sewing center, their bakery, their gym, their library, their "House of Life" (there is no need for a hospital in a land without sickness)—all of this was built from scratch in thirty-some-odd years. These people make their own clothes, grow most of their own food, and, most important, govern themselves.

Where the Beta Israel represent the bitterness, disorientation, and disillusionment of Zionism's dream deferred, members of the African Hebrew Israelite community believe, or are indoctrinated to believe, that they have fully arrived in Canaan. Because the Israeli Rabbinate has never acknowledged them as Jews, they've never enjoyed any of the rights of citizenship that Israel has to offer. This rejection has forced them to fashion their own Zion. Because they've never been forced to assimilate to dominant Orthodox Judaism, they've managed to maintain and forge their own unique Judaic identity. Theirs is truly a fully operable, self-sustained nation-inside-a-nation, with one interesting concession—about seventy African Hebrew Israelite youth are enlisted in the Israel Defense Forces.

I asked Dr. Khazriel if their participation in the IDF conflicted with the African Hebrew Israelites' governing practice of promoting life. "The priest said it was sick for a child to play with a toy gun, but some of your young people are handling real guns right now in Lebanon. What are they fighting for?"

"That's a good question, Sister Emily. I see you have a sharp mind. What you see surrounding you is our spiritual home but it's also a physical realm. We have to protect our village. We're a spiritual entity in a secular world with social realities. Those scuds and rockets are real. Outside of a war atmosphere, killing is not acceptable, but we live in a punishing atmosphere of war. We're not disconnected from greater Israel," Dr. Khazriel reasoned. "We live here, and so we have to show solidarity. But our involvement in the army is only transitional."

I told him I'd been witness to the hard transition Beta Israel was making into Zion. "It's truly a shame what's happening to them," he said, shaking his head. "They're African Hebrew Israelites too. We all descend from Judea, but when they returned home, they began to lose their original form."

We arrived at the guesthouse. "There used to be a baseball diamond scratched in the sand right here," Dr. Khazriel said. "The day I arrived, there was a pick-up game going on. My aunt said, 'Boy, this is the kingdom of heaven, and these are the saints.' I said, 'If this is heaven, then where's Jesus?' She pointed at the pitcher and said, 'Right there.' Do you know who she was pointing at?"

"Abba?" I guessed.

"See that, Aturah? She's sharp as a sword." He laid his hand on my shoulder. "We could use a mind like yours in the Kingdom."

Abba stood in a resplendent, canary-yellow robe, in the center of a large painting hanging above the table in the conference room of the School of the Prophets where Dr. Khazriel sat me down to instruct me further in his beliefs. Twelve other men figured in the painting, just like the apostles at the last supper. The other decorations of note in the classroom were a picture of Martin Luther King, Jr., and a world map.

"Do you really believe Ben Ammi is the Messiah?" I asked.

Dr. Khazriel gestured at the painting. "Those men represent our governing body," he began. "Our government must remain in a prophetic mode. Many men have had visions—Frederick Douglass, Martin Delaney, Father Divine, Garvey, King, Malcolm—and all of their visions failed. Why? Because all black visionaries in America become martyrs. The man who can electrify and unify a black movement is an automatic target. We had to authenticate Ben Ammi's vision by calling him the *Messiah*. That title gives him absolute authority."

"As the son of God?"

"As the anointed leader of the Kingdom of Yah. He's our ruler. We couldn't be free until we had our own nation. 'He who rules Jerusalem rules the world.' "

"Sounds like a crusade."

"It is. All men have focused on Jerusalem since the dawn of mankind. Do you know why?"

"Your priest said Jerusalem is the center of the universe."

"Good listening. Israel began with correct socialist aims, but you don't see too many *kibbutzim* anymore. Jerusalem has fallen under the control of profane and perverted European empires. Their dominion has brought the world to darkness. Euro-gentiles have corrupted earth-centered concepts more than any other people. They have distorted the institutions of liberalism and democracy. You'd have to be blind not to recognize this as a fallen world." Dr. Khazriel pushed up the loose sleeves of his *dashiki* and counted out a list of recent calamities on his fingers: tsunami, Katrina, global warming. . . . The list had more than ten items and it included the present war with Lebanon. He fisted and unfisted his hands.

"We're at a time of transition. Those empowered to administrate the earth are about to have a rude awakening. Their time of rule is up." He pounded the table with his fists. "Our purpose is to restore

Jerusalem, Africa, and the earth. The diaspora cannot save Africa, but Africa can save the diaspora."

"Can you repeat that?"

"There's no spiritual impetus for the black diaspora to save Africa. With all its resources, scholars, and religious leaders, the black diaspora is out of focus. Sister Emily, let me ask you a question. Do you think of Africa as a prophetic or pathetic realm?"

"Um . . ."

"You can admit it."

"Well, I've never been there."

"You're there right now! This is it. You're in Africa." He swiveled his chair and pointed a pen at little Israel on the world map, hanging off Egypt like an earlobe. "All that separates you from the mother continent is the Suez Canal. The Kingdom of Yah is the New Jerusalem. We're not built out of brick and mortar alone. We're building a new mind beyond the shackles we once knew. We've recovered from chattel slavery. We've saved ourselves from stress and harm, trauma and drama, from the dialysis machine, hypertension and heart attack, from kidney failure, self-hatred, and jail. We've reversed all that impurity by restoring Hebraic concepts of interdependent community, love, and humanity. By doing that, we're restoring Africa, which will in turn restore the earth populace. No brag, just fact."

Dr. Khazriel held out his hand. "This hand is humble. This hand reaching out to save the earth is black. People don't want to hold this hand. They are selective about salvation. Look at this mess." He brought out a copy of the *Economist* and slapped it on the table. Bill Gates was on the cover, holding a black baby. "What does that say?"

"Billanthropy."

"That man has thirty-four *billion* dollars. His impulse is greed, profit, big business, tax-deductible philanthropy. When is it enough? There is no possibility for contentment in the framework of capitalism. Do you know why they crucified *him*?"

Dr. Khazriel signaled the picture of Martin Luther King, Jr., which was the same image as the one in Tezeta's office, only much bigger. "Because he was a Hebrew. Their edict was to stop the rise of the black messiah."

"COINTELPRO?"

"Yes, Sister. They got rid of him, of our king, because he spoke the powerful phrase 'Promised Land.' That's a Hebrewism. It comes from Old Testament theology. Hebrewisms are the basis of all black protest social movements. Did you ever read about us in school? Had you ever heard of a black Jew?"

"No," I admitted.

Dr. Khazriel shook his head, sadly. "We've been omitted from the annals of history. But I want you to see that we're not a fringe. We're not a myth blown out of a vacuum. I want you to read this," he held up the holy book, "as a history text. Begin with Genesis. That's our history."

Sister Aturah, in a purple robe and a matching head wrap, entered the room quietly to serve us watermelon. "This was grown on our farm," she whispered, setting it down. "It's very sweet."

"Thank you, Aturah," said Dr. Khazriel. "Do you have something you want to tell Sister Emily on her search for truth?"

"Yes, I do."

"Tell it."

"This is an island of sanity. This is the place our soul was crying out for."

"Aturah might also have said that we see ourselves as the fulfillment of Dr. King's dream," Dr. Khazriel added. "Isn't that right?"

"Yes," she answered, looking at her feet.

I began picking out the little black seeds from the fruit. Pathetic and prophetic. To me their world was both. "So this is Canaan Land?" I asked Dr. Khazriel. The reason I didn't put my question to his wife was that I didn't think she was at liberty to say "No."

"I was born into a Detroit ghetto," he answered, biting into a slice of watermelon. "If I wasn't here, I would be dead."

———

On my last day before leaving Israel, Tamar and I walked Nina through a mob of displaced Israeli settlers dressed in orange. It was *Tisha B'Av*, the Fast of the Ninth of Av, a holiday which observes the many tragedies that have stricken Jews throughout history, including the destruction of the first Temple, the second Temple, and the expulsion of the Jews from Spain. These settlers were using the day to mourn the loss of their homes in Palestinian territory. We hadn't foreseen the march, and soon we were tangled in its masses. There were thousands of settlers, shouting, singing, waving the Israeli flag, flooding us in a rage of orange.

"I can't believe these people," Tamar said, plowing her way through the crowd with the stroller. "Move!"

We escaped behind the walls of the Old City, wended through the maze of its narrow, cobbled streets, bypassed all of its wares—the blue and white Armenian ceramics, the backgammon sets inlaid with mother of pearl, the beads, the baklava, the incense sticks, and *doumbek* drums. We wound up outside the compound of St. Anne's Church. This compound contains the ruins of the curative Bethesda pool, where, according to the Gospel of John, Jesus is said to have performed a miracle of faith. "Do you want to be healed?" Jesus asked a lame man with useless legs. The man said, "Yes." "Then get up and walk!" Christ commanded. Which is just what the invalid did.

"I want to show you something special," said Tamar, leading me into the basilica. Except for two middle-aged French women sitting with their hands folded in the back pew, the church was empty. Tamar unstrapped Nina from her stroller. "This church has a fifteen-second echo," she whispered. Nina squealed and her voice ballooned outward to fill the unadorned space, as high as the vaulted ceilings. She widened her eyes in wonder.

"*Excusez-moi. Êtes-vous américaines?*" asked the French woman with the paisley silk scarf at her throat.

"Sort of," said Tamar.

Sort of.

Sort of.

"Ah!" clapped the woman, and her clap became a cannon's boom. "Do you know how to sing?"

"*Dites-leur de chanter* 'Amazing Grace,' " her friend suggested. The last word bloomed from her lipsticked mouth.

Grace.

Grace.

"*J'aime cette chanson.*"

"We know it." Tamar smiled.

We know it.

We know it.

We know it.

We do. We walked up the aisle side-by-side, sat Nina in the first pew with her quilt, took our places at the altar, looked at each other and began. We sang that mournful hymn composed by a white man who'd sailed the seas on slave ships, witnessed the shackled hold, and attempted to expiate the sin of his complicity through the act of composition.

We sang it in two-part harmony. Our voices cast out like fishing lines into the void where they unraveled. They unraveled into water and swam back to us, doubling and quadrupling in volume, backward and forward, a current running in all directions. This was our sweet sound. Wanting to be cradled in it, the baby scooted backwards off the pew and crawled toward us in her sagging diaper across the marble floor.

We transposed from major to minor key. Nina stopped three feet from us and stood. In the end, this is Zion: the song about our wretchedness lifting up to save us, our voices leashing us together, the child walking towards us on unsteady legs. Two steps. Her first. She will fall down, but right now our song holds her up like hands, and this is Zion, right here, in the moment before she does.

LAST THOUGHTS OF
AN IRAQ "EMBED"

Brian Palmer

Al Asad Air Base
Anbar Province, Iraq
02/24/06

This is my Iraq swansong, Inshallah. I depart soon with the 230+ US Marines and sailors of C Company—Charlie Co.—an infantry element in the 2300-strong 22nd Marine Expeditionary Unit. They are moving on to other military tasks after conducting two months of stability and support and counterinsurgency operations in and around Hit, a city in western Iraq. I will leave my "embed" and return to the predictable comforts of Brooklyn, NY.

Outside my tent the sun rises orange from behind an enormous dirt and gravel berm. The landscape illuminated by the faint sunlight has been scraped and scarred into ugly functionality by earthmoving vehicles. Long cream-colored canvas tents and squat white trailers are nestled behind razor-wire topped fortifications—Hesco barriers, metal mesh frames lined with gray fabric and filled with tons of dirt. Hescos can absorb mortar blasts, rockets, and small-arms fire, and they catch shrapnel well, but they are unsightly reminders that this is not a peaceful environment. The only thing pretty about the vista is the sun and how it colors the morning sky.

Al Asad Air Base is an American bubble dug into the Iraqi desert. Other than a token force of Iraqi soldiers, the people of Iraq are kept at a safe, stand-off distance by miles of desert, guard towers, and checkpoints. At Charlie Company's base back in Hit, the call to prayer from the local mosque easily penetrated the sandbagged window next to my cot. I could step outside and see and hear the city and its inhabitants. I knew I was in Iraq, even though the same Hescos and guard towers separated me. At Asad, I hear whirring generators around the clock and jet aircraft tearing through the sky. I hear helicopter rotors beating the air above this tent, sometimes so close I fear the blades will slash through the canvas. I hear the chatting and bullshitting of grunts and the hum of vehicles whizzing by. But I don't hear Iraq, and I certainly can't see it.

A couple of days ago in Samarra, a city to the east, dozens of people died in violence following the bombing of the Askariya Shrine. Revenge killing now spreads through central Iraq, but I would wager that few on this base other than senior officers know much about what's going on. We're connected to that Iraq only tenuously. Most of the soldiers, sailors, Marines, and airmen don't venture beyond the wire. They're transiting to or from the States and just killing time until their flights. Issues of *Stars & Stripes,* the only independent newspaper that's widely distributed, get here a week late. The best source of news is the TV in the chowhall, which is permanently tuned to the Armed Forces Network. AFN airs American cable news broadcasts in a rotating, equal-time format—CNN (I breakfast with Anderson Cooper), Fox, MSNBC, and ABC.

I learned about Samarra last night during dinner, beef curry and salad (I passed on the corndogs and ham). This morning I came back for more information on the violence and got only a brief hit. CNN was fixated on a Phoenix hostage-taking and the Dubai Ports kerfuffle—this as central Iraq burns.

Yesterday on the tube I caught a too-brief vignette about the recent spate of insurgent violence from a news conference with General Peter Pace, Chairman of the Joint Chiefs of Staff, and Secretary of Defense Donald Rumsfeld. Then I read the transcript of the presser.

"[T]o isolate out violence today and say, 'Oh, my goodness, there's violence today, isn't that different'—which you did not do, of course, but I'm stating it myself—would be out of context, because in fact there's been incredible violence in that country for year after year after year. And that does not minimize what's taking place today, but at least it puts it in a broader context and—one would think," Secretary Rumsfeld said, responding to a reporter who asked about the strength of the insurgency.

"Oh my goodness" indeed. The fact that Iraq was cracked, bruised, and brutalized before the US invasion doesn't matter. The Bush Administration cast America as Iraq's savior, so we must either save the nation—the hope of so many Iraqis back in 2003—or admit that we cannot. But instead of an honest admission of US obligations and missteps, a clear breakdown of Iraq's security situation, or a sensible plan for future operations, the administration offers artful rhetoric about the impending triumph of Iraqi democracy, as illustrated by the success of the nation's three elections.

Unfortunately, and self-servingly, they don't remind us that before each election, US troop strength was increased. Units were put on high alert. Many conducted extra "surge patrols" through cities and towns to deter potential attackers from launching embarrassing election day assaults. During the January 2005 election, I accompanied Marines on such patrols through Musayyib, a city just south of Baghdad. The grunts didn't venture inside polling stations on the day of the vote, as the Bush Administration likes to point out, but they weren't too far away: US troops, armor, and aircraft formed a steel and flesh curtain around the weak and tactically inept Iraqi Army and police force.

The only sure thing about security in Iraq is that US units come and US units go. Some, like Charlie Co. and the other infantry companies in the MEU's ground combat element, Battalion Landing Team ½, round up enough suspected insurgents and capture enough weapons to lower the level of violence in their area of operation. And then they leave. The transition between units usually creates a brief slowdown in operations that the antioccupation and sectarian forces exploit.

Two examples: BLT ½ pulled out of Iskandariya, Musayyib, and the surrounding towns of Babil province in February 2005 and turned it over to a Mississippi National Guard unit. Just days after the rollover, the area was rocked by a wave of IED blasts and suicide bombings. In one attack in Musayyib, a bomb exploded on streets I had walked just a few days earlier with grunts from the BLT's Bravo Company. The explosion ignited a fuel tanker truck. Roughly 100 people were killed. This year in Hit, insurgents launched their biggest and boldest attack in months just moments after Marines handed the Army control of the area. The antioccupation fighters knew a transition was happening, and they took advantage of it. The same process happens in other troubled cities across the country.

Furthermore, a new unit is under no obligation to continue the previous unit's initiatives or successes. To the extent that rules and regs allow, its commanders can damn-near reinvent the wheel if they choose to. If their strategy doesn't work, Iraqi citizens are back to square one.

It would be disingenuous to assert that such insurgent resurgence reflects poorly on the US Marines I am embedded with—and I don't say this because I have been stricken with Stockholm Syndrome. The Marines of Charlie Co., BLT ½ and the 22nd MEU were given orders, which they followed. They conducted sweeps through Hit for guns and anti-US fighters, and they found some. Most of the grunts I watched performed professionally—Staff Sergeant David Marino, Lance Corporal William Whitted, Lance Corporal Adrian Bobadilla, and so many others spring to mind. Some Marines didn't. But all in all, the grunts did the best they could with what little they were given.

While there may have been some flaws in the Marines' execution of orders, the fundamental flaw lies in the orders themselves and in the planning for their execution. The architects, the strategists, and the tacticians of the US endeavor in Iraq have handed US troops a catalogue of Sisyphean tasks—install a democracy; help restore infrastructure (and protect it); build an Army and security apparatus from scraps and dregs; crush a disparate horde of mostly invisible enemies. Add to this the burden of force protection, steps troops must take to guard themselves and their bases against attacks. The 20-somethings of the Army and the Marine Corps (and their older counterparts in the Reserves and the Guard) are neither trained nor equipped to tackle all of this. Finally, throw on top of this pile the instability that transitions between US units inevitably cause and you have a recipe for continuing disaster.

The Administration's response to this reality is to prematurely offload responsibility for Iraq's fate on the nascent and shaky government and on the incipient Iraqi Army, which relies on the US for everything—food, weapons, vehicles, training, command and control, air and heavy-weapon support.

"[I]t will be up to the Iraqi government and the Iraqi people to seize the opportunity they have right now and to allow their people to have jobs and a future that would tell their people that the insurgency offers nothing and that the new government is the way ahead," JCS Chairman General Pace told reporters at a February 21 news conference. Would that the "opportunity" the general describes actually existed.

Stop Trying to "Save" Africa

—⁂—

Uzodinma Iweala

Last fall, shortly after I returned from Nigeria, I was accosted by a perky blond college student whose blue eyes seemed to match the "African" beads around her wrists.

"Save Darfur!" she shouted from behind a table covered with pamphlets urging students to TAKE ACTION NOW! STOP GENOCIDE IN DARFUR!

My aversion to college kids jumping onto fashionable social causes nearly caused me to walk on, but her next shout stopped me.

"Don't you want to help us save Africa?" she yelled.

It seems that these days, wracked by guilt at the humanitarian crisis it has created in the Middle East, the West has turned to Africa for redemption.

Idealistic college students, celebrities such as Bob Geldof, and politicians such as Tony Blair have all made bringing light to the dark continent their mission.

This is the West's new image of itself: a sexy, politically active generation whose preferred means of spreading the word are magazine spreads with celebrities pictured in the foreground, forlorn Africans in the back. Perhaps most interesting is the language used to describe the Africa being saved. For example, the Keep a Child

Alive/"I am African" ad campaign features portraits of primarily white, Western celebrities with painted "tribal markings" on their faces above "I AM AFRICAN" in bold letters. Below, smaller print says, "help us stop the dying."

Such campaigns, however well intentioned, promote the stereotype of Africa as a black hole of disease and death. News reports constantly focus on the continent's corrupt leaders, warlords, "tribal" conflicts, child laborers, and women disfigured by abuse and genital mutilation. These descriptions run under headlines such as "Can Bono Save Africa?"

The relationship between the West and Africa is no longer based on openly racist beliefs, but such articles are reminiscent of reports from the heyday of European colonialism, when missionaries were sent to Africa to introduce us to education, Jesus Christ, and "civilization."

There is no African, myself included, who does not appreciate the help of the wider world, but we do question whether aid is genuine or given in the spirit of affirming one's cultural superiority. My mood is dampened every time I attend a benefit whose host runs through a litany of African disasters before presenting a (usually) wealthy, white person, who often proceeds to list the things he or she has done for the poor, starving Africans. Every time a Hollywood director shoots a film about Africa that features a Western protagonist, I shake my head—because Africans, real people though we may be, are used as props in the West's fantasy of itself. And not only do such depictions tend to ignore the West's prominent role in creating many of the unfortunate situations on the continent, they also ignore the incredible work Africans have done and continue to do to fix those problems.

Why do the media frequently refer to African countries as having been "granted independence from their colonial masters," as opposed to having fought and shed blood for their freedom? How is it that a former mid-level US diplomat receives more attention for his cowboy antics in Sudan than do the numerous African Union countries that have sent food and troops and spent countless hours trying to negotiate a settlement among all parties in that crisis?

Two years ago I worked in a camp for internally displaced people in Nigeria, survivors of an uprising that killed about 1,000 people and displaced 200,000. True to form, the Western media reported on the violence but not on the humanitarian work the state and local governments—without much international help—did for the survivors. Social workers spent their time, and in many cases their own salaries, to care for their compatriots. These are the people saving Africa, and others like them across the continent get no credit for their work.

Last month the Group of Eight industrialized nations and a host of celebrities met in Germany to discuss, among other things, how to save Africa. Before the next such summit, I hope people will realize Africa doesn't want to be saved. Africa wants the world to acknowledge that through fair partnerships with other members of the global community, we ourselves are capable of unprecedented growth.

WE ARE AMERICANS

⁓⅏◯

Jerald Walker

I was midair, somewhere above the Atlantic, when I stopped being black. I was informed of it two days later. "Now you are colored," I was told.

"What does that mean," I asked, " 'colored'?"

"It means you are not black, like you were in America."

"Am . . . am I . . . *white?*"

"No, but you are very, very close. Close enough that the blacks here will hate you."

"Here" was Harare, Zimbabwe, where my wife, Brenda, was to conduct her dissertation research. Her goal was to document the murals women painted on their homes in the rural areas, but first we had to live in the capital city so she could work in the National Archives. During the two days since our arrival, I'd noticed that some of the locals weren't particularly friendly; I'd just asked our hostess about our rude reception. She was surprised that we hadn't been warned, especially by Brenda's father, a native Zimbabwean. He'd married a white American English teacher and they had moved with Brenda to the States when she was three. Our hostess, Farai, was her cousin.

"Oh, yes," Farai continued. "Your time here with the blacks will be very, very difficult."

"What about with the whites?" Brenda asked.

Farai smiled. "They will hate you as well, but not as much."

Just like that, I'd been cast in *The Twilight Zone,* in an episode on racial purgatory. Brenda had had experience with this sort of thing, being a child of a mixed marriage, but both my parents were black, certified Negroes from lands of "chitlins" and cotton. I had been black for thirty-one years, and now my caramel complexion and nappy hair had somehow betrayed me. I was stunned, confused beyond measure. Farai offered us some tea.

This was 1995, fifteen years after the start of Zimbabwe's democratic rule. Prior to that, it had been an apartheid state. Whites had controlled the country, despite being less than five percent of the population, and they'd decided that an even smaller percentage of the population, people of mixed ancestry, the coloreds, should be next in line. Coloreds were provided good schools and housing. They were hired for cushy jobs. They were granted the right to vote. And, according to Farai, they exercised their right to be snide. Now blacks were in power. It was payback time.

"But, but . . ." I stammered, "we are Americans."

"All the worse," Farai responded.

"Why?"

"Blacks hate Americans, too."

"*Why?*"

"Because Americans are rich."

"Not all of them," I told her, but by comparison this wasn't true. Seventy percent of black Zimbabweans were poor, poor in a way that I had not understood, even though I'd been raised in projects and slums. Harare was full of beggars, more naked than not, smelly, dirty, sick, and occasionally missing limbs. Those who could walk had followed us for long periods with their hands extended, and those who could not tugged at our pants legs or called out to us as we passed. I had made a concerted effort to ignore these things, since the African experience I had envisioned for myself had been entirely uplifting, bordering on the spiritual, much in the way that visiting Mecca had been for Malcolm X. Only better. After all, I, a descendant of African slaves, was returning to the motherland, home of the men and women who had endured the middle passage's horrors to bequeath me their genes. And now I was returning to claim my long-denied birthright—

a sense of belonging, a sense of place. Just the thought of it had brought me to tears.

And it had brought my sister, Linda, to tears too. In recent years, she'd become obsessed with her ancestral roots, filling her apartment with items purchased from African art peddlers who traveled through black communities like gypsies, doing brisk business from the trunks of their cars. Her walls held a number of imposing masks, their backs scrawled with the name of a country and an exotic-sounding tribe. Brenda, who was completing her doctorate in African art, knew instantly that all the items were fakes, but she didn't have the heart to tell my sister, as I would later not have the heart to tell her that Africa—at least the one of our imaginations—wasn't real either. "And *this* one," Linda would say to us, pointing towards a lopsided wooden head with the teeth of a walrus and the horns of a ram, "was made by the Pee-*ack*-boo of Nigeria." While we nodded thoughtfully, she'd stand there beaming in her mud-cloth gown, leaning on one of her intricately carved canes, the small head of a god snug in the palm of her hand.

A week before we'd left, Linda had thrown a "Back to Africa" party in my honor. She'd spent hours making an "African feast" of fried chicken and catfish, collard greens, neck bones, oxtails, sweet potatoes, and potato salad. Standing at the head of the picnic table, she'd raised her forty ounces of malt liquor high in the air and spoken passionately of how important it was to maintain our bond with our ancestors, how fortunate I was to be able to take the trip, and how, thanks to me, the severed link with our African kin would soon be restored. And then she tilted the bottle to offer libations, which evoked a gasp from our brother Tim, who staggered drunkenly towards the falling liquid with cupped hands.

I think I cried during her speech. I *know* I cried on the plane. When our slow descent at last brought the motherland into view, I wiped my eyes and tried to say the words "I'm home" but found I was too emotional to speak. By the time our wheels skipped across the tarmac, I sobbed openly; this, I imagined, was what it felt like for a long-held hostage to at last be freed. And so it was difficult to accept Farai's view that, while I had been away in captivity, the locks on the homeland's doors had been changed.

That night, as Brenda and I lay in bed trying to make sense of all that her cousin had told us, we decided to reject our colored status. We would simply explain, as often as necessary, that Zimbabwe's system of racial classification did not apply to us, that we had always been and would always be black. I fell asleep convinced that this would suffice, and the next morning, I woke with so much of my idealism about Africa restored that it would take a full three weeks for it to be thoroughly shattered.

The first crack occurred the next day. After spending six hours at the archives, we were driving home when we came upon a military blockade. There were a half-dozen cars ahead of us in the queue, and one by one the officers, unsmiling with rifles strapped over their torsos like guitars, interrogated the occupants and sometimes searched their vehicles. When it was our turn, an officer approached me and barked, "Open the boot!"

I did not know what a boot was or how to open one. "Open the *what*?" I asked.

He did a double take, caused either by my ignorance or accent. I drew back as he rested his hands on the door and leaned closer, looking from me to Brenda to me again and smelling strongly of tobacco. "Why do you speak this way?" he asked. "Who do you think you are fooling?"

"No . . . no one," I said. "We're Americans."

He grinned. "Ah, but you are a liar! You live in Chitungwiz. I have seen you there myself many times before."

"No, no," I insisted, "we *really* are Americans. It's true!"

"Show me your documentation then, *Mr. America*."

I retrieved my passport from my backpack and handed it to him. He looked at it only briefly before saying, "But this is not you. This is a *white* man."

It was, I admit, an unflattering picture. The flash of the camera had bathed my face in light, making me appear even more pale than had Iowa's overcast winter. Moreover, hours of intense Zimbabwean sun had given me a rich tan. The guard's confusion was understandable. "I'm not white," I politely explained. "I'm not colored either, actually. I'm black."

He exploded in violent laughter. He waved the other officers over and showed them my passport. "This man says he is *black*," he told them, and while the others laughed he composed himself enough to light a cigarette. Smoke puffed from his mouth as he demanded more documentation. I gave him my driver's license. He held it close to his face. The other men peered over his shoulders, all eyes darting between the two pictures and me. After a short debate in *Shona*, I was handed my identification. The officers stepped back from the car, and the one who had stopped me, frowning now, waved me forward with the barrel of his rifle.

"This sucks," I said as we drove away.

"Yes, it does," Brenda agreed. "And now you know what it's like to be me. Sometimes I'm white, sometimes I'm black, sometimes I'm both, sometimes I'm neither. I've also been Indian, Pakistani, and Moroccan." She laughed devilishly, clearly enjoying my indoctrination into her strange world of racial schizophrenia. It *was* kind of funny, I had to confess, and soon I was laughing too.

For a while, it was our laughter that sustained us. We laughed when we were ignored in restaurants and retail stores; we laughed when pedestrians deliberately bumped into us; we laughed when we arrived at the hotels of tourist sites and were told that we had no reservations. For two weeks we laughed at every slight and insult that came our way, and we might have laughed for the rest of our trip had we not made the mistake one afternoon of ordering ice cream at an outdoor café, right in the heart of Harare.

We'd just started eating our sundaes when two boys sat at our table. Shocked by their boldness, Brenda and I looked around, hoping one of the employees would chase them off, but no one paid us any attention. We tried ignoring our uninvited guests, as we had ignored countless other beggars, but the stench radiating from them pulled our gaze to its source like a magnet. They could not have been older than ten. Neither one had a shirt or shoes; their skin was covered with open sores. Things moved in their hair. The boys said nothing, understanding, perhaps, that there was nothing to say. They were starving. We were not. They were poor. We were rich. They felt wronged. We felt guilty. We gave them our sundaes. It helped none of us very much.

Sometimes we'd be driving and see on the roadside women and small children selling tomatoes. We'd stop and buy them all. We bought things obsessively, loaves of bread from old men on bicycles, potatoes from little girls who pulled them in wagons, and, from street vendors, dozens of knickknacks carved in stone. But that didn't help either. In the end, to save ourselves, we learned to look through our guilt, as if it were no more than a dirty window, and concentrate on pleasant things in the distance. We let ourselves be colored.

We started patronizing businesses staffed by whites because whites treated us better. We sought out white convenience stores, white malls, white gas stations. We preferred the company of whites when we should have despised it. Once, while eating in a white restaurant, the waiter asked where we were headed. We mentioned a certain park we'd heard was nice. "Oh, *don't* go there," he warned us. "It's overrun by blacks." We did not go.

The friendliest white person we met there wasn't from there at all. He was from Tyler, Texas, on safari with his family. He approached us while we were on a game reserve watching a giraffe nibble tree leaves. "I know Americans when I see them!" he boomed, grinning, vigorously shaking my hand. "The minute I saw y'all, said to my wife, 'I bet you they're Americans!'" Southern drawls had always raised the hair on my neck and arms, but his was as comforting as a favorite song. I wanted nothing more, at that moment, than to board the nearest U.S.-bound plane.

For six weeks, while Brenda studied in the National Archives, we learned the rules of this new race game, and we played it as best we could. But those were city rules. The rules in the *Matebeland* countryside, where we went when Brenda was ready to leave the city, were different. To many of the people living in thatched, clay homes, whose annual income was less than five dollars, we were *amakiwa*, white people, people whose likely purpose for being there was to make their fortunes rise or fall. This knowledge made me uneasy, because I knew, on some level, their kindness was based on fear or desire. And it also made me thankful, because whatever it was we inspired, it got us what we wanted. No one refused an interview. We took pictures at will.

One day while we were taking pictures, a young boy sprinted over to us and began speaking hurriedly in *isiNdebele* to our translator. After he finished, our translator said, "We are wanted by the headman. Over there." He pointed towards a gazebo-like structure a hundred yards away. We could not see anyone from our distance, but when we arrived, we found four men inside, sitting on straw mats and playing *mancala,* a popular game made of carved wood and plant seeds. The men continued to play with intense purpose, as if something so costly were at stake they could not pause to acknowledge our arrival. Our translator sat along the base of the wall and watched quietly. Brenda and I followed his lead.

One of the men made a move that ended the game. As the good-natured banter that followed tapered off, the man who had won said something to our translator. When the response included the word "Americans," the man's eyes sparkled. "Welcome!" he said, speaking to me but not Brenda, as rural men often did. "I am Msizi Nkosi, the headman of this village." I had not expected him to speak English. He seemed proud of this fact, and after his greeting—and after every question he subsequently asked—he offered his comrades a quick wink.

Most of what he wanted to know was aimed at confirming or dispelling rumors about American culture, things about gangsters, Madonna, and sports. "This Michael Jordan is better than all the others," he said. "You see, he is like me playing *mancala* with these men here." He laughed heartily before his face settled on the wry smile that never left, even when his questions took a twisted turn. "Tell me, my friend. Are you happy that your ancestors were taken to be slaves to America?"

"Of *course* not," I said.

"Ah, but I wish *my* ancestors were made slaves there," he said. "Because then I would be living the good life, like you."

I had heard variations of this reasoning before, the notion that blacks should view their history through the lens of capitalism, a lens that often values means less than ends, humanity less than goods. What about the brutality the slaves endured? The suffering? The rapes and murders? I tried to make this point but the headman was having none of it. "Ah, but you must not dwell on these things," he countered. "You are in America, so just be happy. Or would you rather be here, losing games of *mancala* to me?" I did not respond. He winked at the other men. I looked towards our translator, lifting and lowering my eyebrows, trying to communicate nonverbally that we should go. When I caught his attention, he nodded, but I wasn't sure if it was to say, "Yes, let's get away from this crazy person," or "Yes, you are in America, so just be happy."

"Tell me," the headman continued. "Why do you people call yourselves *African* Americans?"

I considered explaining that it was a way to offer a sense of belonging to a displaced people, but my heart wasn't in the argument, so I said nothing.

"You are *not* Africans," he said. His smile remained, but his voice had a sharp edge to it now. "Do you know that you *insult* Africans when you say that you are one of us?" I still did not respond.

But I did wonder, during our ride back into town, what the headman's definition of an African was. I wondered how he viewed his white countrymen, people whose ancestors arrived from England two centuries prior and had taken over the land. Maybe he didn't see them as Africans either. Or maybe they were the *only* Africans, while the blacks were something else, *something more*—perhaps that was what was being conveyed by the phrase "indigenous peoples" that Brenda and I had heard frequently since our arrival. I wondered, too, what the headman would have thought of Farai, a black native who had made a fortune in banking, now owned a taxi service and rental properties, and lived in a house that could have passed for a small Marriott. What would the headman have thought of her Olympic-sized pool, her tennis court, the crystal chandeliers and marble floors and ceilings made of inlaid cedar? What would he have thought watching her field servants toil all day in rows of maize and potatoes, or watching her house servants cooking, cleaning, babysitting, and laundering until they collapsed in the shacks behind the house that had neither electricity nor running water?

And what, I wondered, would the headman have thought of "African night"?

"*What* night?" Brenda had said at its first mention. We had been in the country for about ten days then.

"African night," Farai said. "I have invited some of my friends to join us for a girl's night out, and we have decided to call it *African* night." This, she explained while giggling, would entail wearing traditional African clothes. Farai did not own any of these clothes, nor did any of her friends; they had to go to the mall to purchase them explicitly for this occasion. It was the same mall to which they'd return for dinner, where there was a restaurant popular among tourists because it served *mopane,* a local delicacy of deep-fried caterpillars. When the plates of *mopane* arrived, the women shrieked and gasped and refused to eat them. And then they went back to their vodka martinis while the cook prepared their new orders of apricot-glazed chicken with peaches and raisins.

I'd thought of my sister Linda, and all the other people I knew who regularly wore African garments, and here were these genuine Africans, these indigenous peoples, wearing the clothing as if for Halloween or a masquerade. Brenda and I had found the irony of all this hilarious. When she'd returned from the restaurant, her head and body still adorned in yards of colorful patterned cotton, we'd stayed up late into the night laughing until our eyes watered, because so many things were still funny then. But not much was funny anymore. Just confusing. The only thing that was clear was that, whatever the definition of an African was, it did not apply to me. Neither did the words "colored" or *amakiwa*. I was black, plain and simple, and in the days leading up to our departure, I looked forward to reclaiming this identity because, before I actually boarded the plane, I still thought I could.

But the truth hit me during the flight, bringing with it that sickening feeling I sometimes get while driving to a new destination when I suddenly realize that I am lost. Occasionally the source of the error can be traced to someone's faulty directions, though usually the mistake is mine for not paying attention. I prefer when it's the former so I can dole out rather than accept the blame. Now, cruising at thirty thousand feet, I considered the directions I had been given regarding race, which made no mention of how unfixed it is, how fluid, how utterly *unscientific* the process by which we assign and accept racial labels. *Who*, I wondered, could I blame for this?

When I reached a few tentative conclusions, I shook Brenda's shoulder, waking her. She turned to face me—wide-eyed, I could see from the dim light of the cabin—and asked me what was wrong.

"My parents," I said, "messed me up."

After a brief pause, just long enough for the pupils of her widened eyes to roll, she mumbled, "How *this* time?"

"I'm not entirely sure."

"Well, when you are entirely sure, let me know." She turned away, burrowing her head back into the pillow she'd propped between her shoulder and the window.

"*You* messed me up too," I added, but I'd whispered it so she could not hear, since I wasn't entirely sure how she had done so either. But I suspected it was related to a story she'd once told me about a boy named Billy. When she met him, she was six years old, living in the suburbs of Chicago and attending a mostly white school. Besides her, Billy was the only other black student. When some of the other children refused to play with him because of his race, Brenda refused too, banding with the white kids who had accepted her as one of their own. That night at dinner, she told her parents, "We didn't play with Billy today because he's black," thereby triggering an enlightening discussion about race in general, her African father in particular, and her own fifty percent blackness.

I remembered this story making me sad—not for Brenda; she was fine, even playing with Billy the next day and persuading her friends to do the same—but because my parents had never had such a discussion with my siblings and me. There was never a moment when they told us we were black, or that they were, or what that designation meant for any of us. Race, in fact, was rarely discussed in the household of my youth. It was only while in the company of friends and relatives that I overheard grown-ups pontificate on racial matters, often concluding their observations with a shake of the head and the phrase, "Black folks are *something else*."

When I was very young, I thought this was an unkind reference to the prostitutes and addicts who shared our housing project stairwell, but by the time I turned ten, in 1974, when a new positive racial awareness was at its height, I understood it to mean that blacks were beautiful. Blacks were cool. Blacks had style and nerve and they could dance, dribble balls, and sing. Being black also now meant being African, a descendant of kings and queens, and while we did not learn that from our parents either, many people we knew spoke of it in the same breath they said that whites were evil. A few altercations I subsequently had with white teens would reinforce this latter view; a few altercations with white police would confirm it.

But my exposure over time to a wider variety of people chipped away at all of these stereotypes; not many remained, I felt, by the time I turned twenty-five. By age thirty I was convinced they were completely gone, only to have them surface, one year later, in a country not my own, like a suddenly remembered dream. As soon as Brenda and I were told we were colored, I realized how many negative beliefs

I had internalized about white people, beliefs that were still very much with me, whether consciously or not. But if my race could change so easily without any fundamental change in me, then race had no meaning, other than the false or superficial ones assigned it. All human behavior associated with race was a myth, a lie. I have found nothing in life more unsettling, or more liberating, than that discovery.

Except for maybe this: I now understood that my parents knew all along what they were doing by not engaging us in discussions about race. They were trying to teach us, through their silence, that race was insignificant, that it shouldn't and ultimately didn't matter. They were trying to teach us to see character, not skin. These, I realized on that long flight home, were my parents' directions for how to be an American. And I had not paid attention.

ACTIVISM/POLITICAL THOUGHT

Jena, O.J. and the Jailing of Black America

Orlando Patterson

Cambridge, Mass.

The miscarriage of justice at Jena, La.—where five black high school students arrested for beating a white student were charged with attempted murder—and the resulting protest march tempts us to the view, expressed by several of the marchers, that not much has changed in traditional American racial relations. However, a remarkable series of high-profile incidents occurring elsewhere in the nation at about the same time, as well as the underlying reason for the demonstrations themselves, make it clear that the Jena case is hardly a throwback to the 1960s, but instead speaks to issues that are very much of our times.

What exactly attracted thousands of demonstrators to the small Louisiana town? While for some it was a simple case of righting a grievous local injustice, and for others an opportunity to relive the civil rights era, for most the real motive was a long overdue cry of outrage at the use of the prison system as a means of controlling young black men.

America has more than two million citizens behind bars, the highest absolute and per capita rate of incarceration in the world. Black Americans, a mere 13 percent of the population, constitute half of this country's prisoners. A tenth of all black men between ages 20 and 35 are in jail or prison; blacks are incarcerated at over eight times the white rate.

The effect on black communities is catastrophic: one in three male African-Americans in their 30s now has a prison record, as do nearly two-thirds of all black male high school dropouts. These numbers and rates are incomparably greater than anything achieved at the height of the Jim Crow era. What's odd is how long it has taken the African-American community to address in a forceful and thoughtful way this racially biased and utterly counterproductive situation.

How, after decades of undeniable racial progress, did we end up with this virtual gulag of racial incarceration?

Part of the answer is a law enforcement system that unfairly focuses on drug offenses and other crimes more likely to be committed by blacks, combined with draconian mandatory sentencing and an absurdly counterproductive retreat from rehabilitation as an integral method of dealing with offenders. An unrealistic fear of crime that is fed in part by politicians and the press, a tendency to emphasize punitive measures and old-fashioned racism are all at play here.

But there is another equally important cause: the simple fact that young black men commit a disproportionate number of crimes, especially violent crimes, which cannot be attributed to judicial bias, racism or economic hardships. The rate at which blacks commit homicides is seven times that of whites.

Why is this? Several incidents serendipitously occurring at around the same time as the march on Jena hint loudly at a possible answer.

In New York City, the tabloids published sensational details of the bias suit brought by a black former executive for the Knicks, Anucha Browne Sanders, who claims that she was frequently called a "bitch" and a "ho" by the Knicks coach and president, Isiah Thomas. In a video deposition, Thomas said that while it is always wrong for a white man to verbally abuse a black woman in such terms, it was "not as much . . . I'm sorry to say" for a black man to do so.

Across the nation, religious African-Americans were shocked that the evangelical minister Juanita Bynum, an enormously popular source of inspiration for churchgoing black women, said she was brutally beaten in a parking lot by her estranged husband, Bishop Thomas Weeks.

O.J. Simpson, the malevolent central player in an iconic moment in the nation's recent black-white (as well as male-female) relations, reappeared on the scene, charged with attempted burglary, kidnapping and felonious assault in Las Vegas, in what he claimed was merely an attempt to recover stolen memorabilia.

These events all point to something that has been swept under the rug for too long in black America: the crisis in relations between men and women of all classes and, as a result, the catastrophic state of black family life, especially among the poor. Isiah Thomas's outrageous double standard shocked many blacks in New York only because he had the nerve to say out loud what is a fact of life for too many black women who must daily confront indignity and abuse in hip-hop misogyny and everyday conversation.

What is done with words is merely the verbal end of a continuum of abuse that too often ends with beatings and spousal homicide. Black relationships and families fail at high rates because women increasingly refuse to put up with this abuse. The resulting absence of fathers—some 70 percent of black babies are born to single mothers—is undoubtedly a major cause of youth delinquency.

The circumstances that far too many African-Americans face—the lack of paternal support and discipline; the requirement that single mothers work regardless of the effect on their children's care; the hypocritical refusal of conservative politicians to put their money where their mouths are on family values; the recourse by male youths to gangs as parental substitutes; the ghetto-fabulous culture of the streets; the lack of skills among black men for the jobs and pay they want; the hypersegregation of blacks into impoverished inner-city neighborhoods—all interact perversely with the prison system that simply makes hardened criminals of nonviolent drug offenders and spits out angry men who are unemployable, unreformable and unmar-riageable, closing the vicious circle.

Jesse Jackson, Al Sharpton and other leaders of the Jena demon-stration who view events there, and the racial horror of our prisons, as solely the result of white racism are living not just in the past but in a state of denial. Even after removing racial bias in our judicial and prison system—as we should and must do—disproportionate num-bers of young black men will continue to be incarcerated.

Until we view this social calamity in its entirety—by also ac-knowledging the central role of unstable relations among the sexes and within poor families, by placing a far higher priority on moral and social reform within troubled black communities, and by greatly ex-panding social services for infants and children—it will persist.

One Nation . . . Under God?

DEMOCRACY DEMANDS THAT RELIGIOUS AMERICANS TRANSLATE THEIR CONCERNS INTO UNIVERSAL VALUES—AND THAT SECULARISTS MAKE ROOM FOR FAITH AND MORALITY.

Sen. Barack Obama

I'd like to look at the connection between religion and politics and offer some thoughts about how we can sort through some of the often-bitter arguments that we've been seeing over the last several years. We can raise up the religious call to address poverty and environmental stewardship all we want, but it won't have an impact unless we tackle head-on the mutual suspicion that sometimes exists between religious America and secular America—a debate we've been having in this country for the last 30 years over the role of religion in politics.

For some time now, there has been plenty of talk among pundits and pollsters that the political divide in this country has fallen sharply

"One Nation . . . Under God?" by Barack Obama. This excerpt was first published in *Soujourners Magazine*, November 2006. Barack Obama, a U.S. senator from Illinois, delivered the speech from which it was adapted at the *Sojourners*/Call to Renewal–sponsored Pentecost conference in June 2006. The whole transcript can be found at www.sojo.net/obama. This article is reprinted with permission from Sojourners, (800) 714-7474, www.sojo.net.

along religious lines. Indeed, the single biggest "gap" in party affilia-
tion among white Americans today is not between men and women, or
those who reside in so-called Red States and those who reside in Blue,
but between those who attend church regularly and those who don't.
Conservative leaders have been all too happy to exploit this gap, consistently reminding evangelical Christians that Democrats disrespect
their values and dislike their church, while suggesting to the rest of the
country that religious Americans care only about the issues of abortion and gay marriage, school prayer and intelligent design.

Democrats, for the most part, have taken the bait. At best, we may
try to avoid the conversation about religious values altogether, fearful
of offending anyone and claiming that—regardless of our personal
beliefs—constitutional principles tie our hands. At worst, there are
some liberals who dismiss religion in the public square as inherently irrational or intolerant, insisting on a caricature of religious Americans
that paints them as fanatical, or thinking that the very word "Christian"
describes one's political opponents, not people of faith.

Such strategies of avoidance may work for progressives in some
circumstances. But over the long haul, I think we make a mistake when
we fail to acknowledge the power of faith in the lives of the American
people, and I think it's time that we join a serious debate about how to
reconcile faith with our modern, pluralistic democracy.

If we're going to do that then we first need to understand that
Americans are a religious people. Ninety percent of us believe in God,
70 percent affiliate themselves with an organized religion, 38 percent
call themselves committed Christians, and substantially more people
in America believe in angels than in evolution. This religious tendency
is not simply the result of successful marketing by skilled preachers or
the draw of popular mega-churches. In fact, it speaks to a hunger
that's deeper than that, a hunger that goes beyond any particular issue
or cause.

Each day, it seems, thousands of Americans are going about their
daily rounds—dropping off the kids at school, driving to the office,
shopping at the mall, trying to stay on their diets—and they're coming
to the realization that something is missing. They are deciding that
their work, their possessions, their diversions, their sheer busyness, is
not enough. They want a sense of purpose, a narrative arc to their

lives. They're looking to relieve a chronic loneliness, so they need an assurance that somebody out there cares about them, that they are not just destined to travel down that long highway toward nothingness.

———————

I speak with some experience on this matter. It wasn't until after college, when I went to Chicago to work as a community organizer for a group of Christian churches, that I confronted my own spiritual dilemma. I was working with churches, and the Christians who I worked with recognized themselves in me. They saw that I knew their Book and that I shared their values and sang their songs. But they sensed that a part of me remained removed, detached, that I was an observer in their midst. In time, I came to realize that something was missing as well—that without a vessel for my beliefs, without a commitment to a particular community of faith, at some level I would always remain apart and alone.

As the months passed in Chicago, I found myself drawn not just to work with the church, but to be in the church. For one thing, I believed and still believe in the power of the African-American religious tradition to spur social change. Because of its past, the black church understands in an intimate way the biblical call to feed the hungry and clothe the naked and challenge powers and principalities. In its historical struggles for freedom and human rights, I was able to see faith as more than just a comfort to the weary or a hedge against death, but rather as an active, palpable agent in the world, as a source of hope.

Perhaps it was out of this intimate knowledge of hardship—the grounding of faith in struggle—that the church offered me a second insight. You need to come to church in the first place precisely because you are first of this world, not apart from it. You need to embrace Christ precisely because you have sins to wash away—because you are human and need an ally in this difficult journey.

It was because of these newfound understandings that I was finally able to walk down the aisle of Trinity United Church of Christ on the South Side of Chicago one day and affirm my Christian faith. It came about as a choice and not an epiphany. I didn't fall out in church. The questions I had didn't magically disappear. But kneeling beneath that cross on the South Side, I felt that I heard God's spirit beckoning me. I submitted myself to God's will and dedicated myself to discovering God's truth.

That's a path that has been shared by millions upon millions of Americans—evangelicals, Catholics, Protestants, Jews, and Muslims alike; some since birth, others at certain turning points in their lives. It is not something they set apart from the rest of their beliefs and values. In fact, it is often what drives their beliefs and their values.

That is why, if we truly hope to speak to people where they're at—to communicate our hopes and values in a way that's relevant to their own—then as progressives we cannot abandon the field of religious discourse. Because when we ignore the debate about what it means to be a good Christian or Muslim or Jew; when we discuss religion only in the negative sense of where or how it should not be practiced, rather than in the positive sense of what it tells us about our obligations towards one another; when we shy away from religious venues and religious broadcasts because we assume that we will be unwelcome—others will fill the vacuum, those with the most insular views of faith or those who cynically use religion to justify partisan ends.

In other words, if we don't reach out to evangelical Christians and other religious Americans and tell them what we stand for, then the Jerry Falwells and Pat Robertsons and Alan Keyeses will continue to hold sway.

More fundamentally, the discomfort of some progressives with any hint of religion has often prevented us from effectively addressing issues in moral terms. If we scrub language of all religious content, we forfeit the imagery and terminology through which millions of Americans understand both their personal morality and social justice. Imagine Lincoln's Second Inaugural Address without reference to "the judgments of the Lord," or King's "I Have a Dream" speech without references to "all of God's children." Their summoning of a higher truth helped inspire what had seemed impossible and move the nation to embrace a common destiny.

Our failure as progressives to tap into the moral underpinnings of the nation is not just rhetorical, though. Our fear of getting "preachy" may also lead us to discount the role that values and culture play in some of our most urgent social problems. After all, the problems of poverty, racism, the uninsured, and the unemployed are not simply technical problems in search of the perfect 10-point plan. They are rooted in both societal indifference and individual callousness—in the imperfections of humanity.

Solving these problems will require changes in government policy, but it will also require changes in hearts and a change in minds. I believe in keeping guns out of our inner cities, but I also believe that when a gang-banger shoots indiscriminately into a crowd because he feels somebody disrespected him, we've got a moral problem. There's a hole in that young man's heart—a hole that the government alone cannot fix.

I am not suggesting that every progressive suddenly latch on to religious terminology—that can be dangerous. Nothing is more transparent than inauthentic expressions of faith. Some politicians come and clap—off rhythm—to the choir. We don't need that. In fact, because I do not believe that religious people have a monopoly on morality, I would rather have someone who is grounded in morality and ethics, and who is also secular, affirm their morality and ethics and values without pretending that they're something they're not.

What I am suggesting is this: Secularists are wrong when they ask believers to leave their religion at the door before entering into the public square. Frederick Douglass, Abraham Lincoln, William Jennings Bryan, Dorothy Day, Martin Luther King—indeed, the majority of great reformers in American history—were not only motivated by faith but repeatedly used religious language to argue for their cause. To say that men and women should not inject their "personal morality" into public policy debates is a practical absurdity. Our law is by definition a codification of morality, much of it grounded in the Judeo-Christian tradition.

Moreover, if we progressives shed some of these biases, we might recognize some overlapping values that both religious and secular people share when it comes to the moral and material direction of our country. We might recognize that the call to sacrifice on behalf of the next generation, the need to think in terms of "thou" and not just "I," resonates in religious congregations all across the country. And we might realize that we have the ability to reach out to the evangelical community and engage millions of religious Americans in the larger project of American renewal.

Some of this is already beginning to happen. Pastors, friends of mine such as Rick Warren and T. D. Jakes, are wielding their enormous influence to confront AIDS, Third World debt relief, and the genocide in Darfur. Religious thinkers and activists such as our good friend Jim Wallis and Tony Campolo are lifting up the biblical injunction to help the poor as a means of mobilizing Christians against budget cuts to social programs and growing inequality. Across the country, individual churches are sponsoring day care programs, building senior centers, helping ex-offenders reclaim their lives, and rebuilding our gulf coast in the aftermath of Hurricane Katrina.

The question is, how do we build on these still-tentative partnerships between religious and secular people of good will? It's going to take a lot more work than we've done so far. The tensions and the suspicions on each side of the religious divide will have to be squarely addressed.

I also want to look at what conservative leaders need to do, some truths they need to acknowledge. For one, they need to understand the critical role that the separation of church and state has played in preserving not only our democracy but the robustness of our religious practice. Folks tend to forget that during our founding, it wasn't the atheists or the civil libertarians who were the most effective champions of the First Amendment. It was the forebears of the evangelicals who were the most adamant about not mingling government with religion, because they did not want state-sponsored religion hindering their ability to practice their faith as they understood it.

Moreover, given the increasing diversity of America's population, the dangers of sectarianism have never been greater. Whatever we once were, we are no longer just a Christian nation; we are also a Jewish nation, a Muslim nation, a Buddhist nation, a Hindu nation, and a nation of nonbelievers.

And even if we did have only Christians in our midst, if we expelled every non-Christian from the United States, whose Christianity would we teach in the schools? Would we go with James Dobson's or Al Sharpton's? Which passages of scripture should guide our public policy? Should we go with Leviticus, which suggests slavery is okay and that eating shellfish is abomination? How about Deuteronomy, which suggests stoning your child if he strays from the faith? Or should we just stick to the Sermon on the Mount—a passage that is so radical that it's doubtful that our own Defense Department would survive its application?

Democracy demands that the religiously motivated translate their concerns into universal, rather than religion-specific, values. It requires that their proposals be subject to argument and amenable to reason. I may be opposed to abortion for religious reasons, but if I seek to pass a law banning the practice, I cannot simply point to the teachings of my church or evoke God's will. I have to explain why abortion violates some principle that is accessible to people of all faiths, including those with no faith at all.

This is going to be difficult for some who believe in the inerrancy of the Bible, as many evangelicals do. But in a pluralistic democracy, we have no choice. Politics depends on our ability to persuade each other of common aims based on a common reality. It involves compromise, the art of what's possible. At some fundamental level, religion does not allow for compromise. It's the art of the impossible. If God has spoken, then followers are expected to live up to God's edicts, regardless of the consequences. To base one's life on such uncompromising commitments may be sublime, but to base our policy-making on such commitments would be a dangerous thing.

Finally, any reconciliation between faith and democratic pluralism requires some sense of proportion. But a sense of proportion should also guide those who police the boundaries between church and state. Not every mention of God in public is a breach to the wall of separation—context matters. It is doubtful that children reciting the Pledge of Allegiance feel oppressed or brainwashed as a consequence of muttering the phrase "under God." I didn't. Having voluntary student prayer groups use school property to meet should not be a threat, any more than its use by the High School Republicans should threaten Democrats.

We all have some work to do here. But I am hopeful that we can bridge the gaps that exist and overcome the prejudices each of us bring to this debate. I have faith that millions of believing Americans want that to happen. No matter how religious they may or may not be, people are tired of seeing faith used as a tool of attack. They don't want faith used to belittle or to divide. They're tired of hearing folks deliver more screed than sermon. Because in the end, that's not how they think about faith in their own lives.

Many Americans are looking for a deeper, fuller conversation about religion in this country. They may not change their positions, but they are willing to listen and learn from those who are willing to speak in fair-minded words, those who know of the central and awesome place that God holds in the lives of so many and who refuse to treat faith as simply another political issue with which to score points.

I have a hope for America that we can live with one another in a way that reconciles the beliefs of each with the good of all. It's a prayer worth praying and a conversation worth having in this country in the months and years to come.

Americans Without Americanness

IS OUR NATION NOTHING MORE THAN AN ADDRESS?

~✦~

John McWhorter

I will never forget a conversation I had with two twentysomething Muslims not long after 9/11. One had been born and raised in the United States, the other had come here at a young age. It was clear from our conversation, though they gingerly avoided putting it explicitly, that neither of them entirely disapproved of what Osama bin Laden had done. There were, of course, multiple recitations of "I think what he did was terrible"—but delivered with a certain lack of emotional commitment. What came through was a sentiment that, in the end, something terrible had been necessary for bin Laden to get across a valuable message. I did not find it hard to imagine that the two young Muslims would have been more explicit about this with each other had I not been present.

The late Arthur Schlesinger Jr. is reported to have said that he could not walk down Fifth Avenue without wondering what it and the people on it would have looked like a century before. I share that type of historical curiosity—and it occurs to me that this conversation with the Muslims would have been very unlikely before about 30 years ago. There was a time when immigrants, if residing in America permanently, unhesitatingly embraced becoming Americans. Any sentiment that, say, Pearl Harbor was "understandable" would have been kept very, very quiet.

These two Muslims, however, thought of America as an opportunity, but not as an identity. Orientations like theirs are, in today's America, perfectly normal—even among the unhyphenated, as I have learned in assorted conversations since 9/11. Among a vast proportion of Americans, one of the very defining traits of being an American is to lack pride in being one. One either has no conscious sense of American identity or, if one is given to lending the issue more attention, is ashamed of being American. To celebrate America, meanwhile, is considered naive and peculiar; one gets a pass by defining America as the sum of competing "diversities"—witness claims that Barack Obama represents "what America is"—which means that America is no one thing, and thus nothing, finally, but an address.

AT HOME IN AMERICA

One thing that an American sent back in time to 1907 would have to get used to is how much prouder the American identity was among people of all walks of life. The term *American* carried a warmth and a swagger. People often referred to English spoken in our country as "American," and were not always joking: H. L. Mencken titled his scholarly masterpiece *The American Language,* a highly unlikely title for a similar work today. The American Beauty Rose was named in 1875; today one imagines a new rose being given a name like Suri. The Gershwin brothers titled an early hit "The Real American Folk Song Is a Rag" in a spirit of jolly celebration. A series of revues called *Americana*—unironically—ran on Broadway starting in the late Twenties.

There was, to be sure, an element of parochialism in this apple-pie patriotism, and too often it shaded into an unreflective George M. Cohan–style jingoism. A century from now, though, what will appear equally unreflective is the opposite sentiment now held up as a sign of enlightenment: active contempt for the American experiment.

Nowhere is this contempt more explicit than among our intelligentsia. The humanities and social sciences enshrine the examination of power relations (or, more specifically, injustice) obsessively. The endless explorations of the *subordination* of the *subaltern,* and the possibilities of *contesting* and *transgression,* are a stark abbreviation of human curiosity. Legions of scholars nevertheless devote careers to this narrow conception of scholarship, out of a fundamental commitment to revealing our Powers That Be as frauds. There is little room for love of country in this view of the world.

Obviously, it is old news for intellectuals to be gadflies. In the 1922 anthology *Civilization in the United States,* editor Harold Stearns blasted "emotional and aesthetic starvation," "the mania for petty regulation," "the driving, regimentating, and drilling" of society. Strong drink, but these scholars were mostly opposed to how the lesser sides of human nature gum up the works in a country that could do better. One searches this book in vain for the kind of bone-deep, utterly dismissive contempt for all that America stands for that is now common coin in academia.

For example, a cherished observation on a certain circuit is that "America was founded upon racism from its very beginnings," which regularly cops vigorous applause from white as well as black audience members. There's some truth to this, to be sure—but in that we cannot change it, the charge implies that it would have been better if Jamestown and Plymouth had never been settled and Africans had remained in their villages. Patriotism, obviously, does not apply here.

Certainly one would not expect scholarly people to devote careers to mere celebration. But one might imagine them fashioning a nuanced but vigorous brand of patriotism, calling America on its weaknesses with a basic pride in what we do right. A model would be typical intellectuals in France. Instead, we are taught that the enlightened orientation to our native land ought be more like the one that reigns in Germany, so deeply embarrassed about the Holocaust as to recoil at any prideful view of their *Vaterland.* The enlightened soul must therefore sneer at such notions as a U.S. policy titled *Homeland* Security.

The extreme nature of modern leftist academics' writings suggests that empirical engagement with reality is not the driving force in such ideology. For example, most of this work, while presented as advocacy for the downtrodden, reveals a curious lack of genuine commitment to change. The tacit assumption is that nothing could make America a

worthy project short of a seismic transformation in its operating pro-
cedures and in the fundamental psychologies of its inhabitants. No
reasonable person could have any hope that this could actually happen, and this can only mean that people who think this way maintain
their opinions for reasons other than practical ones.

Those reasons are emotional rather than political—a desire to
wear alienation from the Establishment as a badge of insight and so-
phistication. It reaffirms that the wearers are good people, good in a
way unavailable to those less learned and aware. This cynicism is cal-
isthenic: It benefits its bearer rather than the people it purports to be
concerned about. It is something I have elsewhere termed *therapeutic
alienation*.

Therapeutic alienation is not, however, confined to the ivory
tower. Beyond the campus, explicit, acrid contempt for the
Establishment is a fringe taste—but the therapeutic alienation at the
roots of this contempt is now widespread, and has equally dire consequences for proud American identity. Existential alienation and oppositional sentiment for their own sake have a way of discouraging
people from saluting a flag.

CHAFING AGAINST "THE MAN"

In 1964, 76 percent of Americans reported trust in the government; by
2000—long before the Iraq War—only 44 percent, fewer than half,
did. The dishonesty of the Johnson and Nixon administrations about
the Vietnam War and the awakening of the country to the unjust treatment of blacks sparked this change. But that was a long time ago, and
alienation has come to reign even among people too young to recall
that era. The alienation has raged unchecked even as blacks have become steadily more central to even the highest realms of American
life, and even under a Clinton administration that liberals did not consider arrantly mendacious about policy. It is no longer a response, but
a self-standing gesture. Initiated by an external stimulus, this alienated
posture has settled in as what one is born to and inhales as a norm, one
readily embraced because of its self-congratulatory appeal.

An example is the howling antiestablishment despair typical of
heavy-metal music, embraced even by the mild-mannered as "cool."
Similar is the "gangsta" strain of hip-hop, full of excoriations of the
police and celebrations of black people as "niggers" engaged in eter-

nal battle against a racist AmeriKKKa, now a staff of life among legions of blacks under 50 and supported by a 70 percent white buyer-
ship. The modern American, having never known a time when music
like this was not a norm, is given to assuming that it is, in the first
case, a natural reflection of the rebelliousness inherent to youth, and,
in the second, the inevitable reaction of blacks who have suffered the
abuse of racism. Yet hungry Okie migrants knew no such music, nor
did the black sharecroppers watching lynchings year by year. No, music like this is the product of an attitudinal tic specific to our times.

Therapeutic alienation sends ripples throughout the culture. The
late comedian Sam Kinison built a career in the Eighties on delighting
audiences with tirades capped by open-throated screaming about The
Man. Barbie is now fighting for her life against Bratz dolls, provoca-
tively clad with smirky facial expressions hinting that they are not un-
familiar with sex. This is alienation and oppositionalism as fetish,
posture, performance.

Alienation as performance, to be sure, began the first time an early
Homo sapiens child had a tantrum. But under ordinary conditions of
human society, this behavior, while more typical of some individuals
than others, does not become a zeitgeist. It is treated as an emotional
indulgence that real-life exigencies must keep in check. Societies living
on the land, ever in fear that weather or warfare will leave them in danger of starvation, do not know of alienation as sport. Modern
America, however, is a wealthy society where few are hungry, and
where there has not been a war on our own soil in 150 years (and not
one that all able-bodied men were required to participate in in 40
years). Under these conditions, the tantrum no longer constitutes a
threat to survival. Enter, then, alienation embraced as a cathartic pose.
It is no accident that America saw a preview of the same in the prosperous Twenties, when the Smart Set went about with their copies of
the studiously cynical *American Mercury,* whose editor, Mencken, was
devoted more to the rhetorical sonority of trashing the powers that be
than fashioning a coherent political alternative.

THE ALIENATED MINORITY
The reign of therapeutic alienation has also upended black America's
orientation to being American. A time traveler to 1907 would find
peculiar how openly the black people, just a decade past *Plessy* v.

Ferguson, were striving toward being "American." At all-black Dunbar High School in Washington, D.C., students were learning Latin. W.E.B. DuBois taught Greek, and those who cherish his Marxist tilt later in life are often unaware that he could have conversed with Marx in German.

In their smash-hit musical *Shuffle Along* (1921), Eubie Blake and Noble Sissle included a ballad with language straight out of the operettas popular at the time: "Love will find a way / though now skies are gray / Love like ours can never be ruled / Cupid's not schooled that way." A photograph of black women protesting lynching in front of the White House in the Thirties includes a placard reading "Kentucky women demand justice for all American citizens"—as opposed to the more likely version in our own times, which would demand justice for "Black People."

Since the Sixties, black Americans are much more concerned with maintaining a "black identity"—a term unknown to Victorian-era DuBois—than with being "American." Many would claim that this is because being black in America is to experience an ongoing assault from racist actions. But striving for Americanness was typical among a great many blacks in an era starkly racist to a degree we are blissfully past, when, as Richard Wright once put it, successful blacks were rare "single fishes that leap and flash for a split second above the surface of the sea," "fleeting exceptions to that vast, tragic school that swims below in the depths."

Of course, quite a few blacks and white fellow-travelers insist that little has changed since Wright wrote; they willfully neglect the fact that today there are more middle-class blacks than poor ones. Ideology also trumps empiricism in the insistences that (a) it's school underfunding that keeps black grades and test scores down (when many black students are amply documented as thinking of doing well in school as a "white" characteristic) and (b) the reason black men are overrepresented in the prison population must be "the prison-industrial complex" (when black men also commit violent crimes in vast disproportion to their percentage of the population). .

The dogged insistence on chronicling "racism"—when the larger problem today is so clearly cultural, and *not* caused by racism—only makes sense as another manifestation of therapeutic alienation. Again, improved prospects ironically pave the way for staged grievance. When barriers to black advancement were concrete and pitiless, there was no room for poses about an all-too-real injustice. Only now can such routines thrive, lending passing pleasure to a people otherwise rising by the year. The result is that amidst musings on what black identity should be, Africa plays a large part while being "American" is considered beside the point—even though America is the only homeland black Americans have known for centuries, or ever will.

ROOTS OF DISASTER

There certainly exist people in the United States who have a self-conscious and positive sense of their identity as Americans. They are more likely to be military than civilian, conservative rather than liberal, working-class rather than upper-middle. They are on the defensive, regularly dismissed as maudlin and uninformed.

Could there ever again be in the U.S. a widespread sense of pride in a single culture, as has been typical of Greece, China, Thailand, or most other nations in human history? Sadly, I can think of nothing that could create such an America other than a sustained violent attack upon our country. Apparently, the single one that already happened has left the self-medicating oppositional impulse intact. Leftist intellectuals like Noam Chomsky and Susan Sontag were fashioning 9/11 as our just deserts for imperialism even while Ground Zero was still aglow. Chomsky's pamphlet on the issue sold like hotcakes. Good-thinking people have been taught to view al-Qaeda as freedom fighters sticking a thumb in our eye for our government's support of Israel.

Yet if we suffered a string of brutal nuclear bombings of several American cities à la television's *24*, in which it became a typical American experience to lose a relative or friend in carnage wrought by fundamentalist Arabs reviling America as the Great Satan, we would suddenly be back to the old days. Tragic, mercilessly concrete reality—maimed corpses, attending funerals as a monthly ritual—would make self-medicating iPod theatrics seem instantly trivial. The urgency of defending the life we know, American life, against murderous barbarians would instantly wake us up to the value of what America, its flaws acknowledged, is, and what it has achieved.

I regret to say that short of that, to be American will continue to be, for most who bother to think about it, what one might term a postmodern position: nurturing a sense of personal legitimacy upon a willful, bitter ambivalence toward a land one has no intention of leaving.

BARACK OBAMA

Michael Eric Dyson

Ever since he thundered into our collective consciousness with an electrifying speech before the 2004 Democratic National Convention, Barack Obama has breathed new life into American politics. He has revived the hope of millions that their elected leaders would dare to dream outside the rigid categories and earthbound aspirations that hold too many politicians captive. Though his written word sings and his spoken word soars on the wings of renewed faith in the democratic process—and how we need such renewal in an ugly age of despotic indifference to freedom's true creed—Obama's eyes are fixed on what we can make together of our national future.

For a clue to what makes Obama stick and tick, one need look no further than his training in the trenches of community organizing. As Ronald Reagan practiced what Vice President George Bush would call "voodoo economics"—supply-side theories wrapped in tax cuts for the wealthy—Obama exited the Ivy League corridors of Columbia University in 1983 and, after a brief and unsatisfying stint on Wall Street, headed straight for the 'hood. On the South Side of Chicago, he worked with a church-based group that sought to speak to poverty by understanding the language of its painful expression in crime and high unemployment. Obama rolled up his sleeves—something he was used to in satisfying his basketball jones on the courts of many a concrete jungle—and applied elbow grease and hard thinking to the persistent ills and unjust plight of the poor. Such practical training in relieving the burdens of the beleaguered will stand him in good stead as leader of the free world—as the poignant memory of the most afflicted replays in his mind.

Young Obama soon learned the limits of local remedies, however, and imagined how law and politics might help him positively change the lives of the vulnerable at the national level. While Reagan spread skepticism about government as a political mantra, Obama's hopeful—but far from naïve—belief in the political process sent him to Harvard Law School in the late '80s, with a round-trip ticket back to Chicago, where he served as an Illinois State Senator for eight years before entering the U.S. Senate in 2004.

If Obama's community organizing and work in the Illinois Senate—especially his bipartisan efforts to earn families across the state more than $100 million in tax cuts, his advocacy of legislation in support of early childhood education and his opposition to racial profiling—offer a glimpse into his political pedigree, so does his stay in the U.S. Senate. Obama has fought for disability pay for veterans, worked to boost the nonproliferation of deadly weapons and advocated the use of alternative fuels to cure our national addiction to oil. He has spoken out against the vicious indifference of the Bush Administration to the poor—and to political competence—in the aftermath of Hurricane Katrina, and he has rallied against genocide in Darfur. Long before it was popular, he stood against the war in Iraq as a futile gesture of American empire that would do little to beat back the threat of terror. Sadly, he has been proved prophetic.

If Obama's credentials for the highest office in the land have been gained in the give-and-take of community organizing and power politics, his belief in the American people—a reflection, in part, of the profound belief they have invested in him—derives from his molding in the crucible of various cultures, colors and communities. Obama's multiracial roots and multicultural experiences are not a liability; instead, they offer him an edge in the national effort to overcome the poisonous divisions that plague the American soul. His fascinating mix of race and culture shows up in lively fashion—including his love for the upper reaches of Abraham Lincoln's emancipating political vision, as well as his compassion for the black boys and girls stuck on the lowest rung of the ladder of upward mobility. That he is aware of race without being its prisoner—that he is rooted in, but not restricted by, his blackness—challenges orthodoxies and playbooks on all sides of the racial divide and debate. But it also makes him curiously effective in the necessary pledge to overcome our racial malaise by working to deny it the upper hand in restoring our national kinship.

Barack Obama has come closer than any figure in recent history to obeying a direct call of the people to the brutal and bloody fields of political mission. His visionary response to that call gives great hope that he can galvanize our nation with the payoff of his political rhetoric: a substantive embrace of true democracy fed by justice—one that balances liberty with responsibility. It is ultimately the hard political lessons he has learned, and the edifying wisdom he has earned—and is willing to share—that make Obama an authentic American. He is our best hope to tie together the fraying strands of our political will into a powerful and productive vision of national destiny.

Standing Up for "Bad" Words

Stephane Dunn

It took me five years to finally tell my conservative religious mother and my pastor stepfather the title of my book, which at that time was *"Baad Bitches" & Sassy Supermamas: Race, Gender, & Sexuality in Black Power Action Fantasies.* I figured it was unfair to wait until I sent it to her in the mail or she strolled past it in Barnes & Noble, or, even worse, some concerned church folk called her on the phone about it. Now, my mother was a woman once known to backhand-slap bad words and cussin' right out of your mouth. So I sat across from them at the dining-room table, giggling nervously, and hurriedly blurted out the first two words of the title. Mama looked at me, her left eyebrow raised way too high. My stepfather looked at her, then glanced at me and took over the nervous grinning.

I rambled on some more about how it was a study about race and gender, underlining women's representations in some 70s action movies associated with the blaxploitation genre. ("Blaxploitation" was a controversial label for these movies aimed at black audiences; the genre emerged after the commercial success of *Sweet Sweetback's Baadasssss Song* in 1971.) Mama rescued me: "Well, they used that word all the time in them movies. Mmmmph, guess we won't be taking it to church. We'll just say the second part and people can look it up."

My mother loved the actress Pam Grier back in the day, when *Coffy* and *Foxy Brown* came out, but she found them disturbing for the same reasons that I did. I exhaled.

A year later, I received a seemingly innocuous e-mail message from my editor with a line about possibly shortening the book's title. The press was squeamish about the B-word in the wake of the Don Imus scandal last spring, when Imus called the Rutgers University women's basketball team "nappy-headed hos." What were my thoughts? I sent a reply, trying to explain why the title fit. But I was so pleased that my book was finally on its way to publication that I suggested a compromise: What about bleeping the letters following an uppercase B and substituting asterisks or dashes, as is often done with words deemed profane? I didn't even like my own suggestion. Until then there'd never been a hint of distaste for the title from the press or readers; I'd heard only how much people liked saying, "How's the 'baad bitches' project going?"

Imus's careless and racist, and sexist, reference to Rutgers' black basketball players infuriated me; it was personal and political. The controversy turned up the heat about the use of racialized words. I was surprised, though, to find myself debating my book's title with my publisher. I've always loved those 70s films, which have become so much a part of our cultural fabric, and been fascinated with their problematic portrayals of women and with the connections between the hip-hop and blaxploitation subcultures, particularly in how they use the word "bitch." While the word "bitch"—and its variants—has long been a derogatory reference to "difficult" women and femininity generally, it has been flipped and claimed by women to signify female empowerment and to celebrate tough women who don't accept subordinate positions easily.

Films like *Cleopatra Jones* and *Foxy Brown* came out in an era of rising black and second-wave feminism, which produced manifestoes like Jo Freeman's "The BITCH Manifesto" (1968) in praise of just such a model of womanhood. This was also an era in which "nigger" became a politicized term in black poetry, sometimes used to call out black folk who were, in the words of the Last Poets—a group of radical black artists that formed in 1968—too "scared of revolution." The term "bad nigger" signified a strong black man—portrayed by black male action heroes in blaxploitation movies—who did not accept racial subordination. Hence that last line emblazoned across the screen in *Sweet Sweetback's Baadasssss Song*: "WATCH OUT—A BAADASSSSS NIGGER'S COMING BACK TO COLLECT SOME DUES!"

My book title was not born out of any attempt to be racy. Rather, I wanted to signal the problems as well as the sassiness of a group of films that offered the first and only "bad" black female action heroes in a genre in which women were called, and primarily thought of, as "bitches" with a small "b." These primarily male-oriented movies represented both conservative and radical perspectives. On the one hand, they upset notions of black disempowerment and the racial status quo, but on the other, they often portrayed very disturbing, traditional representations of patriarchal power. Thus, while Foxy Brown got to kick butt, she was also subject to racist and sexist abuse.

Another e-mail message came from my supportive editor. Some folks at the press were still squeamish. They offered a few lifeless alternatives, none of which came close to signifying my intent and the book's content. I fired off a second response, which essentially was a manifesto.

I criticized Imus for personifying the cultural disrespect for black women. I have been just as concerned about the uncritical use of words like "bitch" and "nigga" within hip-hop, a music culture I love and that defined my adolescence. However, I do not promote the wholesale banning or erasure of "bad" words without consideration of their context. When I began writing my book in 2002, I did not know that the clamor over words like "bitch" and "ho" would grow so loud as an extension of the rap-music and N-word debate. (In fact, the B-word is frequently slung around on mainstream television sitcoms, dramas, and soap operas, without any apparent controversy.)

I was concerned about the move to ban the N-word before my book title became an issue, and not because I use the word freely in personal or professional speech or because I don't grasp the problems and limitations of trying to reinterpret, rename, and reclaim words that have traditionally demeaned a people's identity. Extreme, reactionary responses to historically "bad" words are not the answer. Context matters; how is the historian, artist, conscious consumer, scholar, or activist to engage reality without being able to use the words that reveal history and contemporary culture? How are those who teach and write about, say, Mark Twain's *Adventures of Huckleberry Finn* or Dick Gregory's *Nigger* to do so without fearlessly engaging that N-word? Of course, we absolutely should investigate why and how we use words that are racist or sexist. But we need to engage in critical dialogue about such words to increase our understanding of their historical or contemporary usage, not merely condemn or censor them, or attempt to erase them.

Fighting for my book title was useful. I should be discomforted by the problematic racial and patriarchal connotations of the word "bitch" and question the contexts in which I use it. My book emerged from my own conflict between loving a particular film culture on the one hand and, on the other, being disturbed by the sexual and racial politics of that culture. I tried to keep it as real as I knew how. Luckily, my press came around: I now believe the editors were just trying to be sensitive. I don't mind the shortened version of my book title, but I would have minded a lite version. It's definitely personal, and absolutely political.

Debunking "Driving While Black" Myth

~✦~

Thomas Sowell

Twice within the past few years, I have been pulled over by the police for driving at night without my headlights on. My car is supposed to turn on the headlights automatically when the light outside is below a certain level, but sometimes I accidentally brush against the controls and inadvertently switch them to manual.

Both times I thanked the policeman because he may well have saved my life. Neither time did I get a ticket or even a warning. In each case, the policeman was white.

Recently a well-known black journalist told me of a very different experience. He happened to be riding along in a police car driven by a white policeman. Ahead of them was a car driving at night with no headlights on, and in the dark, it was impossible to see who was driving it.

When the policeman pulled the car over, a black driver got out and, when the policeman told him that he was driving without his lights on, the driver said, "You only pulled me over because I am black!"

Reprinted by permission of Thomas Sowell and Creators Syndicate, Inc.

This was said even though he saw the black man who was with the policeman. The driver got a ticket.

Later, when the journalist asked the cop how often he got such responses from black drivers, the reply was "About 80% of the time."

When the same journalist asked the same question of black cops, the answer was about 30% of the time—lower, but still an amazing percentage under the circumstances.

Various black "leaders" and supposed friends of blacks have in recent years been pushing the idea that "driving while black" is enough to get the cops to pull you over for "one flimsy reason or another."

Heather MacDonald of the Manhattan Institute wrote a book titled *Are Cops Racist?* that examined the empirical evidence behind similar claims. The evidence did not support the claims that had been widely publicized in the media. But her study was largely ignored by the media. Maybe it would have spoiled their stories.

Even before reading MacDonald's book, I found it hard to accept the sweeping claims about the dangers of "driving while black."

Looking back over a long life, I could think of a number of times that I had been pulled over by the police in a number of states, without any of the things happening that are supposed to happen when you are "driving while black." Nor could I recall any member of my family who had told me of any such experiences with the police. It was hard to believe that we had all just led charmed lives all these years.

Only about half the times that I was pulled over did I end up being given a ticket. Once a policeman who pulled me over and asked for my driver's license said wearily, "Mr. Sowell, would you mind paying some attention to these stop signs, so that I don't have to write you a ticket?"

Recently, I pulled off to the side of a highway to take a picture of the beautiful bay below, in Pacifica, Calif. After I had finished and was starting to pack up my equipment, a police car pulled off to the side of the highway behind me.

"What's going on here?" the policeman asked.

"Photography," I said.

"You are not allowed to park here," he said. "It's dangerous."

"All right," I said. "I am packing to leave right now."

"Incidentally," he said as he turned to get back in his car, "you can get a better view of the bay from up on Roberts Road."

I then drove up on Roberts Road and, sure enough, got a better view of the bay. And I didn't get a ticket or a warning.

In a world where young blacks are bombarded with claims that they are being unfairly targeted by police and where a general attitude of belligerence is being promoted literally in word and song, it is hard not to wonder whether some people's responses to policemen do not have something to do with the policemen's responses to them.

Neither the police nor people in any other occupation always do what is right but automatic belligerence is not the answer.

GOODBYE TO ALL THAT: WHY OBAMA MATTERS

~%%◎

Andrew Sullivan

The logic behind the candidacy of Barack Obama is not, in the end, about Barack Obama. It has little to do with his policy proposals, which are very close to his Democratic rivals' and which, with a few exceptions, exist firmly within the conventions of our politics. It has little to do with Obama's considerable skills as a conciliator, legislator, or even thinker. It has even less to do with his ideological pedigree or legal background or rhetorical skills. Yes, as the many profiles prove, he has considerable intelligence and not a little guile. But so do others, not least his formidably polished and practiced opponent Senator Hillary Clinton.

Obama, moreover, is no saint. He has flaws and tics: Often tired, sometimes crabby, intermittently solipsistic, he's a surprisingly uneven campaigner.

A soaring rhetorical flourish one day is undercut by a lackluster debate performance the next. He is certainly not without self-regard. He has more experience in public life than his opponents want to acknowledge, but he has not spent much time in Washington and has never run a business. His lean physique, close-cropped hair, and stick-out ears can give the impression of a slightly pushy undergraduate. You can see why many of his friends and admirers have urged him to wait his turn. He could be president in five or nine years' time—why the rush?

But he knows, and privately acknowledges, that the fundamental point of his candidacy is that it is happening now. In politics, timing matters. And the most persuasive case for Obama has less to do with him than with the moment he is meeting. The moment has been a long time coming, and it is the result of a confluence of events, from one traumatizing war in Southeast Asia to another in the most fractious country in the Middle East. The legacy is a cultural climate that stultifies our politics and corrupts our discourse.

Obama's candidacy in this sense is a potentially transformational one. Unlike any of the other candidates, he could take America—finally—past the debilitating, self-perpetuating family quarrel of the Baby Boom generation that has long engulfed all of us. So much has happened in America in the past seven years, let alone the past 40, that we can be forgiven for focusing on the present and the immediate future. But it is only when you take several large steps back into the long past that the full logic of an Obama presidency stares directly—and uncomfortably—at you.

At its best, the Obama candidacy is about ending a war—not so much the war in Iraq, which now has a momentum that will propel the occupation into the next decade—but the war within America that has prevailed since Vietnam and that shows dangerous signs of intensifying, a nonviolent civil war that has crippled America at the very time the world needs it most. It is a war about war—and about culture and about religion and about race. And in that war, Obama—and Obama alone—offers the possibility of a truce.

The traces of our long journey to this juncture can be found all around us. Its most obvious manifestation is political rhetoric. The high temperature—Bill O'Reilly's nightly screeds against anti-Americans on one channel, Keith Olbermann's "Worst Person in the World" on the other; MoveOn.org's "General Betray Us" on the one side, Ann Coulter's *Treason* on the other; Michael Moore's accusation of treason at the core of the Iraq War, Sean Hannity's assertion of treason in the opposition to it—is particularly striking when you examine the generally minor policy choices on the table. Something deeper and more powerful than the actual decisions we face is driving the tone of the debate.

Take the biggest foreign-policy question—the war in Iraq. The rhetoric ranges from John McCain's "No Surrender" banner to the "End the War Now" absolutism of much of the Democratic base. Yet the substantive issue is almost comically removed from this hyperventilation. Every potential president, Republican or Democrat, would likely inherit more than 100,000 occupying troops in January 2009; every one would be attempting to redeploy them as prudently as possible and to build stronger alliances both in the region and in the world. Every major candidate, moreover, will pledge to use targeted military force against al-Qaeda if necessary; every one is committed to ensuring that Iran will not have a nuclear bomb; every one is committed to an open-ended deployment in Afghanistan and an unbending alliance with Israel. We are fighting over something, to be sure. But it is more a fight over how we define ourselves and over long-term goals than over what is practically to be done on the ground.

On domestic policy, the primary issue is health care. Again, the ferocious rhetoric belies the mundane reality. Between the boogeyman of "Big Government" and the alleged threat of the drug companies, the practical differences are more matters of nuance than ideology. Yes, there are policy disagreements, but in the wake of the Bush administration, they are underwhelming. Most Republicans support continuing the Medicare drug benefit for seniors, the largest expansion of the entitlement state since Lyndon Johnson, while Democrats are merely favoring more cost controls on drug and insurance companies. Between Mitt Romney's Massachusetts plan—individual mandates, private-sector leadership—and Senator Clinton's triangulated update of her 1994 debacle, the difference is more technical than fundamental. The country has moved ever so slightly leftward. But this again is less a function of ideological transformation than of the current system's failure to provide affordable health care for the insured or any care at all for growing numbers of the working poor.

Even on issues that are seen as integral to the polarization, the practical stakes in this election are minor. A large consensus in

America favors legal abortions during the first trimester and varying restrictions thereafter. Even in solidly red states, such as South Dakota, the support for total criminalization is weak. If *Roe* were to fall, the primary impact would be the end of a system more liberal than any in Europe in favor of one more in sync with the varied views that exist across this country. On marriage, the battles in the states are subsiding, as a bevy of blue states adopt either civil marriage or civil unions for gay couples, and the rest stand pat. Most states that want no recognition for same-sex couples have already made that decision, usually through state constitutional amendments that allow change only with extreme difficulty. And the one state where marriage equality exists, Massachusetts, has decided to maintain the reform indefinitely.

Given this quiet, evolving consensus on policy, how do we account for the bitter, brutal tone of American politics? The answer lies mainly with the biggest and most influential generation in America: the Baby Boomers. The divide is still—amazingly—between those who fought in Vietnam and those who didn't, and between those who fought and dissented and those who fought but never dissented at all. By defining the contours of the Boomer generation, it lasted decades. And with time came a strange intensity.

The professionalization of the battle, and the emergence of an array of well-funded interest groups dedicated to continuing it, can be traced most proximately to the bitter confirmation fights over Robert Bork and Clarence Thomas, in 1987 and 1991 respectively. The presidency of Bill Clinton, who was elected with only 43 percent of the vote in 1992, crystallized the new reality. As soon as the Baby Boomers hit the commanding heights, the Vietnam power struggle rebooted. The facts mattered little in the face of such a divide. While Clinton was substantively a moderate conservative in policy, his countercultural origins led to the drama, ultimately, of religious warfare and even impeachment. Clinton clearly tried to bridge the Boomer split. But he was trapped on one side of it—and his personal foibles only reignited his generation's agonies over sex and love and marriage. Even the failed impeachment didn't bring the two sides to their senses, and the election of 2000 only made matters worse: Gore and Bush were almost designed to reflect the Boomers' and the country's divide, which deepened further.

The trauma of 9/11 has tended to obscure the memory of that unprecedentedly bitter election, and its nail-biting aftermath, which verged on a constitutional crisis. But its legacy is very much still with us, made far worse by President Bush's approach to dealing with it. Despite losing the popular vote, Bush governed as if he had won Reagan's 49 states. Instead of cementing a coalition of the center-right, Bush and Rove set out to ensure that the new evangelical base of the Republicans would turn out more reliably in 2004. Instead of seeing the post-'60s divide as a wound to be healed, they poured acid on it.

With 9/11, Bush had a reset moment—a chance to reunite the country in a way that would marginalize the extreme haters on both sides and forge a national consensus. He chose not to do so. It wasn't entirely his fault. On the left, the truest believers were unprepared to give the president the benefit of any doubt in the wake of the 2000 election, and they even judged the 9/11 attacks to be a legitimate response to decades of U.S. foreign policy. Some could not support the war in Afghanistan, let alone the adventure in Iraq. As the Iraq War faltered, the polarization intensified. In 2004, the Vietnam argument returned with a new energy, with the Swift Boat attacks on John Kerry's Vietnam War record and CBS's misbegotten report on Bush's record in the Texas Air National Guard. These were the stories that touched the collective nerve of the political classes—because they parsed once again along the fault line of the Boomer divide that had come to define all of us.

The result was an even deeper schism. Kerry was arguably the worst candidate on earth to put to rest the post-1960s culture war—and his decision to embrace his Vietnam identity at the convention made things worse. Bush, for his part, was unable to do nuance. And so the campaign became a matter of symbolism—pitting those who took the terror threat "seriously" against those who didn't. Supporters of the Iraq War became more invested in asserting the morality of their cause than in examining the effectiveness of their tactics. Opponents of the war found themselves dispirited. Some were left to hope privately for American failure; others lashed out, as distrust turned to paranoia. It was and is a toxic cycle, in which the interests of the United States are supplanted by domestic agendas born of pride and ruthlessness on the one hand and bitterness and alienation on the other.

––––––––––

This is the critical context for the election of 2008. It is an election that holds the potential not merely to intensify this cycle of division but to bequeath it to a new generation, one marked by a new war that need not be—that should not be—seen as another Vietnam. A Giuliani-Clinton matchup, favored by the media elite, is a classic intragenerational struggle—with two deeply divisive and ruthless personalities ready to go to the brink. Giuliani represents that Nixonian disgust with anyone asking questions about, let alone actively protesting, a war. Clinton will always be, in the minds of so many, the young woman who gave the commencement address at Wellesley, who sat in on the Nixon implosion and who once disdained baking cookies. For some, her husband will always be the draft dodger who smoked pot and wouldn't admit it. And however hard she tries, there is nothing Hillary Clinton can do about it. She and Giuliani are conscripts in their generation's war. To their respective sides, they are war heroes.

In normal times, such division is not fatal, and can even be healthy. It's great copy for journalists. But we are not talking about routine rancor. And we are not talking about normal times. We are talking about a world in which Islamist terror, combined with increasingly available destructive technology, has already murdered thousands of Americans, and tens of thousands of Muslims, and could pose an existential danger to the West. The terrible failure of the Iraq occupation, the resurgence of al-Qaeda in Pakistan, the progress of Iran toward nuclear capability, and the collapse of America's prestige and moral reputation, especially among those millions of Muslims too young to have known any American president but Bush, heighten the stakes dramatically.

Perhaps the underlying risk is best illustrated by our asking what the popular response would be to another 9/11–style attack. It is hard to imagine a reprise of the sudden unity and solidarity in the days after 9/11, or an outpouring of support from allies and neighbors. It is far easier to imagine an even more bitter fight over who was responsible (apart from the perpetrators) and a profound suspicion of a government forced to impose more restrictions on travel, communications, and civil liberties. The current president would be unable to command the trust, let alone support, of half the country in such a time. He could even be blamed for provoking any attack that came.

Of the viable national candidates, only Obama and possibly McCain have the potential to bridge this widening partisan gulf. Polling reveals Obama to be the favored Democrat among Republicans. McCain's bipartisan appeal has receded in recent years, especially with his enthusiastic embrace of the latest phase of the Iraq War. And his personal history can only reinforce the Vietnam divide. But Obama's reach outside his own ranks remains striking. Why? It's a good question: How has a black, urban liberal gained far stronger support among Republicans than the made-over moderate Clinton or the southern charmer Edwards? Perhaps because the Republicans and independents who are open to an Obama candidacy see his primary advantage in prosecuting the war on Islamist terrorism. It isn't about his policies as such; it is about his person. They are prepared to set their own ideological preferences to one side in favor of what Obama offers America in a critical moment in our dealings with the rest of the world. The war today matters enormously. The war of the last generation? Not so much. If you are an American who yearns to finally get beyond the symbolic battles of the Boomer generation and face today's actual problems, Obama may be your man.

What does he offer? First and foremost: his face. Think of it as the most effective potential re-branding of the United States since Reagan. Such a re-branding is not trivial—it's central to an effective war strategy. The war on Islamist terror, after all, is two-pronged: a function of both hard power and soft power. We have seen the potential of hard power in removing the Taliban and Saddam Hussein. We have also seen its inherent weaknesses in Iraq, and its profound limitations in winning a long war against radical Islam. The next president has to create a sophisticated and supple blend of soft and hard power to isolate the enemy, to fight where necessary, but also to create an ideological template that works to the West's advantage over the long haul.

There is simply no other candidate with the potential of Obama to do this. Which is where his face comes in.

Consider this hypothetical. It's November 2008. A young Pakistani Muslim is watching television and sees that this man—Barack Hussein Obama—is the new face of America. In one simple image, America's soft power has been ratcheted up not a notch, but a logarithm. A brown-skinned man whose father was an African, who grew up in Indonesia and Hawaii, who attended a majority-Muslim school as a boy, is now the alleged enemy. If you wanted the crudest but most effective weapon against the demonization of America that fuels Islamist ideology, Obama's face gets close. It proves them wrong about what America is in ways no words can.

The other obvious advantage that Obama has in facing the world and our enemies is his record on the Iraq War. He is the only major candidate to have clearly opposed it from the start. Whoever is in office in January 2009 will be tasked with redeploying forces in and out of Iraq, negotiating with neighboring states, engaging America's estranged allies, tamping down regional violence. Obama's interlocutors in Iraq and the Middle East would know that he never had suspicious motives toward Iraq, has no interest in occupying it indefinitely, and foresaw more clearly than most Americans the baleful consequences of long-term occupation.

This latter point is the most salient. The act of picking the next president will be in some ways a statement of America's view of Iraq. Clinton is running as a centrist Democrat—voting for war, accepting the need for an occupation at least through her first term, while attempting to do triage as practically as possible. Obama is running as the clearer antiwar candidate. At the same time, Obama's candidacy cannot fairly be cast as a McGovernite revival in tone or substance. He is not opposed to war as such. He is not opposed to the use of unilateral force, either—as demonstrated by his willingness to target al-Qaeda in Pakistan over the objections of the Pakistani government. He does not oppose the idea of democratization in the Muslim world as a general principle or the concept of nation building as such. He is not an isolationist, as his support for the campaign in Afghanistan proves. It is worth recalling the key passages of the speech Obama gave in Chicago on October 2, 2002, five months before the war:

I don't oppose all wars. And I know that in this crowd today, there is no shortage of patriots, or of patriotism. What I am opposed to is a dumb war. What I am opposed to is a rash war . . . I know that even a successful war against Iraq will require a U.S. occupation of undetermined length, at undetermined cost, with undetermined consequences. I know that an invasion of Iraq without a clear rationale and without strong international support will only fan the flames of the Middle East, and encourage the worst, rather than best, impulses of the Arab world, and strengthen the recruitment arm of al-Qaeda. I am not opposed to all wars. I'm opposed to dumb wars.

The man who opposed the war for the right reasons is for that reason the potential president with the most flexibility in dealing with it. Clinton is hemmed in by her past and her generation. If she pulls out too quickly, she will fall prey to the usual browbeating from the right—the same theme that has played relentlessly since 1968. If she stays in too long, the antiwar base of her own party, already suspicious of her, will pounce. The Boomer legacy imprisons her—and so it may continue to imprison us. The debate about the war in the next four years needs to be about the practical and difficult choices ahead of us—not about the symbolism or whether it's a second Vietnam.

A generational divide also separates Clinton and Obama with respect to domestic politics. Clinton grew up saturated in the conflict that still defines American politics. As a liberal, she has spent years in a defensive crouch against triumphant post-Reagan conservatism. The mau-mauing that greeted her health-care plan and the endless nightmares of her husband's scandals drove her deeper into her political bunker. Her liberalism is warped by what you might call a Political Post-Traumatic Stress Syndrome. Reagan spooked people on the left, especially those, like Clinton, who were interested primarily in winning power. She has internalized what most Democrats of her generation have internalized: They suspect that the majority is not with them, and so some quotient of discretion, fear, or plain deception is required if they are to advance their objectives. And so the less-adept ones seem deceptive, and the more-practiced ones, like Clinton, exhibit the plastic-ness and inauthenticity that still plague her candidacy. She's hiding her true feelings. We know it, she knows we know it, and there is no way out of it.

Obama, simply by virtue of when he was born, is free of this defensiveness. Strictly speaking, he is at the tail end of the Boomer generation. But he is not of it.

"Partly because my mother, you know, was smack-dab in the middle of the Baby Boom generation," he told me. "She was only 18 when she had me. So when I think of Baby Boomers, I think of my mother's generation. And you know, I was too young for the formative period of the '60s—civil rights, sexual revolution, Vietnam War. Those all sort of passed me by."

Obama's mother was, in fact, born only five years earlier than Hillary Clinton. He did not politically come of age during the Vietnam era, and he is simply less afraid of the right wing than Clinton is, because he has emerged on the national stage during a period of conservative decadence and decline. And so, for example, he felt much freer than Clinton to say he was prepared to meet and hold talks with hostile world leaders in his first year in office. He has proposed sweeping middle-class tax cuts and opposed drastic reforms of Social Security, without being tarred as a fiscally reckless liberal. (Of course, such accusations are hard to make after the fiscal performance of today's "conservatives.") Even his more conservative positions—like his openness to bombing Pakistan, or his support for merit pay for public-school teachers—do not appear to emerge from a desire or need to credentialize himself with the right. He is among the first Democrats in a generation not to be afraid or ashamed of what they actually believe, which also gives them more freedom to move pragmatically to the right, if necessary. He does not smell, as Clinton does, of political fear.

There are few areas where this Democratic fear is more intense than religion. The crude exploitation of sectarian loyalty and religious zeal by Bush and Rove succeeded in deepening the culture war, to Republican advantage. Again, this played into the divide of the Boomer years—between God-fearing Americans and the peacenik atheist hippies of lore. The Democrats have responded by pretending to a public religiosity that still seems strained. Listening to Hillary Clinton detail her prayer life in public, as she did last spring to a packed house at George Washington University, was at once poignant and repellent. Poignant because her faith may well be genuine; repellent because its Methodist genuineness demands that she not profess it so tackily. But she did. The polls told her to.

Obama, in contrast, opened his soul up in public long before any focus group demanded it. His first book, *Dreams from My Father*, is a candid, haunting, and supple piece of writing. It was not concocted to solve a political problem (his second, hackneyed book, *The Audacity of Hope*, filled that niche). It was a genuine display of internal doubt and conflict and sadness. And it reveals Obama as someone whose "complex fate," to use Ralph Ellison's term, is to be both believer and doubter, in a world where such complexity is as beleaguered as it is necessary.

This struggle to embrace modernity without abandoning faith falls on one of the fault lines in the modern world. It is arguably the critical fault line, the tectonic rift that is advancing the bloody borders of Islam and the increasingly sectarian boundaries of American politics. As humankind abandons the secular totalitarianisms of the last century and grapples with breakneck technological and scientific discoveries, the appeal of absolutist faith is powerful in both developing and developed countries. It is the latest in a long line of rebukes to liberal modernity—but this rebuke has the deepest roots, the widest appeal, and the attraction that all total solutions to the human predicament proffer. From the doctrinal absolutism of Pope Benedict's Vatican to the revival of fundamentalist Protestantism in the U.S. and Asia to the attraction for many Muslims of the most extreme and antimodern forms of Islam, the same phenomenon has spread to every culture and place.

You cannot confront the complex challenges of domestic or foreign policy today unless you understand this gulf and its seriousness. You cannot lead the United States without having a foot in both the religious and secular camps. This, surely, is where Bush has failed most profoundly. By aligning himself with the most extreme and basic of religious orientations, he has lost many moderate believers and alienated the secular and agnostic in the West. If you cannot bring the agnostics along in a campaign against religious terrorism, you have a problem.

Here again, Obama, by virtue of generation and accident, bridges this deepening divide. He was brought up in a nonreligious home and converted to Christianity as an adult. But—critically—he is not born-again. His faith—at once real and measured, hot and cool—lives at the center of the American religious experience. It is a modern, intellectual Christianity. "I didn't have an epiphany," he explained to me. "What I really did was to take a set of values and ideals that were first instilled in me from my mother, who was, as I have called her in my book, the last of the secular humanists—you know, belief in kindness and empathy and discipline, responsibility—those kinds of values. And I found in the Church a vessel or a repository for those values and a way to connect those values to a larger community and a belief in God and a belief in redemption and mercy and justice . . . I guess the point is, it continues to be both a spiritual, but also intellectual, journey for me, this issue of faith."

The best speech Obama has ever given was not his famous 2004 convention address, but a June 2007 speech in Connecticut. In it, he described his religious conversion:

> One Sunday, I put on one of the few clean jackets I had, and went over to Trinity United Church of Christ on 95th Street on the South Side of Chicago. And I heard Reverend Jeremiah A. Wright deliver a sermon called "The Audacity of Hope." And during the course of that sermon, he introduced me to someone named Jesus Christ. I learned that my sins could be redeemed. I learned that those things I was too weak to accomplish myself, he would accomplish with me if I placed my trust in him. And in time, I came to see faith as more than just a comfort to the weary or a hedge against death, but rather as an active, palpable agent in the world and in my own life.
>
> It was because of these newfound understandings that I was finally able to walk down the aisle of Trinity one day and affirm my Christian faith. It came about as a choice and not an epiphany. I didn't fall out in church, as folks sometimes do. The questions I had didn't magically disappear. The skeptical bent of my mind didn't suddenly vanish. But kneeling beneath

that cross on the South Side, I felt I heard God's spirit beckoning me. I submitted myself to his will, and dedicated myself to discovering his truth and carrying out his works.

To be able to express this kind of religious conviction without disturbing or alienating the growing phalanx of secular voters, especially on the left, is quite an achievement. As he said in 2006, "Faith doesn't mean that you don't have doubts." To deploy the rhetoric of Evangelicalism while eschewing its occasional anti-intellectualism and hubristic certainty is as rare as it is exhilarating. It is both an intellectual achievement, because Obama has clearly attempted to wrestle a modern Christianity from the encumbrances and anachronisms of its past, and an American achievement, because it was forged in the only American institution where conservative theology and the Democratic Party still communicate: the black church.

And this, of course, is the other element that makes Obama a potentially transformative candidate: race. Here, Obama again finds himself in the center of a complex fate, unwilling to pick sides in a divide that reaches back centuries and appears at times unbridgeable. His appeal to whites is palpable. I have felt it myself. Earlier this fall, I attended an Obama speech in Washington on tax policy that underwhelmed on delivery; his address was wooden, stilted, even tedious. It was only after I left the hotel that it occurred to me that I'd just been bored on tax policy by a national black leader. That I should have been struck by this was born in my own racial stereotypes, of course. But it won me over.

Obama is deeply aware of how he comes across to whites. In a revealing passage in his first book, he recounts how, in adolescence, he defused his white mother's fears that he was drifting into delinquency. She had marched into his room and demanded to know what was going on. He flashed her "a reassuring smile and patted her hand and told her not to worry." This, he tells us, was "usually an effective tactic," because people

were satisfied as long as you were courteous and smiled and made no sudden moves. They were more than satisfied; they were relieved—such a pleasant surprise to find a well-mannered young black man who didn't seem angry all the time.

And so you have Obama's campaign for white America: courteous and smiling and with no sudden moves. This may, of course, be one reason for his still-lukewarm support among many African Americans, a large number of whom back a white woman for the presidency. It may also be because African Americans (more than many whites) simply don't believe that a black man can win the presidency, and so are leery of wasting their vote. And the persistence of race as a divisive, even explosive, factor in American life was unmissable the week of Obama's tax speech. While he was detailing middle-class tax breaks, thousands of activists were preparing to march in Jena, Louisiana, after a series of crude racial incidents had blown up into a polarizing conflict.

Jesse Jackson voiced puzzlement that Obama was not at the fore-front of the march. "If I were a candidate, I'd be all over Jena," he remarked. The South Carolina newspaper *The State* reported that Jackson said Obama was "acting like he's white." Obama didn't jump into the fray (no sudden moves), but instead issued measured statements on Jena, waiting till a late-September address at Howard University to find his voice. It was simultaneously an endorsement of black identity politics and a distancing from it:

> When I'm president, we will no longer accept the false choice between being tough on crime and vigilant in our pursuit of justice. Dr. King said: "It's not either/or, it's both/and." We can have a crime policy that's both tough and smart. If you're convicted of a crime involving drugs, of course you should be punished. But let's not make the punishment for crack cocaine that much more severe than the punishment for powder cocaine when the real difference between the two is the skin color of the people using them. Judges think that's wrong. Republicans think that's wrong. Democrats think that's wrong, and yet it's been approved by Republican and Democratic presidents because no one has been willing to brave the politics and make it right. That will end when I am president.

Obama's racial journey makes this kind of both/and politics something more than a matter of political compromise. The paradox of his candidacy is that, as potentially the first African American president in a country founded on slavery, he has taken pains to downplay the racial catharsis his candidacy implies. He knows race is important, and yet he knows that it turns destructive if it becomes the only important thing. In this he again subverts a Boomer paradigm, of black victimology or black conservatism. He is neither Al Sharpton nor Clarence Thomas; neither Julian Bond nor Colin Powell. Nor is he a post-racial figure like Tiger Woods, insofar as he has spent his life trying to reconnect with a black identity his childhood never gave him. Equally, he cannot be a Jesse Jackson. His white mother brought him up to be someone else.

In *Dreams from My Father,* Obama tells the story of a man with an almost eerily nonracial childhood, who has to learn what racism is, what his own racial identity is, and even what being black in America is. And so Obama's relationship to the black American experience is as much learned as intuitive. He broke up with a serious early girlfriend in part because she was white. He decided to abandon a post-racial career among the upper-middle classes of the East Coast in order to reengage with the black experience of Chicago's South Side. It was an act of integration—personal as well as communal—that called him to the work of community organizing.

This restlessness with where he was, this attempt at personal integration, represents both an affirmation of identity politics and a commitment to carving a unique personal identity out of the race, geography, and class he inherited. It yields an identity born of displacement, not rootedness. And there are times, I confess, when Obama's account of understanding his own racial experience seemed more like that of a gay teen discovering that he lives in two worlds simultaneously than that of a young African American confronting racism for the first time.

And there are also times when Obama's experience feels more like an immigrant story than a black memoir. His autobiography navigates a new and strange world of an American racial legacy that never quite defined him at his core. He therefore speaks to a complicated and mixed identity—not a simple and alienated one. This may hurt him among some African Americans, who may fail to identify with this fellow with an odd name. Black conservatives, like Shelby Steele, fear he is too deferential to the black establishment. Black leftists worry that he is not beholden at all. But there is no reason why African Americans cannot see the logic of Americanism that Obama also represents, a legacy that is ultimately theirs as well. To be black and white, to have belonged to a nonreligious home and a Christian church, to have attended a majority-Muslim school in Indonesia and a black church in urban Chicago, to be more than one thing and sometimes not fully anything—this is an increasingly common experience for Americans, including many racial minorities. Obama expresses such a conflicted but resilient identity before he even utters a word. And this complexity, with its internal tensions, contradictions, and moods, may increasingly be the main thing all Americans have in common.

None of this, of course, means that Obama will be the president some are dreaming of. His record in high office is sparse; his performances on the campaign trail have been patchy; his chief rival for the nomination, Senator Clinton, has bested him often with her relentless pursuit of the middle ground, her dogged attention to her own failings, and her much-improved speaking skills. At times, she has even managed to appear more inherently likable than the skinny, crabby, and sometimes morose newcomer from Chicago. Clinton's most surprising asset has been the sense of security she instills. Her husband—and the good feelings that nostalgics retain for his presidency—has buttressed her case. In dangerous times, popular majorities often seek the conservative option, broadly understood.

The paradox is that Hillary makes far more sense if you believe that times are actually pretty good. If you believe that America's current crisis is not a deep one, if you think that pragmatism alone will be enough to navigate a world on the verge of even more religious warfare, if you believe that today's ideological polarization is not dangerous, and that what appears dark today is an illusion fostered by the lingering trauma of the Bush presidency, then the argument for Obama is not that strong. Clinton will do. And a Clinton-Giuliani race could be as invigorating as it is utterly predictable.

But if you sense, as I do, that greater danger lies ahead, and that our divisions and recent history have combined to make the American polity and constitutional order increasingly vulnerable, then the calculus of risk changes. Sometimes, when the world is changing rapidly, the greater risk is caution. Close-up in this election campaign, Obama is unlikely. From a distance, he is necessary. At a time when America's estrangement from the world risks tipping into dangerous imbalance, when a country at war with lethal enemies is also increasingly at war with itself, when humankind's spiritual yearnings veer between an excess of certainty and an inability to believe anything at all, and when sectarian and racial divides seem as intractable as ever, a man who is a bridge between these worlds may be indispensable.

We may in fact have finally found that bridge to the 21st century that Bill Clinton told us about. Its name is Obama.

THE HIGH GROUND

_✦✦✦_

Stanley Crouch

One of Michelle Obama's favorite points is that for too long we have been manipulated by the fear that has been imposed on us about almost everything. "Be not afraid" are watchwords that rise through her speeches and seem to exit into the air from a hot spring of ideas and feeling bubbling beneath her hair.

That combination of ideas and feeling touches something more than a little important in the charred heart of the American populace because it is grounded in a far-from-naive optimism. It is the optimism that any scrapper has to have when entering a fight. That optimism is as old as the republic itself and is, again, providing a sensational skin graft that always must be performed when the heart of the country has been charred by the lies and corruption giving fuel to the latest version of an incapacitating cynicism we know quite well. It has become famous because it burns away more of our democratic distinctions.

Opponents want to dismiss that optimism as "false hope" because they think—or pretend to think—that Barack Obama represents no more than a charismatic political slogan that has even less value than one of the worthless products brilliantly hawked around the clock throughout our media. But Barack Obama is actually a bluesman from Chicago whose big stage is not in a nightclub or a concert hall but the huge national podium on which politics are argued. Obama knows that the blues always presents the unvarnished problem and provides a solution through the rhythms and tones of engagement. It is, as the writer Albert Murray has observed, a music of confrontation and it is presented in what amounts to a purification ritual.

———————

Americans have longed for the purification ritual that they sense in Obama's campaign because it faces what they feel is wrong with this country and allows them to believe, once again, that they can do something substantial about it. An important part of this purification ritual is the presentation of an American history that is common to us all. Obama does that by building a blues- and glory-bound train. He has shown himself to be the master of making couplers that should have functioned before—and would have if someone had seen to it that they were strong enough to hold all of the cars in line, no matter how they were made or what they contained, as long as none of it was trivia and none of it should be misplaced or forgotten. He takes his listeners to the station and shows them how well the train is built and how all of the cars are linked to each other by importance. The couplers of perception that Obama has designed link the Revolutionary War to the abolition movement against slavery. Those two are coupled to Abraham Lincoln and the Civil War. He then couples those four to women getting the vote and the emergence of organized labor. The train has become more impressive as those six are linked to defeating European fascism during World War II, saving the world from people driven mad by the superstitions of bigotry. That's seven cars held together by strong couplers made from facts, not dreams; timeless actualities, not nostalgia. The last car so far is the Civil Rights struggle in which black and white people, some young, some not, brought this country much closer to its democratic destiny.

When they can stand in that station and walk from car to car and see how well they are held together, Americans feel both purified and closer to each other. They notice that each of the cars and each of the couplers has nothing to do with special interest groups; they are made and held together by perpetually vital American principles which can extend themselves into newly designed cars whenever absolutely necessary. Those cars can seat everyone because that is what a democracy returning to its power always does. It knows how to make room for one more. But, as Americans, we are continually learning that the extra person, even if different on the surface, is never less than ourselves.

I was once told that there is a tale in the Talmud about a man somewhere in the desert who sees an animal on the horizon. As the animal comes closer, he realizes that it is a man. When it gets even closer, he recognizes that the man is his brother. That is the story that is forever learned in the United States; it is the meaning of that blues-and-glory train, of every car, and every coupler. Once the people realize it, they want to get on board that train and travel on out: into the world.

That is what no presidential candidate has been able to do in many, many years: make people FEEL that e pluribus unum is not only alive and well but is the foundation of the strategy that will get us out of our messes. As Billie Holiday once said of a good night when she communicated perfectly with her audience, "Then we felt as though we were all in the same storm."

When Barack Obama dismisses superficial differences as confidently as scientists do the superstitions of bigotry and blood libel, Americans begin to believe in the country as a whole again. They feel liberated from identity politics and any other form of segregation in which distinctions never rise free of one form or another of separatist politics.

Americans have longed for this feeling throughout all of the sellouts to the Christian right, to the remaining reptilian rednecks of the bigoted South, to the big-money special interests and their lobbyists, and to the general incompetence and lack of integrity that have left the greasy fingerprints of self-interest and the squalor of greed on our national policies.

That is why Obama has created a movement no one knew was possible and that our pundits still fail to understand because they reduce it to something neither he nor his followers are interested in: race.

Our nation has talked that talk for a long time but now is the time to finally put up or shut up. Barack Obama will not shut up because he is in the business of acting as though e pluribus unum is the connecting foundation upon which all necessary change must be built, and his supporters obviously agree with him.

We are all joined at the American heart, and the superficial cacophony of its beat disguises a central pulse of irrepressible vitality. Barack Obama and his supporters have built a movement because they can hear the brightness of that heartbeat and intend to get everyone else to hear it as well.

PERMISSIONS AND CREDITS

Dances with Daffodils by Jamaica Kincaid. Copyright © 2007 by Condé Nast Publications. Originally published in *Architectural Digest*, April 2007. All rights reserved. Reprinted by permission.

The Coincidental Cousins: A Night Out with Artist Kara Walker by James Hannaham. First published in *The Village Voice*, December 4, 2007. Copyright © 2007 by James Hannaham. Reprinted by permission of the author.

Music: Bodies in Pain by Mark Anthony Neal. First published on SeeingBlack.com, June 20, 2007. Copyright © 2007 by Mark Anthony Neal. Reprinted by permission of the author.

When Tyra Met Naomi: Race, Fashion, and Rivalry by Hawa Allan. First published in *Bitch: Feminist Response to Pop Culture*, issue no. 34, Winter 2007. Copyright © 2007 by Hawa Allan. Reprinted by permission of the author.

Dancing in the Dark by Gerald Early. First published in *The Oxford American*, Issue 56, 2007. Copyright © 2007 by Gerald Early. Reprinted by permission of the author.

Modern-Day Mammy? by Jill Nelson. First published in *Essence*, May 2007. Copyright © 2007 by Essence Communications Inc. Reprinted by permission of Essence Communications Inc. All rights reserved.

Broken Dreams by Michael A. Gonzales. First published in *Vibe* magazine, October 2007. Copyright © 2007 by *Vibe* magazine. Reprinted by permission of the editors.

SCIENCES, TECHNOLOGY, EDUCATION

None of the Above: What I.Q. Doesn't Tell You About Race by Malcolm Gladwell. First published in *The New Yorker*, December 17, 2007. Copyright © 2007 by Malcolm Gladwell. Reprinted by permission of the author.

Driving by Kenneth A. McClane. Originally published in *The Antioch Review*, vol. 64, no. 4, Fall 2006. Copyright © 2006 by *The Antioch Review*, Inc. Reprinted by permission of the editors.

Part I: I Had a Dream by Bill Maxwell. First published in *The St. Petersburg Times*, May 13, 2007. Copyright © 2007 by *The St. Petersburg Times*. Reprinted by permission of *The St. Petersburg Times*.

Part II: A Dream Lay Dying by Bill Maxwell. First published in *The*

St. Petersburg Times, May 20, 2007. Copyright © 2007 by *The St. Petersburg Times.* Reprinted by permission of *The St. Petersburg Times.*

Part III: The Once and Future Promise by Bill Maxwell. First published in *The St. Petersburg Times,* May 27, 2007. Copyright © 2007 by *The St. Petersburg Times.* Reprinted by permission of *The St. Petersburg Times.*

GAY

Get Out of My Closet: Can You Be White and "On the Down Low"? by Benoit Denizet-Lewis. First published on Slate.com, August 29, 2007. Copyright © 2007 by Benoit Denizet-Lewis. Reprinted by permission of the author.

Girls to Men: Young Lesbians in Brooklyn Find That a Thug's Life Gets Them More Women by Chloé A. Hilliard. First published in *The Village Voice,* April 11–17, 2007. Copyright © 2007 by Chloé A. Hilliard. Reprinted by permission of the author.

INTERNATIONALLY BLACK

A Slow Emancipation by Kwame Anthony Appiah from *Buying Freedom* by Kwame Anthony Appiah (ed.) and Martin Bunzl (ed.). Copyright © 2007 by Princeton University Press. Reprinted by permission of Princeton University Press.

Searching for Zion by Emily Raboteau. First published in *Transition Magazine,* 2007. Copyright © 2007 by Emily Raboteau. Reprinted by permission of the author.

Last Thoughts of an Iraq "Embed" by Brian Palmer. First published in the *Huffington Post,* February 24, 2006. Copyright © 2006 by Brian Palmer. Reprinted by permission of the author.

Stop Trying to "Save" Africa by Uzodinma Iweala. First published in the *Washington Post,* July 15, 2007. Copyright © 2007 by Uzodinma Iweala. Reprinted with permission of The Wylie Agency, Inc.

We Are Americans by Jerald Walker. Copyright © 2009 by Jerald Walker. Used by permission of the author.

ACTIVISM/POLITICAL THOUGHT

Jena, O.J. and the Jailing of Black America by Orlando Patterson. From *The New York Times,* September 30, 2007. Copyright © 2007 by

One Nation . . . Under God? by Barack Obama. This excerpt was first published in *Soujourners Magazine,* November 2006. Barack Obama, a U.S. senator from Illinois, delivered the speech from which it was adapted at the *Sojourners/*Call to Renewal–sponsored Pentecost conference in June 2006. The whole transcript can be found at www.sojo.net/obama. This article is reprinted with permission from Sojourners, (800) 714-7474, www.sojo.net.

Americans Without Americanness: Is Our Nation Nothing More Than an Address? by John McWhorter. First published in *The National Review,* April 16, 2007. Copyright © 2007 by John McWhorter. Reprinted by permission of the author.

Barack Obama by Michael Eric Dyson. Copyright © 2007 by *The Nation.* Reprinted with permission from the November 26, 2007, issue of *The Nation* magazine.

Standing Up for "Bad" Words by Stephane Dunn. First published in *The Chronicle Review,* March 14, 2008. Copyright © 2008 by Stephane Dunn. Reprinted by permission of the author.

Debunking "Driving While Black" Myth by Thomas Sowell. First published in *Human Events,* November 12, 2007. Copyright © 2007 by Thomas Sowell. Reprinted by permission of Thomas Sowell and Creators Syndicate, Inc.

Goodbye to All That: Why Obama Matters by Andrew Sullivan. First published in *The Atlantic,* December 2007. Copyright © 2007 by Andrew Sullivan. Reprinted by permission of the author.

The High Ground by Stanley Crouch. Copyright © 2009 by Stanley Crouch. Used by permission of the author.

ABOUT THE EDITORS

GERALD EARLY is a noted essayist and American culture critic. A professor of English, African and African American Studies, and American Culture Studies at Washington University in St. Louis, Early is the author of several books, including *The Culture of Bruising: Essays on Prizefighting, Literature, and Modern American Culture,* which won the 1994 National Book Critics Circle Award for criticism, and *This Is Where I Came In: Black America in the 1960s.* He is also editor of numerous volumes, including *The Muhammad Ali Reader* and *The Sammy Davis, Jr. Reader.* He served as a consultant on four of Ken Burns's documentary films, *Baseball, Jazz, Unforgivable Blackness: The Rise and Fall of Jack Johnson,* and *The War,* and appeared in the first three as an on-air analyst.

DEBRA J. DICKERSON was educated at the University of Maryland, St. Mary's University, and Harvard Law School. She has been both a senior editor and a contributing editor at *U.S. News & World Report,* and her work has also appeared in *The New York Times Magazine, The Washington Post, The New Republic, Slate, The Village Voice,* and *Essence.* She is the author of *The End of Blackness* and *An American Story.* She lives in Albany, New York.

To view the contributors' bios, visit www.bantamdell.com.